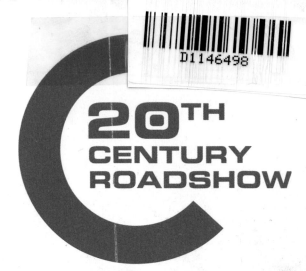

D1146498

# 20TH CENTURY ROADSHOW

## Collectables Price Guide

Judith Miller & Mark Hill

Foreword by Alan Titchmarsh

A DORLING KINDERSLEY BOOK

LONDON, NEW YORK,
MELBOURNE, MUNICH AND DELHI

A joint production from DORLING KINDERSLEY
and THE PRICE GUIDE COMPANY

**THE PRICE GUIDE COMPANY LIMITED**

**Publisher** Judith Miller

**Collectables Specialist** Mark Hill

**Publishing Manager** Julie Brooke

**Managing Editor** Carolyn Madden

**Senior Editors** Emma Clegg,
Sara Sturgess

**Digital Image Co-ordinator**
Ellen Spalek

**Sub-editors** Jessica Bishop,
Dan Dunlavey, Sandra Lange

**Design and DTP**
Tim Scrivens, TJ Graphics

**Photographers** Graham Rae, John
McKenzie, Byron Slater, Steve Tanner,
Heike Löwenstein, Andy Johnson,
Adam Gault

**Indexer** Hilary Bird

**Workflow Consultant** Bob Bousfield

**Business Advisor** Nick Croydon

**DORLING KINDERSLEY LIMITED**

**Senior Editor** Dawn Henderson

**Designer** Katie Eke

**Managing Art Editor**
Heather McCarry

**Managing Editor** Julie Oughton

**Publishing Director** Jackie Douglas

**Category Publisher** Stephanie Jackson

**Publishing Manager** Adele Hayward

**DTP Designer** Adam Walker

**Production** Melanie Dowland

**Production Manager** Sarah Coltman**

---

While every care has been taken in the compilation of this guide,
neither the authors nor the publishers accept any liability for any
financial or other loss incurred by reliance placed on the information
contained in *20th Century Roadshow Collectables Price Guide*

---

First published in 2005 by
Dorling Kindersley Limited
80 Strand, London WC2R 0RL

A Penguin Company

The Price Guide Company (UK) Ltd
Studio 21, Waterside
44–48 Wharf Road
London N1 7UX
info@thepriceguidecompany.com

2 4 6 8 10 9 7 5 3 1

A CIP catalogue record for this book is available from the British Library.

1 4053 0995 4

Printed and bound in Germany by GGP Media GmbH

Discover more at
**www.dk.com**

# CONTENTS

# FOREWORD

THE COLLECTING BUG is something that bites most of us at some point in our lives. In spite of the fact that I try to tell myself that material possessions are not important, I still find myself hankering after bits of this and that, simply because I want to have them about me. It's a comfort thing, rather than a miserly acquisitiveness. At least, that's what I tell myself.

The trouble with presenting *20th Century Roadshow* is that it has made me far more aware of what is out there, and also of what is collectable. Over the time we've been making the series I've handled everything from Marilyn Monroe's dresses, which are beyond the financial scope of most of us, to comics that are well within reach of kids with very little pocket money.

Above all, I've discovered the tremendous variety of things that people collect and the fact that, unlike most antiques, they can be very affordable. This will be seen as a great disadvantage to the other members of my family who are more attracted to minimalist living than I am.

But, you see, I treasure the pot ginger beer bottle that comes from just down the road in Portsmouth; the inkwell with the brass lid that the lady next door gave me when I was a nipper in Yorkshire, and the signed photograph of Alec Guinness from *The Bridge On The River Kwai* that I found in an old bookshop.

Ah yes, books have always been a passion, and every now and then I run out of shelves and have to have a clean out. You can disappear into a book and inhabit another world. I suppose it's the same with memorabilia – be it film posters, theatre programmes or signed photos – you can touch the coat-tails of the famous for as long as you have them by you.

The value of all these bits and pieces is as variable as the objects themselves, but then the 20th century went from the last year of Queen Victoria's reign through the Edwardian era, Art Nouveau, Art Deco, the roaring twenties, the fabulous fifties, the swinging sixties and ... well, you know the rest.

Fads and fashions come and go in popularity by their very nature. But somewhere, you can be certain, there is someone who treasures their own little collection of postcards or tins or handbags, Toby jugs or Dinky toys or Poole Pottery. Some of them may have little value, except that of sentimentality, but every now and again the last century, which ended only moments ago, will throw up something relatively commonplace, which is of surprising value.

With any luck, this book will help you to sort the wheat from the chaff; the collectable from the binable. But, then, if everybody bins the binable, it will suddenly become collectable.

Collect what you love, and love what you collect. It's only by looking at our past that we can see how we have come to be where we are today. They say nostalgia is not what it was, but *20th Century Roadshow* has proved otherwise. Nostalgia has never been more alive, or more varied, and I for one can't get enough of it.

ALAN TITCHMARSH

# INTRODUCTION

COLLECTING HAS NOW become an important and exciting part of our culture. Our exposure to TV programmes, collectables fairs, car-boot sales and internet auction sites makes us more sensitive to the objects that surround us in our homes, and invites us to question whether they might be valuable.

The 20th century covers an immense range of visual styles and fashions, with something for everyone. It's all a question of taste. Whether it's the early passenger cruise liners that float your boat, costume jewellery from the 1930s that makes your eyes sparkle, the colourful lure of 1930s Art Deco that makes you swing or 1960s music memorabilia that unleashes your passion, each collection is eclectic, highly personal and has the potential to grow.

As some of you already know, or will come to know, collecting is incredibly addictive. The inspiration that leads us to collect can be as much for the sheer pleasure we derive from the pieces we have around us as for nostalgic reasons where the faces, brands and styles of a particular decade evoke our childhoods or fond memories. Truth be known, many also collect for financial gain. Even if you take tremendous pride in your collection of Elvis memorabilia and would never consider selling it, you will probably also have a

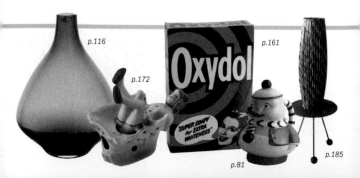

*p. 237*

*p.116*

*p.172*

*p.161*

*p.185*

*p.81*

*p.244*

good understanding of its market value. In most cases, however, it is most likely to be a combination of all these factors, and perhaps others. Building a good working knowledge of your subject is key. Price guides such as this are an invaluable resource to keep up to date with market trends, or if you aren't yet sure what to focus on, or have wide-ranging interests. Auction catalogues and the accompanying price lists published after the sale also allow you to track changing values, as will internet sites such as eBay, and even collectors' clubs. Don't let 'hands-on' experience fall behind, however, as this is often the most useful. Visit pre-auction views, dealers and collectors' fairs to carefully handle and examine as many different items as you can. This will enable you to develop an experienced 'eye', which will help you spot both fakes and rarities in the future.

If you're new to collecting, look first in your own home or relatives' homes for any undiscovered modern valuables. Scouring advertisements in local papers, charity shops, jumble sales and car-boot sales can yield surprising results. Although it is a little harder today than it once was, the thrill of the hunt is still there! In all cases except charity shops, try to haggle over the price – sellers will expect this. Do so sensibly, politely and respectfully and most will be prepared to cut you a deal if they can. Also ask for a written receipt, both for your records and for your security.

*p.180*

*p.189*

*p.288*

*p.322*

Don't be frightened to visit auction houses as they offer amazing variety, and buying and indeed selling at auction really is part of the fun and addiction of the collecting experience. Dealers often focus on specific subjects and building a friendly relationship can be very rewarding – many will help you to develop your knowledge and they may give you insider tips for a specific find. Some trade from shops, whereas others work through fairs and many now have a website and a mail-order service. The internet, in fact, has made it possible to buy and sell from the comfort of your own home computer. At the back of this book, you'll find a directory of auction houses, fairs, antiques centres and useful websites to help you get started.

There are no hard-and-fast rules for establishing any piece's value or desirability over a period of time. This is mainly because changing tastes and fashions dictate what is most sought after and desirable, and thus usually valuable. Scandinavian glass, for example, is a popular collecting area at the moment because the clean lines and often glowing colours fit well with our modern interior tastes. There are still, however, certain guidelines to any object's value that apply to most areas – the quality of design and manufacture, notable names, rarity and condition.

On that note, one of the best tips I learnt was to try to collect items in the best condition possible. Not only are they more visually

*p.67*

*p.54*

*p.162*

*p.167*

*p.325*

attractive, but they are also more likely to command higher prices in the future. This is especially true for items produced in the 20th century, when many were mass-produced or produced in larger numbers than some older 'antiques'. Always look for and ask about any restoration too, as this has a bearing on value. Avoid undertaking any major restoration, other than a gentle clean, yourself. Always entrust this to a professional, as a badly restored piece can be worth less than one in poor but original condition.

Good luck with whatever path your collecting takes – the last century offers so much scope. It's amazing to think that a book published only a couple of years ago can now be worth many times more than an ancient-looking leather bound volume, such as a 19th- century bible. As you'll read later, a true first edition of the first Harry Potter book can fetch up to £20,000! Many were originally sent to libraries and may have now found their way to car-boot sales across the country, waiting to be found. I guess the old phrase 'never judge a book by its cover' continues to apply! I'm sure you'll find a 20th-century passion that will give you constant pleasure and may even make you richer in years to come.

*Judith Miller*

JUDITH MILLER

p.210

p.90

p.158

p.352

# LIST OF CONSULTANTS

## Ceramics

**Beth & Beverley Adams**
Alfies Antique Market, London

**Mick Collins**
SylvaC Collector's Club, UK

**Joy Humphreys**
Feljoy Antiques, London

**Judith Miller**
The Price Guide Company (UK) Ltd

**John Pym**
Hope & Glory, London

## Glass

**Graham Cooley**
Private Collector

**Jeanette Hayhurst**
Jeanette Hayhurst Fine Glass,
London

**Mark Hill**
The Price Guide Company (UK) Ltd

**Chris & Val Stewart**
Cloudglass.com

## Around the House

**Ian Broughton**
Alfies Antique Market, London

**Mark Hill**
The Price Guide Company (UK) Ltd

**David Huxtable**
Huxtins.com

## Books & Ephemera

**Patrick Bogue**
Onslow's, Dorset

**Leo Harrison**
Biblion, London

**Roddy Newlands**
Bloomsbury Auctions, London

## Fashion & Jewellery

**Richard Ball**
richard@lighter.co.uk

**Stephen Miners**
Cristobal, London

**Sparkle Moore**
Alfies Antique Market, London

## Entertainment & Sports

**Sam Sarowitz**
Posteritati, New York, USA

**Russell Singler**
Animation Art Gallery, London

## Toys, Dolls & Teddies

**Glenn Butler**
Wallis & Wallis, Lewes, Sussex

**Hugo Lee Jones**
Electronic Collectables, London

**Barbara Lauver**
Harper General Store, Pennsylvania,
USA

## Technology & Travel

**Victoria Campbell**
Aurora Galleries, California, USA

**Peter Boyd-Smith**
Cobwebs, Portsmouth, Hampshire

*We are also very grateful to our friends
and specialists who gave us so much
help: Michael Bennett-Levy of Early
Technology, Dr Uwe Breker of Auction
Team Cologne, Gary Grant, Sasha Keen
and Stacey LoAlbo, Sharon and Joe
Happle, Andrew Hilton of Special Auction
Sevices, Mark Laino, Simon Smith of
Vectis Auctions Ltd, Alison Snelgrove,
Roxanne Stuart, Vanessa Strougo, Kirsty
Wallace at Gray's and Alfies Antique
Markets and Ron and Ann Wheeler of
artiusglass.co.uk*

# HOW TO USE THIS BOOK

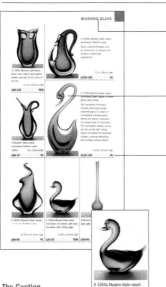

A 1950s Murano triple cased Sommerso duck figure, with green foil sticker with curling edges.

6.25in (16cm) high

£25-35    TGM

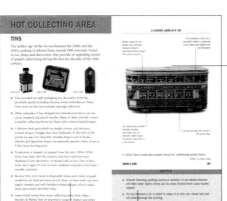

# CERAMICS

Ceramics and collecting have a long and intimate relationship. Even when looking at the 20th century, there is an amazingly diverse range of wares on offer to both the novice and the serious collector.

We all have a deep-seated nostalgia for the objects of our childhood and for anyone given ceramic animals as gifts in the 1950s and 60s, then the cute figures of Beswick, Bunnykins and Pendelfin will all have a special attraction. Another popular area with a nostalgic flavour is commemorative ware, particularly the Charles and Diana memorabilia of the 1980s, but also, now, anything featuring the royal children, William and Harry, is growing in popularity and likely in the future to grow in value.

The brilliant colours and Art Deco designs of Clarice Cliff and Susie Cooper, alongside Keith Murray's clean and minimal 1930s pieces, have been achieving high prices in recent years as our attachment to the style of the 1930s continues. Also typical of the period is Myott ware – although their prices are generally lower as less is known about the company, interest is increasing and prices are beginning to rise. For similar investment potential look, too, to the smaller studio potteries active between the 1950s and 70s such as Rye, Buchan, Hornsea and Troika whose pieces are now attracting significantly more interest.

# HOT COLLECTING AREA

## BESWICK

Beswick has become best known for its range of animal figures, first introduced in the 1930s. Becoming ever more popular with collectors, prices for rare colourways and forms have risen dramatically since production ended in 2002.

*see p.20*          *see p.22*          *see p.23*

■ Beswick produced an extensive range of animals, drawn from both native and foreign species of wild and domestic animals. Familiar animals such as cattle, birds and dogs can be collected alongside more exotic examples, such as a moose or a zebra, that can command higher prices.

■ Collectors tend to specialise in a type of animal, and constantly popular are their ranges of horse and cattle models. Look for unusual colours and for models only produced for short periods, especially during the mid-20th century, as these are often rarer and more desirable.

■ The Beatrix Potter inspired range is also popular. The initial series of 10 characters, including Jemima Puddleduck and Peter Rabbit, was designed by noted Beswick modeller Arthur Gredington and was released in 1948. Its great success saw the range extended to over 40 figures in subsequent years, with over 10 versions.

■ The popularity of the character, the colour and the production period dictate the value of individual pieces, with limited editions and early models generating most enthusiasm.

■ Variations for both types exist in terms of shape, finish and colour, which all changed over the years. Early examples often had protruding features that were easily damaged. That led to the design being changed, so these early examples are sought after. Colours and designs of some clothing also changed, so examine figures carefully.

# A CLOSER LOOK AT A BESWICK ANIMAL FIGURE

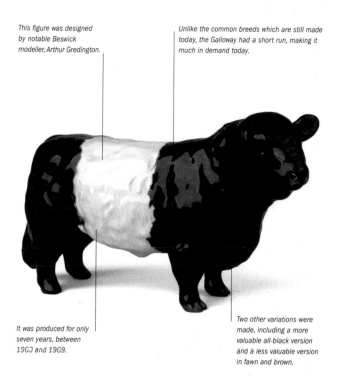

This figure was designed by notable Beswick modeller, Arthur Gredington.

Unlike the common breeds which are still made today, the Galloway had a short run, making it much in demand today.

It was produced for only seven years, between 1963 and 1969.

Two other variations were made, including a more valuable all-black version and a less valuable version in fawn and brown.

A Beswick 'Belted Galloway Bull' figure, No. 1746B.
**£2,000-2,500**

PSA

## TOP TIPS

■ Check Beswick figures carefully for 'crazing', a network of fine cracks in the glaze that will eventually cover the entire piece.

■ Check the protruding parts and freestanding legs of Beswick animals as these are vulnerable to damage.

■ Examine animals closely – some rare and desirable variations have only slightly different elements, such as differently positioned legs.

■ Look for the coveted and valuable 'gold' backstamp that was used on Beatrix Potter figures produced before 1972, when the brown and black stamps were introduced.

A Beswick 'Highland Bull' gloss figure, No. 2008.

£180-220    PSA

A Beswick 'Hereford Bull' first version gloss figure, No. 1363A.

£150-200    PSA

A Beswick 'Aberdeen Angus Calf' gloss figure, No. 1406A.

£280-320    PSA

A rare Beswick 'Aberdeen Angus Calf' special commission gloss figure.

£1,500-2,000    PSA

A Beswick 'Guernsey Cow' version one, gloss figure, No. 1248A.

£200-300    PSA

A Beswick 'Ayrshire Cow Champion Ickham Bessie' gloss figure, No. 1350.

£150-200    PSA

A Beswick 'Dairy Shorthorn Calf' figure, No. 1406C, restored ear.

£300-500    PSA

A Beswick 'Lesser Spotted Woodpecker' gloss figure, No. 2420.

£150-200    PSA

A Beswick 'Zebra' gloss figure, No. 845b.

**£120-180**  PSA

A Beswick 'Faracre Viscount 3rd' saddleback boar gloss figure, No. 1512.

**£200-300**  PSA

A Beswick 'Wall Queen 40th' sow champion gloss figure, No. 1452a.

**£20-30**  PSA

A Beswick 'Pig' gloss figure, No. 832.

**£20-30**  PSA

A Beswick 'Piggy Back' pig and piglet gloss figure, No. 2746.

**£30-50**  PSA

A Beswick 'Corgi' large gloss figure, No. 1299b.

**£40-60**  PSA

A Beswick 'Endon Black Rod' smooth-haired terrier gloss figure, No. 964.

**£300-500**  PSA

A Beswick 'Fireside Black Labrador' gloss figure, No. 2314.

**£220-280**  PSA

A rare Beswick 'Cat' dark pewter satin gloss figure, lying with its left front paw up, No. 1542.

**£400-600**  PSA

A Beswick 'Eagle on a Rock' figure, No. 2307, restored wing tip.

**£80-120**     **PSA**

A Beswick 'Tawny Owl' gloss figure, No. 3272.

**£30-50**     **PSA**

A Beswick 'Mallard Duck' large gloss figure, No. 817.

**£200-250**     **PSA**

A Beswick 'Mallard Duck' large gloss wall plaque, No. 596/0.

**£150-200**     **PSA**

A Beswick set of graduated 'Kingfisher' wall plaques, No. 729, smallest restored.

**£120-180**     **PSA**

A Beswick set of three graduated 'Seagull' wall plaques, No. 922/1/2/3.

**£180-220**     **PSA**

A graduated set of three Beswick models of penguins, the largest with a parasol, each decorated in coloured enamels, printed marks in black.

*4in (10cm) high*

**£40-60**     **LFA**

A Beswick 'Cowboy on Horseback', No. 1377, 'Ghost Rider', restored ears.

**£700-1,000**     **PSA**

A Beswick Thelwell Pony 'Kickstart' grey gloss figure, No. 2769A.

**£150-200**     **PSA**

A Beswick 'Girl on a Pony' gloss figure, No. 1499, at fault.

**£180-220**     **PSA**

A Beswick Beatrix Potter 'Mr Benjamin Bunny figure', with gold back stamp.

*4.25in (11cm) high*

£250-350     **OACC**

A Beswick Beatrix Potter 'Cottontail' figure.

*c1985*    *3.5in (9cm) high*

£50-80     **OACC**

A Beswick Beatrix Potter 'Mrs Flopsy Bunny' figure.

*c1965*    *4in (10cm) high*

£50-70     **OACC**

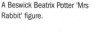

A Beswick Beatrix Potter 'Miss Moppit' figure, with gold back stamp.

*3in (7.5cm) high*

£80-120     **OACC**

A Beswick Beatrix Potter 'Peter Rabbit' figure, with gold back stamp.

*4.5in (11.5cm) high*

£100-150     **OACC**

A Beswick Beatrix Potter 'Mrs Rabbit' figure.

*c1951*    *4in (10cm) high*

£50-80     **OACC**

A Beswick Beatrix Potter 'Ribby' figure.

*c1951*    *3.25in (8.5cm) high*

£50-70     **OACC**

A Beswick Beatrix Potter 'Simpkin' figure with brown backstamp.

*4in (10cm) high*

£40-80     **DN**

A Beswick Beatrix Potter 'Tom Kitten' figure, no. "BP2", slight restoration.

£20-40     **PSA**

A Beswick Beatrix Potter 'Ribby', figure, BP3B.

£30-50       PSA

A Beswick Beatrix Potter 'Ginger' figure, BP3B.

£200-300       PSA

A Beswick Beatrix Potter 'Benjamin Bunny' figure, BP2 GBS, ears out, shoes out.

£150-200       PSA

A Beswick Beatrix Potter 'Mr Benjamin Bunny and Peter Rabbit' figure, BP3B.

£50-80       PSA

A Beswick Beatrix Potter 'Mrs Rabbit' figure, BP2 GBS, umbrella out.

£120-180       PSA

A Beswick 'Mrs Rabbit' large figure, BP6, boxed.

£30-50       PSA

A Beswick Beatrix Potter 'Flopsy, Mopsy and Cottontail' figure, BP2 GBS.

£70-100       PSA

A Beswick Beatrix Potter 'Amiable Guinea Pig' figure, BP2 GBS.

£220-280       PSA

A Beswick Beatrix Potter 'Johnny Townmouse Eating Corn' figure, BP10, boxed.

£30-50       PSA

A Beswick Beatrix Potter 'Old Woman who Lived in a Shoe' figure, BP2 GBS.

£50-80       PSA

A Beswick Beatrix Potter 'Anna Maria' figure, BP2 GBS.

£150-200       PSA

A Beswick Beatrix Potter 'Hunca Munca' figure.

£30-40       AOY

A 1960s Buchan Pottery coaster, hand-painted, unnamed pattern.

*4in (10.5cm) diam*

**£10-15** FFM

A 1960s Buchan Pottery 'Hebrides' pattern coaster, hand-painted.

*4in (10.5cm) diam*

**£10-15** FFM

A 1960s Buchan Pottery coaster, hand-painted, unnamed pattern.

*4.5in (11.5cm) diam*

**£10-15** FFM

A 1950s Buchan Pottery milk jug with hand-painted stylized leaf decoration.

*2.5in (6.5cm) high*

**£12-18** FFM

A 1960s Buchan Pottery jug, hand-decorated.

*5in (13cm) high*

**£20-25** FFM

A 1960s Buchan Pottery jug, hand-decorated.

*5in (13cm) high*

**£15-20** FFM

A 1960s Buchan Pottery tankard, hand-decorated.

*4in (10.5cm) high*

**£12-18** FFM

A 1960s Buchan Pottery teapot, hand-painted.

*8.75in (22cm) high*

**£25-35** FFM

A 1960s Buchan Pottery 'Riviera' pattern oil and vinegar cruet set, hand-decorated.

*5in (13cm) high*

**£20-25** FFM

A Royal Doulton 'Bunnykins' Family Photograph', DB1.

*This example is the first of three colour variations.*

*1972-88 4.5in (11.5cm) high*

**£50-80** PSA

A Royal Doulton 'Billie and Buntie Sleigh Ride' Bunnykins figure, DB4.

*1972-97*                    *3.5in (9cm) high*

**£15-25** PSA

A Royal Doulton 'Mr Bunnykins Autumn Days' figure, DB5, underglaze chip to ear.

*1972-82 4.25in (10.5cm) h*

**£70-100** PSA

A Royal Doulton 'Mrs Bunnykins Clean Sweep' figure, DB6.

*1972-91 4in (10cm) high*

**£50-80** PSA

A Royal Doulton 'Daisy Bunnykins, Spring Time' figure, DB7.

*1972-83 3in (7.5cm) high*

**£80-120** PSA

A Royal Doulton 'Dollie Bunnykins Playtime' figure, DB8.

*1972-93 4in (10cm) high*

**£40-60** PSA

A Royal Doulton 'The Artist' Bunnykins figure, DB13.

*1975-82 3.75in (9.5cm) high*

**£120-180** PSA

A Royal Doulton 'Mr Bunnykins at the Easter Parade' figure, DB18, boxed.

*1982-93 5in (12.5cm) high*

**£50-80** PSA

A Royal Doulton 'King John' Bunnykins figure, DB91.

*This is part of the desirable second series of the Bunnykins Royal Family. Each figure was released in a limited edition of 250 in 1990 only. Designed by Harry Sales and modelled by David Lyttleton and with a UKI Ceramics Special backstamp, they were issued without certificates.*

*1990*  4in (10cm) high

**£200-300**  PSA

A Royal Doulton 'Queen Sophie' Bunnykins figure, DB92, from a limited edition of 250.

*1990*  4in (10cm) high

**£220-280**  PSA

A Royal Doulton 'Prince Frederick' Bunnykins figure, DB94, from a limited edition of 250.

*1990*  3.25in (8cm) high

**£200-250**  PSA

A Royal Doulton 'Harry the Herald' Bunnykins figure, from a limited edition of 250, DB95.

*1990*  3.5in (9cm) high

**£200-250**  PSA

A Royal Doulton 'Hallowe'en' Bunnykins figure, DB132.

*1993-97*  3.25in (8cm) high

**£30-40**  PSA

A Royal Doulton yellow 'Cheerleader' Bunnykins figure, DB143, from a limited edition of 1,000.

*1994*  4.5in (11.5cm) high

**£80-120**  PSA

A Royal Doulton 'Boy Skater' Bunnykins figure, DB152.

*1995-98*  3.75in (9.5cm) high

**£15-25**  PSA

A limited edition Royal Doulton 'Fortune Teller' Bunnykins toby jug, DB157.

*2000*  5.5in (12.5cm) high

**£80-120**  PSA

# HOT COLLECTING AREA

## CARLTON WARE

Founded in 1890, the Carlton Works at Stoke-on-Trent produced numerous varied ranges over more than 70 years. Whilst their 1930s lustre pieces fetch high prices today, floral ranges from the same period and their later stylish 1950s and 1960s ranges are accessible to most collectors and are growing in popularity.

see p.30    see p.32    see p.31

- Lustreware, inspired by Wedgwood's example and produced in the 1920s and 1930s, is one of their most sought after and valued ranges. Flowers, birds and stylised natural themes are typical patterns. Large examples and geometric, Art Deco patterns and shapes are the most sought after.

- Chinoiserie or Persian designs on bold backgrounds such as red, blue and black are also found. These 'Royale' ranges were produced in shapes from dishes to jars to desk bases. Trees, plants, oriental houses and birds are common motifs, many picked out in raised enamels. Egyptian styles are highly desirable.

- During the same period, they released a large range of brightly coloured moulded domestic ware. Decorated with or shaped like flowers, leaves or fruit they were mass-produced and aimed at the middle market. Colour, form and pattern are the primary indicators to value, with rare examples commanding a premium.

- As they were used regularly, undamaged examples will fetch much higher prices today. Some colourways and shapes are rarer than others, leading to higher prices. Ranges produced for short periods such as 'Cherries' are also more desirable today.

- From the 1950s onwards, designs such as the 'Orbit' range followed sophisticated post-war tastes with two-tone colours and clean lines. These are becoming increasingly collectable.

# A CLOSER LOOK AT A CARLTON WARE CHARGER

The 'Handcraft' range was hand painted with freehand designs.

The design of certain elements shows a strong Art Deco influence.

The fairy and entire 'fairy tale' scene shows the influence of Wedgwood's highly successful 'Fairyland Lustre' range, which Carlton Ware aimed to mimic.

This is a large example, and chargers like this, which are easy to display, show off the pattern extremely well.

A Carlton Ware 'Handcraft' charger, painted with a seated faun playing pipes in an exotic floral and foliate landscape, printed marks.

c1932

15in (38cm) diam

**£1,000-1,500**

**L&T**

## TOP TIPS

- Look in particular for any damage to more vulnerable parts, such as lids, rims, spouts and bases, especially on more common 1930s floral ranges.

- Examine enamelled detailing carefully as wear and loss reduce value considerably.

- Examine the entire lustre surface and beware of thin, patchy areas where layers of lustre have been worn off.

- Original boxes for 1930s moulded floral and foliate ranges are much sought after.

A Carlton ware yellow glazed fruit bowl.

*1930s*

£30-50      **AS&S**

An unusual Carlton ware comical dog, decorated in black and white with a brown collar.

*6in (15cm) high*

£100-150      **PSA**

A Carlton ware 'Egyptian Fan' vase.

*7.5in (19cm) high*

£800-1,200      **RH**

A Carlton ware 'Heron and Magical tree' pattern coffeepot, milk jug and sugar server.

*7.5in (19cm) high*

£400-600      **RH**

A Carlton ware 'Barge' pattern bowl.

*10in (25.5cm) diam*

£350-450      **RH**

A 1930s Carlton ware 'springtime' dish.

*6.75in (17cm) wide*

£70-80      **RH**

A Carlton ware 'lily pink' cruet set.

*1.5in (4cm) high*

£100-150      **RH**

A 1930s Carlton ware yellow 'Apple Blossom' pattern bowl.
*9.25in (23.5cm) wide*

**£40-60**     **BEV**

A 1930s Carlton ware 'Daffodil' pattern posy holder.
*4.5in (11.5cm) high*

**£70-100**     **BEV**

A 1930s Carlton ware green 'Waterlilies' pattern jug.
*3.75in (9.5cm) high*

**£80-120**     **BEV**

A 1930s Carlton ware green 'Foxglove' pattern toast rack.
*4.5in (11.5cm) wide*

**£80-90**     **BEV**

An unusual 1930s Carlton ware 'Flower and Basket' pattern jam pot.
*4.5in (11.5cm) high*

**£70-100**     **BEV**

A 1930s Carlton ware 'Fruit Basket' pattern trefoil dish.
*8.75in (22cm) high*

**£40-60**     **BEV**

A 1930s Carlton ware pink 'Buttercup' pattern trefoil dish.
*This pattern is rare in the pink colourway, and more desirable than in the yellow colourway.*
*10.5in (26.5cm) wide*

**£150-250**     **BEV**

A 1930s Carlton ware 'Hydrangea' pattern vase.
*5in (12.5cm) high*

**£80-120**     **BEV**

A 1930s Carlton ware 'Raspberry' pattern bowl.
*10.5in (26.5cm) high*

**£70-90**     **BEV**

A pair of Carlton ware 'Geometric' pattern book ends.
*5.5in (14cm) high*

**£300-400**     **BEV**

A 1930s cream-coloured Carlton ware jug, with gilt painted Art Deco styled handle and foot.

*5.5in (14cm) high*

**£30-50** **AOY**

A light green Carlton ware jug, with gilt detailing and rare factory foil sticker.

*5in (12.5cm) high*

**£30-50** **AOY**

A 1960s Carlton ware 'Orbit' pattern jam pot.

*5.25in (13.5cm) high*

**£50-90** **BEV**

A 1960s Carlton ware 'Orbit' pattern cruet set.

*9.25in (23.5cm) wide*

**£50-80** **BEV**

A 1950s curved Carlton ware dish, with link rim and green leaf design.

*4.75in (12cm) wide*

**£10-15** **AOY**

A 1960s Carlton ware 'Orbit' pattern cheese dish.

*8in (20cm) wide*

**£50-80** **BEV**

A Carlton ware Rouge Royale leaf-shaped dish.

*6.75in (17cm) wide*

**£30-40** **AOY**

A light blue and gilt leaf-shaped Carlton ware dish.

*13.75in (35cm) long*

**£20-30** **AOY**

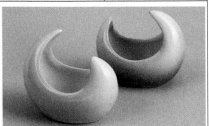

Two Carlton ware napkin rings, dish-shaped on oval bases and decorated in peach, yellow and green glazes.

**£15-25** **D**

A large 'Beethoven' character jug, with box, no. D7021.

£55-65     PSA

A large 'Parson Brown' character jug, no. D5486, small fault to rim.

£45-55     PSA

A large 'Buddy Holly' character jug, limited edition number 1411 of 2500, with box and certificate, glasses broken.

£35-45     PSA

A large 'The Walrus and the Carpenter' character jug, no. D6600.

£80-120     PSA

A large 'Desperate Dan' character jug, with box, no. D7006.

£45-55     PSA

A small Sandland 'Francis Drake' character jug, crazed.

£7-10     PSA

A large Royal Doulton 'Jimmy Durante' character jug, D.6708, from the Celebrity Collection, by S. Biggs.

*1985-1986*

£80-120     DN

A large 'The Gardener' character jug.

£55-65     PSA

A large 'Henry VIII' character jug, no. D6642.

£30-40     PSA

A small Sandland 'Robin Hood' character jug, crazed.

£8-12     PSA

A large 'Sir Henry Doulton' character jug, limited edition number 0365 of 1997, with certificate, no. D7054, style three.

*This character jug was made to commemorate the death of Sir Henry Doulton in 1887.*

£50-80     PSA

A large 'Jarge' character jug, no. D6288.

£120-180     PSA

A large Royal Doulton character jug, 'Groucho Marx', D.6710.

£40-60     DN

A large 'Glenn Miller' character jug, with box, no. D6970.

£120-180     PSA

A large 'Jesse Owens' character jug, with box, no. D7019.

£60-80     PSA

A large 'Chelsea Pensioner' character jug, no. D6817.

£55-65     PSA

A large 'Schubert' character jug, with box, no. D7056.

£70-100     PSA

A rare Beswick 'Aberdeen Angus Calf' special commission gloss figure.

£1,200-1,800     PSA

A large 'Punch and Judy' character jug, with certificate, no. D6946.

£150-200     PSA

A large 'Thomas O' Shanter' character jug, no. D6632.

£50-70     PSA

A Burleigh ware 'General Smuts' character jug.

£400-500     PSA

A Burleigh ware white-glazed 'General Smuts' character jug.

£120-180     PSA

A Royal Doulton 'Sancho Panza', large character jug, D6456.

*1957-83*

**£40-60** PSA

A Royal Doulton 'The Snowman' miniature character jug, D7158, with Christmas cracker handle, with box and certificate.

*This character jug was sold exclusively by UK retailer John Sinclairs as a limited edition of 2,000.*

*c1997*

**£40-60** PSA

A Royal Doulton 'The Viking' miniature character jug, D6526.

*1959-75*

**£50-80** PSA

A SylvaC bright glaze painted 'George Bernard Shaw' character jug, stamped "3279".

*6in (15.5cm) high*

**£50-80** MCOL

A SylvaC cellulose painted 'Neville Chamberlain' character jug, stamped "1463".

*This jug was also available with a green glaze.*

*6.5in (16.5cm) high*

**£80-120** MCOL

A 1960s SylvaC 'John F. Kennedy' character jug, stamped "2899".

*6.25in (16cm) high*

**£50-80** MCOL

A 1960s SylvaC 'Uncle Sam' character jug, stamped "2888".

*6.75in (17cm) high*

**£50-80** MCOL

**£40-60** MCOL

SYLVAC
STAFFORDSHIRE
HAND
PAINTED
MADE IN ENGLAND
MAID MARIAN

A 1970s SylvaC 'Maid Marian' character jug, stamped "5117".

*7in (18cm) high*

A 1970s SylvaC 'Robin Hood' character jug, stamped "5114".

*6.25in (16cm) high*

**£40-60** MCOL

A 1940s/50s Royal Winton Chintz 'Balmoral' pattern sandwich tray.

*These trays would have had six small plates on top of them.*

*10.25in (26cm) wide*

**£50-80** FJA

A 1940s/50s Royal Winton Chintz 'Summertime' pattern sandwich tray.

*12.25in (31cm) wide*

**£50-80** FJA

A 1940s/50s Royal Winton Chintz 'Sweet Pea' pattern sandwich tray.

*12.25in (31cm) high*

**£80-120** FJA

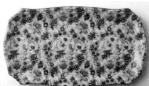

A 1940s/50s Royal Winton Chintz 'Kew' pattern sandwich tray.

*12.25in (31cm) wide*

**£60-90** FJA

A Royal Winton Chintz 'Marion' pattern dish.

*c1950    10.25in (26cm) wide*

**£60-90** FJA

A 1940s/50s Royal Winton Chintz 'Cheadle' pattern plate.

*9in (23cm) wide*

**£50-80** FJA

A Royal Winton Chintz 'Sweet Pea' pattern plate, marked for Australia on the back.

*Pieces with a blue rim are usually earlier than those with a gold rim.*

*8.75in (22.5cm) wide*

**£70-100** FJA

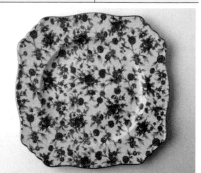

A 1940s/50s Royal Winton Chintz 'Old Cottage Chintz' plate.

*9in (23cm) wide*

**£40-60** FJA

A BCM Nelson Ware Chintz 'Rose Time' pattern plate.

*6.75in (17cm) wide*

**£20-30** FJA

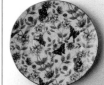

A Royal Tudor Ware Chintz plate, by Barker Bros., decorated with butterflies.

*8in (20.5cm) wide*

**£30-40** FJA

A 1930s James Kent Chintz 'Du Barry' pattern plate.

*8in (20cm) wide*

**£30-50** FJA

A 1940s/50s Royal Winton Chintz 'Marion' pattern bread-and-butter plate, from a tea set.

*9.75in (24.5cm) wide*

**£70-100** FJA

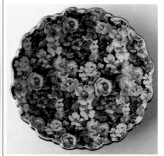

A 1940s James Kent Chintz 'Florita' pattern sweetmeat dish.

*5.25in (13cm) wide*

**£50-80** FJA

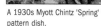

A 1930s Myott Chintz 'Spring' pattern dish.

*11.75in (30cm) wide*

**£50-80** FJA

A 1940s Royal Winton Chintz 'Black Crocus' pattern dish.

*10.75in (27cm) wide*

**£100-150** FJA

A 1940s/50s Royal Winton Chintz 'Somerset' pattern bread-and-butter plate, from a tea set.

*10in (25.5cm) wide*

**£70-100** FJA

A 1930s Wade Chintzware milk jug.

*Note the pattern covers the whole of the handle, not just the outside. Examples such as this are more desirable.*

4.25in (10.5cm) high

£60-90      FJA

A 1940s Royal Winton Chintz 'White Crocus' pattern coffee pot.

8.25in (21cm) high

£300-400      FJA

One of a pair of Mintons Chintzware candlesticks.

*Candlesticks are rare. Matched pairs are very desirable and fetch high prices.*

1890-95   8.75in (22cm) high

£100-150 (PAIR)      FJA

A 1930s Crown Ducal Chintz 'Peony' pattern mint sauce boat.

Tray 5.5in (14cm) wide

£70-100      FJA

A 1930s James Kent Chintz 'Hydrangea' pattern 'tennis' tea set.

Tray 8.75in (22cm) wide

£70-100      FJA

A 1930s Royal Corona Ware Chintz 'Rosetta' pattern jug, by Hancock & Sons.

6.25in (16cm) high

£120-180      FJA

A 1940s/50s Royal Winton Chintz 'Old Cottage Chintz' pattern 'tennis' tea set.

9.5in (24cm) wide

£50-80      FJA

A 1940s/50s Royal Winton Chintz 'Old Cottage Chintz' pattern bedside set, or tea for one set.

*Look at the bottom of each piece to check that they are all of the same period. Pieces were often broken and replaced, or sets 'made up'. Also ensure that the pattern is identical.*

Tray 10.5in (26.5cm) wide

£400-600      FJA

A Royal Winton Chintz 'Fireglow' pattern Ascot-shape sugar bowl.

4.75in (12cm) wide

£30-50      FJA

A Royal Winton Chintz 'Estelle' pattern butter-dish.

6.5in (16.5cm) wide

£80-120      FJA

A 1940s/50s Royal Winton Chintz 'Joyce Lynn' pattern butter-dish.

6.75in (17cm) wide

£100-150      FJA

A 1930s Crown Ducal Chintz 'Primula' pattern sugar sifter.
*5.25in (13.5cm) high*

**£100-150** FJA

A 1940s Royal Winton Chintz 'Kew' pattern sweetmeat basket.
*5in (12.5cm) wide*

**£120-180** FJA

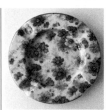

A 1940s/50s Royal Winton Chintz 'Shrewsbury' ashtray.
*4.75in (12cm) wide*

**£30-50** FJA

A Royal Winton Chintz 'Royalty' pattern sugar sifter, with original metal top.
*6in (15cm) high*

**£120-180** FJA

A 1930s James Kent Chintz 'Apple Blossom' toast rack.

*7in (18cm) long*

**£80-120** FJA

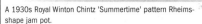

A 1930s Royal Winton Chintz 'Summertime' pattern Rheims-shape jam pot.

*Although original, examples with metal parts are not as desirable as those with transfer-decorated ceramic parts.*

*4.25in (11cm) high*

**£50-80** FJA

A 1920s Copeland late Spode Chintz toothbrush holder, with transfer-printed decoration.

*These toothbrush holders were sold as part of a toilet set and are often mistaken for vases.*

*4.75in (12cm) high*

**£60-90** FJA

A Crown Ducal Chintz 'Ivory Chintz' pattern toothbrush holder, by A.G. Richardson, from a toilet set.

**£80-120** FJA

An unusual 1930s Royal Corona Ware Chintz 'Rosetta' pattern vase, by Hancock & Sons.
*11in (28cm) high*

**£120-180** FJA

# HOT COLLECTING AREA

## CLARICE CLIFF

Clarice Cliff was a prominent and ground-breaking designer who in her heyday was a household name. Her long career ran from the 1920s until after World War II, over which period she designed more than 2,000 patterns and 500 shapes. Her pre-war work was the ultimate in modernity – outrageous, colourful and unrestrained.

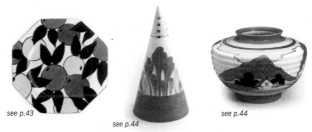

see p.43

see p.44

see p.44

- Inspired by the brilliant colours of contemporary artists, Cliff designed a range of patterns for A. J. Wilkinson Ltd in Burlsem after she joined in 1916. Now greatly in demand, these were produced as hand-painted pieces and were thickly painted with visible brushstrokes.

- Her highly successful 'Bizarre' range was launched in 1928 with A. J. Wilkinson Ltd. Radical for the time, she employed a team of female decorators known as the 'Bizarre Girls'. These 'Bizarre' pieces are probably the most popular in salerooms today, although prices can vary considerably. 'Fantasque' is another popular range.

- In the late 1920s, the tableware range was extended to encompass teapots, bookends, candlesticks and other decorative pieces. Wall masks are particularly desirable, as are any objects in strong geometric shapes and decoration.

- Among Cliff's most popular patterns are 'Crocus', 'May Avenue', 'Sunray', and 'Solitude', along with 'Honolulu' and 'Oranges and Lemons'. Popular shapes are the Art Deco styled cone-shaped bowls and sugar sifters, vases and teaware with triangular handles and feet.

- The value of an individual Cliff piece relates to its combined shape and pattern, with in-demand, highly stylised patterns and scarcer geometric shapes adding value. Chargers, 'Lotus' shape jugs, vases and plates display the pattern well so are very popular and fetch high prices.

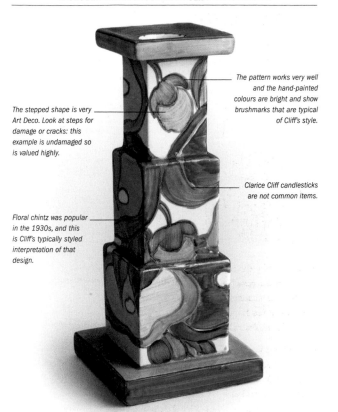

The pattern works very well and the hand-painted colours are bright and show brushmarks that are typical of Cliff's style.

The stepped shape is very Art Deco. Look at steps for damage or cracks: this example is undamaged so is valued highly.

Clarice Cliff candlesticks are not common items.

Floral chintz was popular in the 1930s, and this is Cliff's typically styled interpretation of that design.

A Clarice Cliff 'Blue Chintz' pattern stepped candlestick.

*1932-33*                                         *6.75in (17cm) high*

**£900-1,000**                                                **SCG**

## *TOP TIPS*

- Look for bright, colourful and geometric Art Deco patterns that typify Cliff's style.

- Colourways vary and can affect the price. Also make a point of examining the pattern carefully as colour variations are important.

- If buying a set, check that all the pieces match and are original.

- Most pieces carry a printed mark and signature on the base. Very small pieces such as salt and pepper shakers are often unmarked.

- Fakes are common – look for poor-quality painting, smudged designs and thick, uneven glazes.

A Clarice Cliff 'Idyll' pattern bowl, with original EPNS overlaid rim.
*1930-36    8in (20.5cm) diam*

**£300-500**                                    **SCG**

A Clarice Cliff 'Summerhouse' pattern rose bowl, printed marks.
*1931-33    9in (23cm) diam*

**£250-350**                                    **L&T**

A Clarice Cliff Bizarre 'Tennis' pattern cauldron, printed mark, minor scratches.
*c1931    3in (7.5cm) high*

**£500-800**                                    **WW**

A Clarice Cliff 'Delecia Pansies' pattern bowl.
*1933-34                    7in (18cm) diam*

**£300-500**                                    **SCG**

A Clarice Cliff 'Tulip' pattern cauldron, printed mark.
*1934-35    3in (7.5cm) high*

**£400-600**                                    **WW**

A Clarice Cliff 'Forest Glen' pattern bowl.
*1936-37                    7in (18cm) diam*

**£300-500**                                    **SCG**

A Clarice Cliff 'Newlyn' pattern bowl.
*1935-36    8.5in (21.5cm) diam*

**£500-700**                                    **SCG**

A Clarice Cliff 'Rodanthe' pattern 'Bon Jour' biscuit barrel and cover, printed mark.

*During the second half of the 1930s this pattern overtook Crocus as the top selling design.*

*1934-39                    6in (15cm) high*

**£150-250**                                    **L&T**

A Clarice Cliff Bizarre 'Pine Grove' pattern preserve pot and cover, printed mark.
*c1935                    3.5in (9cm) high*

**£250-350**                                    **WW**

A Clarice Cliff 'Honolulu' pattern side plate.

*1933-34*                     *7in (18cm) diam*

**£220-280**                               **GORL**

A Clarice Cliff 'Rudyard' pattern ribbed, tapered, cylindrical vase, shape 6028.

*This is the blue and green version of Honolulu, named after Rudyard, near Stoke.*

*1933-34*          *7in (18cm) h*

**£700-1,000**            **GORL**

A Clarice Cliff 'Melons' pattern bowl.

*6in (15cm) diam*

**£350-450**              **RH**

A Clarice Cliff 'Rhodanthe' pattern bowl.

*This pattern took over from 'Crocus' as the best-selling design. It was produced by the etching technique.*

*1934-39*     *9in (22.5cm) d*

**£280-320**              **RH**

A Clarice Cliff 'Nuage' pattern conical bowl.

*c1932*                     *7.5in (19cm) diam*

**£800-1,000**                             **SCG**

A Clarice Cliff 'Gibraltar' pattern milk jug.

*1931-35*     *4in (10cm) high*

**£500-1,000**           **FRE**

A Clarice Cliff 'Oranges and Lemons' pattern plate.

*1931-32*     *9.5in (4cm) d*

**£800-1,200**           **SCG**

A Clarice Cliff 'Solomon's Seal' cup and saucer, with solid triangular handle.

*c1930*

**£180-240**           **GORL**

A Clarice Cliff 'Crocus' pattern beehive honey pot.

*3.75in (9.5cm)*

**£150-200** **GORL**

A Clarice Cliff 'Diamonds' pattern jardinière.

*1929-30   9.5in (24cm) diam*

**£1,000-1,400** **FRE**

A Clarice Cliff 'Crocus' pattern conical sugar sifter.

*5.75in (14.5cm) high*

**£80-120** **GORL**

A Clarice Cliff 'Etna' pattern vase, of squat form with ribbed body, hand-painted with stylized mountainous landscape.

*6.75in (17cm) diam*

**£4,000-6,000** **FRE**

A Clarice Cliff Citrus 'Delicia' pattern flower ring.

*1932-34   7in (18cm) diam*

**£350-400** **SCG**

A Clarice Cliff 'Delicia Citrus' pattern Athens shape tea cup and saucer.

*The colourway of this pattern to really look out for is the rare version where the fruit has a silver and gold lustre finish.*

*c1932   cup 2.5in (6cm) high*

**£250-300** **RH**

A Clarice Cliff 'Gayday' pattern cream jug and matching cup and saucer.

*1930-34*

**£120-180** **GORL**

A Clarice Cliff 'Gayday' pattern vase, of lobed bulbous form with colourful daisies between yellow and brown bands.

*1930-34   8in (20.5cm) high*

**£800-1,200** **FRE**

A Clarice Cliff 'Crocus' pattern conical sugar sifter, printed marks.

*c1928   5.25in (13.5cm) high*

**£300-350**   L&T

A Clarice Cliff Fantasque 'Secrets' pattern three-footed sugar caster.

*1933-37   6.75in (17cm) high*

**£350-450**   CLV

A Clarice Cliff Bizarre 'Clematis' pattern sifter, with electroplated mount, printed mark.

*1930s   5.5in (14cm) high*

**£300-350**   WW

A Clarice Cliff Bizarre 'Windbells' pattern conical sugar sifter, printed mark, restored.

*1933-34   5.5in (14cm) high*

**£400-450**   WW

A Clarice Cliff 'Mowcop' pattern conical sugar sifter, printed mark.

*1937   5.5in (14cm) high*

**£250-350**   WW

A Clarice Cliff octagonal plate, painted in a geometric 'Bizarre' pattern, printed marks.

*'Bizarre' is not a specific pattern, but a name for a collection of otherwise unnamed geometric patterns.*

*c1930   8.75in (22cm) diam*

**£180-220**   L&T

A Clarice Cliff 'Comets' pattern plate.

*This is an early abstract pattern, the comets have small floral shapes at their heads.*

*1929-30   10in (25.5cm) diam*

**£800-1,200**   SCG

A Clarice Cliff 'Secrets' pattern Biarritz shape plate.

*Plates with decoration inside the centre as well as around the rim are more desirable.*

*1933-37   9in (23cm) wide*

**£600-800**   SCG

A Susie Cooper for Grays stylized floral coffee set.
*1928*                    *Coffee pot 8in (20.5cm) h*
**£500-800**                                    SCG

A Susie Cooper for Grays
stylized floral box.
*1928*           *2.5in (6.5cm) high*
**£200-250**                    SCG

A Susie Cooper for Grays fruit
bowl.

*1929*    *9.25in (23.5cm) diam*
**£300-400**           SCG

A Susie Cooper for Grays tall jug.

*1928*    *6.75in (17cm) high*
**£300-400**           SCG

A Susie Cooper 'Ross's Belfast'
dish.

*1929*        *5in (13cm) diam*
**£200-250**           SCG

A Susie Cooper hand-painted 'Geometric' coffee pot.
*1928*                  *8in (20.5cm) high*
**£300-500**                             SCG

A Susie Cooper jug, 'Bronze
Chrysanthemum Dutch' pattern.
*1930*       *4.75in (12cm) high*
**£300-400**                SCG

A Susie Cooper jug.
*1930*       *6.75in (17cm) high*
**£300-400**                SCG

A Susie Cooper for Grays
lemonade jug.
*c1928 7.25in (18.5cm) high*

**£300-350** SCG

A Susie Cooper 'Moon and Mountain' pattern jug.
*c1928* 7.5in (12cm) high

**£350-400** SCG

A Susie Cooper 'Cubist'
pattern jug.
*c1929 4.75in (12cm) high*

**£350-400** SCG

A Susie Cooper for Grays cup
and saucer.
*c1929 Saucer 5.5in (14cm) diam*

**£200-250** SCG

A Susie Cooper 'Geometric'
pattern plate.
*c1929*

**£650-750** SCG

A Susie Cooper for Grays
'Quadrupeds' pattern plate.

*c1929 8.75in (22.5cm) diam*

**£180-220** SCG

A Susie Cooper hand-painted
coffee pot.
*c1930 6in (15.5cm) high*

**£200-250** SCG

A 1930s Susie Cooper part coffee service, yellow decoration
with black dot border, comprising coffee pot, six cups, six
saucers, sugar bowl and jug, one cup badly damaged.

**£100-150** AS&S

A Susie Cooper jug.
*c1930 5in (12.5cm) high*

**£300-350** SCG

A Denby mug, made to commemorate the marriage of Prince Charles and Lady Diana Spencer.

*1981* 3.5in (9cm) diam

**£20-25** OACC

An Elizabethan Bone China royal commemorative mug, the marriage of Prince Charles and Lady Diana Spencer.

*1981*

**£18-22** OACC

A Spode bone china mug, made to commemorate the wedding of Prince Charles to Lady Diana Spencer.

*1981* 3.5in (9cm) high

**£40-60** H&G

A Kiln Cottage Pottery earthenware teapot, made to commemorate the wedding of Prince Charles to Lady Diana Spencer.

*1981* 6.75in (17.5cm) high

**£120-180** H&G

A bone china mug, by Chown, to commemorate the divorce of the Prince and Princess of Wales, limited edition of 150.

*1996* 4in (10.5cm) high

**£70-90** H&G

A Kevin Francis 'Charles and Diana' Spitting Image mug, from a limited edition of 350.

**£60-90** PSA

A pair of J. & J. May bone china mugs, made to commemorate the betrothal, on left, and wedding, on right, of Prince Charles and Lady Diana Spencer.

*c1981*                                    *3.75in (9.5cm) high*

**£50-80 (EACH)**                          **H&G**

A Crown Staffordshire bone china loving cup, made to commemorate the wedding of Prince Charles and Lady Diana Spencer.

*1981*          *3.25in (8cm) high*

**£40-60**                    **H&G**

A Royal Doulton bone china beaker, made to commemorate the wedding of the Prince of Wales and Lady Diana Spencer.

*Only six examples of this beaker were made in blue as specimens. As such they are extremely rare and highly sought after. The beaker was released publicly in brown sepia and is worth £30-40 in that colour.*

*c1981*                                    *3.75in (9.5cm) high*

**£400-600**                               **H&G**

A large Paragon bone china lion-handled loving cup, made to commemorate the marriage of the Prince of Wales and Lady Diana, limited edition of 750.

*c1981*          *5in (13cm) high*

**£250-350**                  **H&G**

A J. & J. May bone china mug, made to commemorate the birth of Prince William.

*c1982*          *3.5in (9cm) high*

**£70-100**                   **H&G**

A pair of Royal Crown Derby bone china miniature loving cups, made to commemorate the births of Prince William and Prince Harry respectively.

*c1982-1984*

**£50-80 (EACH)**                          **H&G**

A Caverswall bone china beaker, Prince Charles' 40th birthday, limited edition 250.

*1988*          *4.5in (11.5cm) high*

**£50-80**                    **H&G**

A Wedgwood 1953 coronation mug, designed by Eric Ravilious, of cylindrical form, printed and painted in colours, printed and painted marks.

*4in (10cm) high*

**£350-400** **L&T**

An Arthur Wood earthenware lion-handled mug, made to commemorate the coronation of Queen Elizabeth II.

*c1953 4.75in (12cm) high*

**£50-80** **H&G**

A Wedgwood 1953 coronation mug, designed by Richard Guyatt, of cylindrical form, with printed and painted marks.

*c1953 4in (10cm) high*

**£100-150** **L&T**

A Holkham Pottery mug, made to commemorate the coronation of Queen Elizabeth II.

*c1953 3in (8.5cm) high*

**£30-50** **H&G**

A small Arthur Bowker bone china mug to commemorate the coronation of Queen Elizabeth II.

*c1953 3.25in (8.5cm) high*

**£30-50** **H&G**

A Wedgwood earthenware mug, made to commemorate the coronation of Queen Elizabeth II.

*c1953 4.25in (10.5cm) high*

**£40-60** **H&G**

A Paragon bone china dish, made to commemorate the coronation Queen Elizabeth II.

*c1953 4.25in (10.5cm) diam*

**£30-50** **H&G**

A Paragon 'Coronation' china plate, printed and over-enamelled with the Royal Coat of Arms, within a cobalt blue border inscribed in gilt, printed marks.

*10.5in (26.5cm) diam*

**£80-120** **HAMG**

A Fotostile earthenware plaque, to commemorate Queen Elizabeth II's coronation.

*c1953 6in (15cm) high*

**£40-60** **H&G**

A Bradmere House bone china mug, to commemorate the 99th birthday of H.M. Queen Elizabeth the Queen Mother, from a limited edition of 99.

*1999*        *3.5in (9cm) high*

**£30-50**        **H&G**

A Caverswall bone china lionhead beaker, made to commemorate the 100th birthday of H.M. Queen Elizabeth the Queen Mother, from a limited edition of 500.

*2000*        *4.25in (11cm) high*

**£45-55**        **H&G**

A Chown bone china mug, made to commemorate the 101st birthday of H.M. Queen Elizabeth the Queen Mother, from a limited edition of 70.

*2001*        *3.75in (9.5cm) high*

**£50-80**        **H&G**

A Salisbury bone china mug, made to commemorate the coronation of Queen Elizabeth II.

*1953*        *3in (7.5cm) diam*

**£15-25**        **OACC**

A Caverswall bone china lionhead beaker, made to commemorate the life *in memoriam* of H.M. Queen Elizabeth the Queen Mother, from a limited edition.

*2002*        *4.25in (11cm) high*

**£30-50**        **H&G**

A china mug, made to commemorate the coronation of Queen Elizabeth II, illegible mark, ink stains inside.

*1953*        *3.25in (8cm) diam*

**£10-15**        **OACC**

A Royal Doulton bone china beaker, made to commemorate the coronation of Queen Elizabeth II.

*1953*        *4in (10cm) high*

**£40-60**        **H&G**

An Aynsley mug, made to commemorate the Silver Jubilee of Queen Elizabeth II, with a list of the kings and queens of England on the reverse.

*1977*        *3.25in (8.5cm) diam*

**£30-50**        **OACC**

A Copeland Spode Winston Churchill toby jug.

*As well as this white version, which was made for the home market, there is a coloured version.*

c1942          8in (20cm) h

£150-200          H&G

A Panorama bone china plate, made to commemorate Harold Wilson's second term as Prime Minister, from a limited edition of 50.

1974    10.5in (26.5cm) diam

£70-90          H&G

A Caverswall plate, made to commemorate Margaret Thatcher's election on 3rd May, 1979, from a limited edition of 1,979.

1979    10.5in (27cm) diam

£60-90          H&G

A Caverswall mug, made to commemorate the convening of the first European Parliament.

1979    3.75in (9.5cm) high

£25-35          H&G

A Royal Doulton bone china loving cup, to commemorate Margaret Thatcher's election as the first female Prime Minister of Great Britain.

1979    4in (10cm) high

£30-50          H&G

A mug depicting Margaret Thatcher, to commemorate the 50th annual Conservative Women's conference.

1980    3.75in (9.5cm) high

£35-45          H&G

A Coalport bone china goblet, made to commemorate Margaret Thatcher's second election victory, from a limited edition of 500.

1983    4.5in (11.5cm)high

£80-120          H&G

A Caverswall Winston Churchill plate, made to commemorate 50 years since Churchill first became prime minister.

8.5in (22cm) diam

£30-50          H&G

A rare Goss commemorative bowl for the Empire Exhibition, showing Burn's Cottage, a sprig of lucky white heather and a Glasgow thistle.

*1938*                    *3in (7.5cm) high*

**£60-70**                    **AOY**

A Carlton ware oval dish, commemorating the Empire Exhibition, Glasgow.

*1938*                    *8.75in (22.5cm) long*

**£60-80**                    **AOY**

An unmarked ceramic mug commemorating the Empire Exhibition, Glasgow.

*The Tower of Empire depicted on this mug was meant to remain after the Exhibition. However, it was pulled down and, although urban myth whispered that it was used by the German airforce as a landmark, it is more likely that the cost of its upkeep and its presence on Government-owned land led to it being dismantled.*

*1938*                    *3in (7.5cm) high*

**£50-70**                    **AOY**

A Carlton ware pickle jar, commemorating the Empire Exhibition, Glasgow, with pear-shaped handle to lid, with "Supplied by Treron, Glasgow" stamp to base.

*1938*        *3.25in (8.5cm) high*

**£50-60**                    **AOY**

A Carlton ware toast rack, commemorating the Empire Exhibition, in Glasgow, with transfer showing the Tower of Empire and mark to base reading "Supplied by Treron Glasgow".

*1938*        *3.5in (9cm) long*

**£50-60**                    **AOY**

A scarce translucent pressed glass plate, commemorating the Empire Exhibition, Glasgow, showing the Tower of Empire.

*1938*        *6.5in (16.5cm) wide*

**£60-80**                    **AOY**

A Cornish ware 'rice' storage jar with lid, and T. G. Green stamp to base.

*4in (10cm) high*

£50-70       **GA**

A Cornish ware "barley" storage jar with lid, and T. G. Green stamp to base.

*5in (12.5cm) high*

£80-120       **GA**

A Cornish ware 'currants' storage jar with lid, and T. G. Green stamp to base.

*5in (12.5cm) high*

£40-60       **GA**

A Cornish ware "nutmegs" spice jar with lid, and T. G. Green stamp to base.

*2.5in (6.5cm) high*

£50-80       **GA**

A Cornish ware "ginger" spice jar with lid, and T. G. Green stamp to base.

*2.5in (6.5cm) high*

£70-100       **GA**

A Cornish ware "candied-peel" spice jar with lid, and T. G. Green stamp to base.

*2.5in (6.5cm) high*

£100-150       **GA**

A rare Cornish ware 'meal' storage jar, with lid and T. G. Green stamp to base.

*7in (17.5cm) high*

£300-350       **GA**

A Cornish ware jug, with T. G. Green stamp to base.

*4.5in (11.5cm) high*

£35-45       **GA**

A Cornish ware rolling pin.

*Barrel 9.75in (24.5cm) long*

£70-100       **GA**

A Cornish ware "icing sugar" storage jar with lid, and T. G. Green stamp to base.

*5.5in (14cm) high*

A Cornish ware "loaf sugar" storage jar with lid, and T. G. Green stamp to base.

*5in (12.5cm) high*

£100-150      **GA**      £70-100      **GA**

A Cornish ware "olive oil" bottle, made by the Cornish Collectors Club, and with T. G. Green stamp to base.

*7.25in (18.5cm) high*

A Cornish ware "vinegar" bottle, with T. G. Green stamp to base, lacks stopper.

*7.25in (18.5cm) high*

A Cornish ware beaker, with T. G. Green stamp to base.

*4in (10cm) high*

£40-60      **GA**      £70-100      **GA**      £30-50      **GA**

A Cornish ware salt box, with wooden lid, and T. G. Green stamp to base.

*4.5in (11.5cm) high*

A Cornish ware cheese dish, with T. G. Green stamp to base.

*8.5in (21.5cm) wide*

£80-100      **GA**      £40-60      **GA**

A Cornish ware mug, with T. G. Green stamp to base.

*3.5in (9cm) diam*

**£5-10** **GA**

A Cornish ware plate, with T. G. Green stamp to base.

*7.5in (19cm) diam*

**£10-15** **GA**

A Cornish ware sugar sifter.

*5.5in (14cm) high*

**£40-60** **GA**

A Cornish ware teapot, with 'Cloverleas' and T.G. Green stamp to base.

*5in (12.5cm) high*

**£30-40** **GA**

A Cornish ware cafetière, probably 1960s, made for the Australian market.

*7.5in (19cm) high*

**£70-100** **GA**

Two yellow-and-white Cornish ware egg cups.

*2in (5cm) diam*

**£5-10 EACH** **GA**

A yellow and white Cornish ware funnel, a special edition for the Cornish ware Collectors Club.

*3.25in (8.5cm) high*

**£50-75** **GA**

A Cornish ware butter dish with lid, by Judith Onion, with T. G. Green stamp to base.

*5.5in (14cm) wide*

**£40-60** **GA**

A yellow and white Cornish ware plate, with T. G. Green stamp to base.

*9in (23cm) diam*

£10-15                                    GA

A Domino jug, with T. G. Green stamp to base.

*4in (10cm) high*

£35-45                                    GA

A Domino toast rack, with T. G. Green stamp to base.

*6.5in (16.5cm) wide*

£40-50                                    GA

A Domino sugar bowl, with T. G. Green stamp to base.

*3.75in (9.5cm) high*

£20-30                                    GA

A T. G. Green teapot, with stamp to base.

*Although not classed as Cornish ware, this teapot was produced by the same maker, T.G. Green.*

*4.25in (10.5cm) high*

£70-100                                   GA

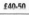

# HOT COLLECTING AREA

## ROYAL DOULTON FIGURINES

Although Doulton was founded in 1815, it was not until the 1920s that the company began in earnest to release the large and varied range of figurines that have become so popular with collectors today. The range now includes more than 2,000 different figures.

see p.62    see p.60    see p.62

- Look on the base as marks include an 'HN' number, which will identify the name of the model, the designer and the dates of the period of production. It is not usually possible to date a figurine to a particular year, except for a few exceptions. Each different figurine, in each colour it was produced in, will bear an individual number.

- 'Fair Ladies' are the most popular collecting subject. Posed in expressive, carefree or romantic postures, Royal Doulton ladies vary tremendously in value depending on the model, date and colour. Other popular subjects include children, character studies such as jesters, and historical and literary personalities.

- Values tend to be high for early figures dating from the 1920s and 30s and for those produced for limited periods. Many of these designs were made in runs of fewer than 2,000, which makes them comparatively rare and valuable today.

- Some collectors focus on figurines in a specific colour. A knowledge of the many colour variations is essential when deciding whether to buy or sell a Royal Doulton figure, as rare colours will increase the value.

- Modellers are also important. Leslie Harradine is perhaps the most notable and is renowned for his stylish 'Fair Ladies'. He released his first figures in 1920 and designed at least one figure per month for 30 years. Mary Nicholl is known for her nautical personalities and characters released during the 1950s and 60s.

## A CLOSER LOOK AT A ROYAL DOULTON FIGURINE

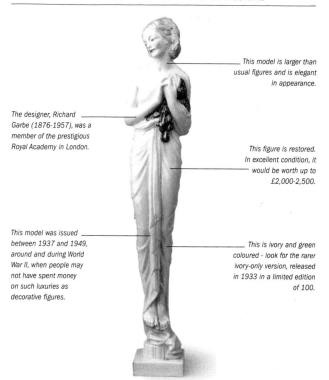

*This model is larger than usual figures and is elegant in appearance.*

*The designer, Richard Garbe (1876-1957), was a member of the prestigious Royal Academy in London.*

*This figure is restored. In excellent condition, it would be worth up to £2,000-2,500.*

*This model was issued between 1937 and 1949, around and during World War II, when people may not have spent money on such luxuries as decorative figures.*

*This is ivory and green coloured - look for the rarer ivory-only version, released in 1933 in a limited edition of 100.*

A rare Royal Doulton 'Spring' figure HN1774, designed by Richard Garbe RA.

*1937-49*

*21in (53.3cm) high*

**£1,200-1,500**

**PSA**

### TOP TIPS

- Look for the 'HN' number on the base as this will identify the model name, the designer and the dates of production.

- Always consider the colour, subject matter and period of production when assessing a figurine.

- Collect models in the best condition - scratches, wear to paint and cracks will reduce value dramatically.

- Look out for the 'Middle Earth' series, inspired by Tolkien's 'Lord of The Rings', which are already becoming harder to find and more valuable due to the films' success.

A Royal Doulton 'Autumn Breezes' figure HN1934, designed by Leslie Harradine.

*Leslie Harradine was one of Royal Doulton's key modellers. He released his first figure in 1920 and, for 30 years, designed at least one figure per month. He is renowned for his stylish ladies which dominated 1930s production.*

*1940-97*                    8in (19cm) high

**£70-100**                    **CLV**

A Royal Doulton 'Top o' the Hill' figure HN1834, designed by Leslie Harradine.
*1937-present*
7.25in (18.5cm) h

**£80-100**                    **CLV**

A Royal Doulton 'Paisley Shawl' figure HN1392, by Leslie Harradine.

*This figure in purple HN1707 can fetch twice the value of this version.*

*1930-1949*                    8.5in (21.5cm) high

**£150-200**                    **D**

A rare Royal Doulton 'Colinette' figure HN 1998, by Leslie Harradine.
*1947-49*    7.25in (18.5cm) h

**£160-200**                    **DN**

A Royal Doulton 'The Mask Seller' figure HN2103, designed by Leslie Harradine, boxed.
*1953-95*    8.5in (21.5cm) h

**£100-150**                    **D**

A Royal Doulton miniature figure 'Sweet Anne' M5, designed by Leslie Harradine.

*1932-45*    4in (10cm) high

**£120-180**                    **DN**

A Royal Doulton 'Mr Pickwick' figure style 3 HN2099, by Leslie Harradine and from the Dickens series.
*1952-67    7.5in (19cm) high*

**£70-90**                              **DN**

A Royal Doulton 'Marie' figure HN1370, designed by Leslie Harradine, restored.
*1930-88    4.75in (12cm) h*

**£20-30**                              **PSA**

A rare Royal Doulton 'Erminie' miniature figure M40, designed by Leslie Harradine.
*1933-45                              4in (10cm) high*

**£400-600**                              **PSA**

A Royal Doulton 'Past Glory' figure HN2484, designed by M. Nicholl.
*1973-79    7.5in (19cm) high*

**£120-170**                              **PSA**

A Royal Doulton 'A Good Catch' figure HN2258, designed by M. Nicholl, from the Sea Characters series.
*1966-86    7.5in (19cm) high*

**£80-120**                              **D**

A Royal Doulton 'The Captain' figure HN2260, designed by M. Nicholl and from the Sea Characters series.
*1965-82    9.5in (24cm) high*

**£160-200**                              **PSA**

A Royal Doulton 'Omar Khayyam' figure HN2247, designed by M. Nicholl.
*1965-83    6.25in (16cm) h*

**£120-180**                              **CLV**

A Royal Doulton 'Sweet Sixteen' figure HN2231, designed by M. Davies and from the Teenagers series.

*Margaret 'Peggy' Davies produced her first figure in 1946 and, working on a contract basis, produced around 250 designs until her retirement in 1984. Dominating the collection as Harradine moved towards retirement, she is known for her 1950s figures in contemporary dress, historical characters and studies of children.*

A Royal Doulton 'The Young Master' figure HN2872, designed by M. Davies, boxed.

*1980-89*    7.5in (19cm) high

**£120-180**                         **D**

*1958-65*    7.25in (18.4cm) h

**£80-120**                       **PSA**

A Royal Doulton 'St George' figure HN2051, designed by M. Davies.

*1950-85*    7.5in (19cm) high

**£250-350**                      **PSA**

A Royal Doulton 'Take Me Home' figure HN3662, designed by N. Pedley, boxed.

*1995-99*    7.5in (19cm) high

**£30-50**                           **D**

A Royal Doulton 'Christine' figure HN3767, designed by N. Pedley.

*1996-98*    8in (20cm) high

**£70-100**                       **CLV**

A Royal Doulton 'The Jester' miniature figure HN3335, designed by C.J. Noke and remodelled by R. Tabbenor.

*1990*    4in (10cm) high

**£100-150**                      **PSA**

A Royal Doulton 'The Genie' figure HN2989, designed by R. Tabbenor, boxed.

*1983-90*    10in (25.5cm) h

**£80-120**                          **D**

A Royal Doulton 'Barbara' figure HN3441, from a limited edition of 9,500, designed by P. Gee.

7.5in (19cm) high

**£70-100**                          **D**

A Royal Doulton 'Amy' figure HN3316, designed by P. Gee. This figure was 'Figure of the Year' in 1991.

*1991*                                    *8in (20.5cm) high*

**£320-380**                                         **PSA**

A Royal Doulton 'Sisterly Love' figure HN3130, designed by P. Parsons, from Reflections Series, boxed.

*1987-95        9in (23cm) high*

**£55-65**                     **D**

A Royal Doulton 'Susan' figure HN3050, designed by P. Parsons, boxed.

*1986-95  8.5in (21.6cm) high*

**£90-110**               **PSA**

A Royal Doulton 'The Wizard' figure HN2877, designed by A. Maslankowski.

*1979+        9in (24cm) high*

**£80-120**               **PSA**

A Royal Doulton 'Partners' figure HN3119, designed by A. Maslankowski.

*1990-92      6in (17cm) high*

**£90-110**               **PSA**

A Royal Doulton 'The Clown' figure HN2890, designed by W.K. Harper.

*1979-99      9in (23cm) high*

**£120-180**              **PSA**

A Royal Doulton 'Grace Darling' limited edition figure HN3089, designed by E.J. Griffiths.

*This model was commissioned by 'Lawleys By Post' in a limited edition of 9,500 and was issued in 1987.*

*1987        9in (23cm) high*

**£150-200**              **PSA**

A Fornasetti Balarms ceramic pot.
*1958*

**£80-120** FM

A Fornasetti limited edition plate, made to celebrate the 45th annual international automobile exhibition at Turin, Italy, 3rd-16th December 1967.
*7.75in (20cm) diam*

**£60-90** FM

A Fornasetti calendar plate.

*1969      9.5in (24cm) diam*

**£100-150** FM

A Fornasetti Astronomers plate, made for annual Christmas release.

*1969      9.5in (24cm) diam*

**£100-150** FM

A Fornasetti limited edition plate, made to celebrate the 3rd international exhibition of industrial vehicles, Turin, Italy, 3rd-11th November 1974.
*7.75in (20cm) diam*

**£60-90** FM

A commemorative Fornasetti plate, made to celebrate 50 years of the company (1925-1975).
*9.5in (24cm) diam*

**£100-150** FM

One of a series of Fornasetti opera plates, featuring José from George Bizet's 'Carmen'.
*10.25in (26cm) diam*

**£120-180** FM

A Fornasetti ceramic paperweight, with crossed keys motif.

*3.5in (9cm) wide*

**£100-150** FM

One of a series of Fornasetti Italian artists plates, featuring Andrea Mantegna.
*10in (25.5cm) diam*

**£100-150** FM

A set of Fornasetti 'Vini & Legumi' coasters, with original box.

*4.25in (10.5cm) wide*

£150-200      FM

A pair of Fornasetti kidney-shaped dishes.

£40-60      FM

A Fornasetti 'crème de cocu' ashtray.

*6in (15cm) diam*

£80-120      FM

A set of six Fornasetti cups.

*2in (5cm) high*

£150-250 (SET)      FM

A rare Fornasetti dish, with sun motifs.

*6.75in (17cm) diam*

£100-150      FM

A Fornasetti 'Al Merito' (For Merit) teacup and saucer.

*Saucer 5.5in (14cm) diam*

£150-200      FM

A pair of Fornasetti dishes.

*5.5in (14cm) long*

£60-90      FM

A Fornasetti ceramic biscuit barrel.

*9.5in (24cm) high*

£600-800      FM

A pair of Fornasetti pen holders.

*2.75in (7cm) high*

£100-150      FM

A 1970s pastel violet Hornsea slipware baluster vase, with zig-zag pattern to neck.

*9.25in (23.5cm) high*

**£70-90** GC

A small light green Hornsea slipware baluster vase, with zig-zag pattern to neck.

*7.5in (19cm) high*

**£50-70** GC

A small light blue Hornsea slipware vase with zig-zag pattern to base of neck.

*4in (10cm) high*

**£20-30** GC

A small ochre yellow Hornsea slipware oval bud vase, with zig-zag pattern to base of neck, with metal flower holder.

*10in (25.5cm) wide*

**£80-100** GC

A large grey Hornsea slipware oval bud vase, with zig-zag pattern to base and metal grid flower holder.

*11.5in (29.5cm) wide*

**£80-120** GC

A Hornsea Pottery flower holder, designed by Marion Campbell, mould no. "302".

*c1957    6in (15.25cm) high*

**£200-250** GGRT

A Hornsea Pottery Home Décor range 'Studio Craft' pattern fluted vase, designed by John Clappison, mould no. "351".

*c1960    11in (28cm) high*

**£280-320** GGRT

A Hornsea Pottery vase, designed by John Clappison, mould no. "382".

*c1960    11in (28cm) high*

**£100-150** GGRT

A Hornsea Studio Craft dish, in the form of a viking longboat.

*c1950    11in (28cm) wide*

**£60-80** MHT

A 1940s Hummel figure, 'Weary Wanderer', restored.

*6in (15cm) high*

**£80-90** **OACC**

A Hummel figure, 'Sister', small restoration to hair.

*5.5in (14cm) high*

**£80-100** **OACC**

A Hummel figure, 'Mother's Darling'.

*1940-56* *6in (15cm) high*

**£80-120** **OACC**

A Hummel Club figure, 'Forever Yours', first issue 1996/7.

*4in (10cm) high*

**£60-80** **OACC**

A Hummel figure, 'For Mother', dated.

*1963* *5in (12.5cm) high*

**£60-80** **PSA**

A Hummel figure, 'Merry Wanderer'.

*4in (10cm) high*

**£60-80** **OACC**

A Hummel figure, 'Meditation'.

*4.5in (11cm) high*

**£40-60** **OACC**

A Hummel figure, 'Cuddles', dated.

*1997* *3.5in (9cm) high*

**£40-60** **OACC**

A Hummel Club figure, 'Garden Treasures', membership year 1998/99.

*3.5in (9cm) high*

**£40-60** **OACC**

A Hummel figure, 'My best friend', first issue 1998.

*3.5in (9cm) high*

**£40-60** **OACC**

A German Hummel-style figure, modelled as a boy with an umbrella, black painted marks to base.

**£5-10** **PSA**

A Goebel Hummel 'Little Pharmacist' figurine, stamped "322".

*c1955    5.75in (14.5cm) high*

**£150-200**    **MAC**

A Goebel Hummel 'Puppy Love' figurine, with some damage.

*c1955    4.75in (12cm) high*

**£120-180**    **MAC**

A Goebel Hummel 'Strolling Along' figurine, stamped "5".

*5in (13cm) high*

**£220-280**    **GCA**

A Goebel Hummel 'Good Friends' figurine, stamped "182".

*4in (10cm) high*

**£120-180**    **GCA**

A Goebel Hummel 'Prayer before Battle', stamped "20".

*4.25in (11cm) high*

**£120-180**    **GCA**

A Goebel Hummel ''Favourite Pet' figurine, stamped "361".

*c1960    4.25in (11cm) high*

**£200-250**    **MAC**

A Goebel Hummel 'Wayside Harmony' figurine, stamped "111 3/0".

*4.25in (10.5cm) high*

**£80-120**    **MAC**

A Goebel Hummel 'Just Resting' figurine, stamped "112 3/0".

*3.75in (9.5cm) high*

**£80-120**    **MAC**

A Goebel Hummel 'Out of Range' figurine, stamped "56/A".

*6.5in (16.5cm) high*

**£200-250**    **MAC**

A Goebel Hummel figurine, of a Scottie dog with a slipper and a girl up a tree.

*6.25in (16cm) high*

**£100-150**    **GCA**

A Goebel Hummel 'Little Bookkeeper' figurine, stamped "306".

*c1965    4.5in (11.5cm) high*

**£300-350**    **GCA**

A Goebel Hummel 'School Girl' figurine, stamped "81 2/0".

*4.5in (11.5cm) high*

**£80-120** GCA

A Goebel Hummel 'Little Gardener' figurine, stamped "74".

*4.25in (11cm) high*

**£70-100** MAC

A Goebel Hummel 'Autumn Harvest' figurine, stamped "355".

*5in (12.5cm) high*

**£100-170** MAC

A Goebel Hummel 'Chimney Sweep' figurine, stamped "12 2/0".

*This model was originally modelled by sculptor Arthur Moeller in 1935 but was remodelled many times following this. The other vintage version on this page has differences including a different mould number and a turned head and is more valuable than this version.*

*4in (10cm) high*

**£70-100** MAC

A Goebel Hummel 'Happy Pastime' figure, stamped "69".

*3.25in (8.5cm) high*

**£80-120** GCA

A Goebel Hummel 'Chimney Sweep' figurine, stamped "12/I".

*5.5in (14cm) high c1940*

**£120-180** GCA

A Goebel Hummel 'Trumpet Boy' figurine, stamped "97".

*4.25in (11cm) high*

**£60-90** MAC

A Midwinter Fashion shape 'Bali H'ai' pattern plate, designed by John Russell, with printed and enamelled decoration.

*c1960  8.75in (22.5cm) diam*

**£5-8**  FFM

A Midwinter Stylecraft shape plate, unnamed designer, transfer-printed with hand-painted banding.

*c1953  6in (15.5cm) diam*

**£3-6**  FFM

A Midwinter Fashion shape 'Magnolia' pattern plate, designed by John Russell, transfer-printed.

*c1955  6in (15.5cm) diam*

**£3-6**  FFM

A Midwinter Stylecraft shape 'Ming Tree' pattern platter, designed by Jessie Tait, with printed and enamelled decoration.

*c1953  12in (30.5cm) wide*

**£20-30**  FFM

A Midwinter Fashion shape 'Falling Leaves' pattern plate, designed by Jessie Tait, with unusual hand-painted background texture and transfer-printed decoration.

*c1955  7.5in (19.5cm) diam*

**£20-30**  FFM

A Midwinter Fashion shape 'Bouquet' pattern meat plate, unnamed designer, transfer-printed.

*c1960  13.75in (35cm) diam*

**£15-25**  FFM

A Midwinter 'Vegetable' pattern plate, designed by Sir Terence Conran, transfer-printed.

*c1955  7.75in (19.5cm) diam*

**£60-80**  REN

A Midwinter Stylecraft shape 'Riviera' pattern meat platter, designed by Sir Hugh Casson, with printed and enamelled decoration.

*c1954  12in (30.5cm) wide*

**£20-30**  FFM

A hand-painted Midwinter Stylecraft shape 'Primavera' pattern plate, designed by Jessie Tait.

*c1954  9.5in (24.5cm) diam*

**£20-35**  FFM

A Midwinter Pottery 'Chequers' pattern plate, designed by Sir Terence Conran.

*c1957*    *8.75in (22cm) diam*

**£70-100**    **GGRT**

A Midwinter Pottery 'Chequers' pattern oval platter, designed by Sir Terence Conran.

*Conran's 'Chequers' pattern began in 1951 as a textile pattern for David Whitehead, having featured in the Festival of Britain.*

*c1957*    *13.75in (35cm) wide*

**£200-300**    **GGRT**

A Midwinter Pottery 'Patio' pattern plate, designed by Jessie Tait.

*c1959*    *9.5in (24cm) diam*

**£75-85**    **GGRT**

A Midwinter Pottery 'Caribbean' pattern plate, designed by Jessie Tait.

*This was the first Midwinter pattern to utilise the innovative Murray Curvex printing method.*

*c1955*    *9.5in (24.5cm) diam*

**£80-120**    **GGRT**

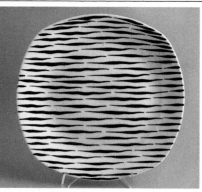

A hand-painted Midwinter Fashion shape 'Zambesi' pattern plate, designed by Jessie Tait.

*This pattern was introduced in 1956 and was so popular that it was widely copied. Beswick's 'Zebrette' range is very similar.*

*c1956*    *8.5in (22cm) diam*

**£10-20**    **FFM**

A Midwinter Pottery 'Savanna' pattern plate, designed by Jessie Tait.

*c1956*   *9.75in (24.5cm) diam*

**£40-60**    **GGRT**

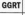

A Midwinter Pottery 'Savanna' pattern bowl, designed by Jessie Tait, with yellow interior.

*c1956*    *10in (25.5cm) diam*

**£80-120**    **GGRT**

Two Midwinter Fashion shape 'Festival' pattern milk or water jugs, designed by Jessie Tait, hand-painted.

*1955   Larger 5.25in (13.5cm) high*

**£20-30 (EACH)**    **FFM**

A Midwinter Fashion shape coffee pot with later version of 'Happy Valley' pattern, designed by Jessie Tait.

c1961    8.5in (22cm) high

**£25-45**    FFM

A Midwinter Fashion shape 'Magic Moments' pattern plate, designed by Jessie Tait, hand-painted.

c1956    6in (15.5cm) diam

**£20-30**    FFM

A Midwinter Fashion shape 'Monaco' pattern plate, designed by Jessie Tait, transfer-printed.

c1956    8.5in (22cm) diam

**£8-15**    FFM

A Midwinter Fashion shape 'Melody' pattern trio set, unnamed designer, transfer-printed.

c1958    6in (15.5cm) diam

**£35-45**    FFM

A Midwinter Stylecraft shape unusual 'Mimosa' pattern trio set, unnamed designer, transfer-printed.

c1953    6in (15.5cm) diam

**£15-20**    FFM

A Midwinter 'Nature Study' pattern plate, designed by Sir Terence Conran, transfer-printed.

c1955    9.5in (24.5cm) diam

**£25-35**    FFM

A Midwinter Fashion shape 'Pierrot' pattern plate, designed by Jessie Tait, transfer-printed.

c1955    6.25in (16cm) diam

**£25-35**    FFM

A Midwinter Fashion shape 'Plant Life' trio set, by Terence Conran, transfer-printed.

c1960    6in (15cm) diam

**£40-50**    FFM

A Midwinter Fashion shape 'Primavera' pattern plate, designed by Jessie Tait, hand-painted, extremely rare, minor crack.

c1954    12.5in (32cm) diam

**£30-50**    FFM

A Midwinter Fashion shape 'Cherokee' pattern trio, designed by Jessie Tait, hand-painted.

*c1957   Plate 6in (15.5cm) diam*

**£30-40**                    FFM

A late 1950s Midwinter Fashion shape 'Contemporary' pattern meat plate, unnamed designer, transfer-printed.

*13.75in (35cm) diam*

**£18-25**                    FFM

A Midwinter Stylecraft shape 'Cottage Ivy' pattern milk jug, designed by Jessie Tait, hand-painted.

*c1953   2.25in (5.5cm) high*

**£15-20**                    FFM

A Midwinter Stonehenge 'Day' pattern trio set, possibly by Eve Midwinter, transfer-printed.

*1970s   6.75in (17.5cm) diam*

**£15-25**                    FFM

A Midwinter Stylecraft shape 'Domino Variant' pattern trio set, designed by Jessie Tait, hand-painted.

*This variation is rarer than the 'Red Domino' pattern.*

*c1954   16in (15.5cm) diam*

**£25-30**                    FFM

A hand-painted Midwinter Stylecraft shape 'Fantasy' pattern plate, designed by Jessie Tait.

*c1953   8.5in (22cm) diam*

**£20-30**                    FFM

A hand-painted Midwinter Fashion shape 'Festival' pattern egg cup, designed by Jessie Tait.

*c1955   1.75in (4.5cm) high*

**£20-25**                    FFM

A Midwinter Fine shape 'Focus' pattern meat plate, designed by Barbara Brown, transfer-printed.

*c1954   15.5in (39.5cm) diam*

**£15-25**                    FFM

A Midwinter Fashion shape 'Happy Valley' pattern plate, designed by Jessie Tait, with printed and enamelled decoration.

*c1959   6in (15.5cm) diam*

**£8-12**                    FFM

A Midwinter Stylecraft shape 'Homeweave' pattern trio set, designed by Jessie Tait, hand painted.

*This is the rare version with coloured holloware.*

*c1960   Plate 6in (15.5cm) diam*

**£25-35**                    FFM

A Keith Murray for Wedgwood matt green fluted vase, with signature mark.

*This shape, known as 3802, was introduced in 1933.*

*c1930*          9in (23cm) high

**£500-800**          SCG

A Keith Murray for Wedgwood matt green bulbous ribbed vase, with signature mark.

*c1932*                    6in (15cm) high

**£600-900**                    SCG

A Keith Murray for Wedgwood matt green ribbed vase, with signature mark.

*c1932*
6in (15cm) high

**£500-800 SCG**

A Keith Murray for Wedgwood matt green ribbed vase, with "KM" mark.

*c1934*          5in (12.5cm) high

**£500-800**          SCG

A Keith Murray for Wedgwood matt green, tall, fluted vase, with "KM" mark.

*c1934*          9.5in (24cm) high

**£400-600**          SCG

A Keith Murray for Wedgwood matt green, tall, fluted vase, with signature mark.

*c1932*          12in (30.5cm) high

**£500-800**          SCG

A Keith Murray for Wedgwood 'Etruscan' white-lined green tall vase, with "KM" mark.

*c1934*          8in (20.5cm) high

**£350-400**          SCG

A Keith Murray for Wedgwood matt green vase, "KM" mark.

*c1934*    6.5in (16.5cm) diam

**£320-380**          SCG

A Keith Murray for Wedgwood matt green plain bowl, with signature mark.

*c1932*          11in (28cm) diam

**£400-600**          SCG

A Keith Murray for Wedgwood matt green sweet dish, with signature mark.

*c1932*          4in (10cm) diam

**£40-60**          SCG

A Keith Murray for Wedgwood matt green lidded sugar bowl, with signature mark.

c1932     4in (10cm) diam

**£180-220**     **SCG**

A Keith Murray for Wedgwood matt green ashtray, with signature mark.

c1932     4.5in (11.5cm) diam

**£50-80**     **SCG**

A Keith Murray and others for Wedgwood matt green tea cup and saucer.

Saucer 5in (12.5cm) diam

**£40-60**     **SCG**

A Keith Murray for Wedgwood matt green dinner plate, with "KM" mark.

c1934     8in (20.5cm) diam

**£20-30**     **SCG**

A Keith Murray for Wedgwood matt green desk tray, with signature mark.

*The value is considerably reduced if the lid or the liners are missing or damaged.*

c1932     10in (25.5cm) wide

**£1,000-1,500**     **SCG**

A Keith Murray for Wedgwood moonstone ribbed vase, with "KM" mark.

c1934     6.5in (16.5cm) high

**£300-500**     **SCG**

A Keith Murray for Wedgwood moonstone ribbed vase, signature mark.

*This shape is hard to find.*

c1932     6in (15cm) high

**£700-1,000**     **SCG**

A Keith Murray for Wedgwood moonstone ribbed vase, with "KM" mark.

c1934     7.25in (18.5cm) high

**£400-600**     **SCG**

A Keith Murray for Wedgwood moonstone bulbous vase, with "KM" mark.

c1934     6.5in (16.5cm) high

**£320-380**     **SCG**

A Keith Murray for Wedgwood moonstone ribbed vase, with "KM" mark.

c1934     5.5in (14cm) high

**£500-700**     **SCG**

A Keith Murray for Wedgwood moonstone vase, with signature mark.
*c1932      7.5in (19cm) high*

**£200-250**                    **SCG**

A Keith Murray for Wedgwood moonstone vase, with signature mark.
*c1932      6.5in (16.5cm) high*

**£400-600**                    **SCG**

A Keith Murray for Wedgwood moonstone ribbed vase, with signature mark.
*This style of mark was introduced from 1932.*
*c1932                    6.5in (16.5cm) high*

**£600-850**                                        **SCG**

A Keith Murray for Wedgwood moonstone tall vase, with signature mark.
*c1932      11in (28cm) high*

**£500-800**                    **SCG**

A Keith Murray for Wedgwood moonstone tankard, printed mark.
*5in (12.5cm) high*

**£50-80**                      **L&T**

A Keith Murray for Wedgwood moonstone tankard, with signature mark.
*c1932      4.75in (12cm) high*

**£30-50**                      **SCG**

A Keith Murray for Wedgwood moonstone coffee pot, with platinum-glazed handle and "KM" mark.

*c1934*

**£200-300**                    **SCG**

A Keith Murray for Wedgwood moonstone milk jug, with platinum-glazed handle and "KM" mark.
*c1934      2.5in (6.5cm) high*

**£40-60**                      **SCG**

A Keith Murray for Wedgwood blue fluted bowl, with "KM" mark.
*c1934*                     10in (25.5cm) diam

**£300-400**                     **SCG**

A Keith Murray for Wedgwood blue bowl, with "KM" mark.

*c1934*     6.5in (16.5cm) diam

**£300-400**                     **SCG**

A Keith Murray for Wedgwood blue bowl, with "KM" mark.

*c1934*     6in (15cm) diam

**£300-400**     **SCG**

A Keith Murray for Wedgwood straw bowl, with "KM" mark.

*c1934*     5.75in (14.5cm) diam

**£300-400**     **SCG**

A Keith Murray for Wedgwood straw bowl, with "KM" mark.

*c1934*     5.75in (14.5cm) diam

**£300-400**     **SCG**

A Keith Murray for Wedgwood matt straw, fluted vase, "KM" mark.
*c1934*                     7.5in (19cm) high

**£500-800**                     **SCG**

A Keith Murray for Wedgwood matt straw melon bowl, with signature mark.
*c1932*     9.5in (24cm) diam

**£200-250**     **SCG**

A Keith Murray for Wedgwood black vase, with ribbed decoration, with signature mark.

4in (10cm) high

**£400-600**     **CLV**

A Myott ware Scroll jug.

*8in (20.5cm) high*

**£300-400**  RH

A Myott ware Trumpet jug.
*8in (20.5cm) high*

**£70-100**  RH

A Myott ware Bowtie jug.
*8in (20.5cm) high*

**£150-200**  RH

A Myott ware jug.
*8.25in (21cm) high*

**£100-150**  RH

A Myott ware Dante jug.
*8.25in (21cm) high*

**£100-150**  RH

A Myott ware Dante jug.
*8.75in (22cm) high*

**£80-120**  RH

A Myott ware Dante jug.
*8.5in (21cm) high*

**£100-150**  RH

A Myott ware square neck jug.
*7.75in (19.5cm) high*

**£120-180** RH

A Myott ware square neck jug.
*7.25in (18.5cm) high*

**£80-120** RH

A Myott ware star vase.
*8.5in (21.5cm) high*

**£120-180** RH

A Myott ware Star vase.
*8.75in (22cm) high*

**£150-200** RH

A Myott ware Diamond planter, without insert.
*6in (15cm) high*

**£100-150** RH

A Myott ware spiderweb jug.
*6.5in (16cm) high*

**£150-200** RH

A Myott ware Bowtie vase.
*8in (20.5cm) high*

**£200-300** RH

A Myott ware round jug.
*6.5in (16cm) high*

**£180-220** RH

A Myott ware apple picker jug.
*8in (20.5cm) high*

**£150-200** RH

A Myott ware castle vase.
*8.5in (21.5cm) high*

**£250-350** RH

A Myott ware cat jug.
*8.25in (21cm) high*

**£1,000-1,500** RH

A 1920s Noritake cup and saucer, with hand-painted gilt decoration and lakeside scene.

*Saucer 5in (12.5cm) wide*

**£80-120** **BAD**

A Noritake hand-painted plate, with desert scene.

*6.75in (19.5cm) wide*

**£70-90** **BAD**

A 1930s hand-painted Noritake vase, decorated with flowers and birds.

*6in (15.5cm) high*

**£80-120** **BAD**

A 1930s Noritake ashtray, with hand-painted geometric pattern.

*4.5in (11.5cm) wide*

**£40-60** **BAD**

An H. & S.L. Oriental hand-painted dressing table box, with floral and gilt motifs.

*3.5in (9cm) wide*

**£40-50** **BAD**

An L. & Co. Nippon small lidded bowl, with hand-painted floral and gilt details.

*3.25in (8cm) high*

**£40-60** **BAD**

A blown-out Nippon vase, hand-painted scenic decoration with three eagles sitting on rocks, signed on bottom with green mark.

*The large size, excellent condition and exquisite detailing of the hand-painted scenic decoration make this a more valuable piece.*

*10in (25.5cm) high*

**£2,000-3,000** **JDJ**

A Nippon large two-handled scenic vase, with gold decoration, lake scene with mountains and trees.

*13in (33cm) high*

**£250-350** **JDJ**

A 1930s Mabel Lucie Attwell for Shelley 'Plane' nursery bowl.

*6in (15cm) diam*

**£120-180**     **SCG**

A 1930s Mabel Lucie Attwell for Shelley 'Good Ned' nursery bowl.

*6in (15cm) diam*

**£100-150**     **SCG**

A 1930s Mabel Lucie Attwell for Shelley 'Man in the Moon' nursery trio set.

*Plate 6in (15cm) diam*

**£350-450**     **SCG**

A 1930s Mabel Lucie Attwell for Shelley 'Man in a Caravan' nursery beaker.

*2.75in (7cm) high*

**£180-220**     **SCG**

A 1930s Mabel Lucie Attwell for Shelley 'Duck' nursery tea set.

**£800-1,200**     **BEV**

A 1930s Mabel Lucie Attwell for Shelley 'Man in the Moon' nursery beaker.

*This is a sought-after design.*

*2.75in (7cm) high*

**£200-250**     **SCG**

A Shelley Nursery tea set, designed by Mabel Lucie Attwell, comprising teapot and cover, milk-jug and sugar basin, printed factory mark, facsimile signature.

*5in (13cm) high*

**£700-800**     **WW**

A Royal Doulton 'Bunnykins' pattern child's breakfast service, comprising plate, cereal bowl and mug, all signed by the artist Barbara Vernon.

*Plate 7in (18cm) diam*

**£40-50**     **DAW**

A 1930s Mabel Lucie Attwell for Shelley nursery chamber pot.

*The mark shown is the mark found on the base of this pot and all of Attwell's ceramics with Shelley.*

**£450-550**     **SCG**

A Pendelfin 'Maud' figure, dressed in pink, chip to ear.

*1967-78    4in (10cm) high*

**£40-60**                    **PSA**

A Pendelfin 'Lucy Pocket' figure, dressed in green, out of production.

*4in (10cm) high*

**£30-40**                    **PSA**

A Pendelfin thin neck 'Mother' figure, dressed in lilac, out of production, minor wear.

*7.5in (12.5cm) high*

**£180-220**                  **PSA**

A Pendelfin 'Midge Rabbit' figure, with two crumbs, dressed in blue, out of production.

*Midge's value depends on how many crumbs are on her dress, which vary between one and three. The more crumbs seen, the more she is worth!*

*1956-65    3.25in (12.5cm) high*

**£80-120**                   **PSA**

A Pendelfin 'Uncle Soames Rabbit' figure, dressed in yellow, out of production.

*Look for the earlier versions produced around 1959 which are less colourful and were unpopular. Their rarity today means their value is usually double that of the colourful versions.*

*1959-85*
*7.25in (12.5cm) high*

**£40-60**                    **PSA**

A Pendelfin 'George And The Dragon' figure, out of production.

*5.25in (13.5cm) high*

**£80-120**                   **PSA**

A Pendelfin 'Gramps' figure, out of production.

*1999    4.5in (11.5cm) high*

**£25-35**                    **PSA**

A Pendelfin 'Treasure' figure, out of production.

*1999-2000    4.5in (11.5cm) high*

**£35-45**                    **PSA**

A limited edition Pendelfin 'The Auctioneer' figure, from the Pendelfin Auction 2000, out of production.

*2000      5in (12.5cm) high*

**£40-60**                          **PSA**

A Pendelfin 'Cracker Rabbit' figure.

*c2000    4.5in (11.5cm) high*

**£18-22**                          **PSA**

A Pendelfin 'The Buffet' figure, out of production.

*c2002      5in (12.5cm) high*

**£50-70**                          **PSA**

A Pendelfin 'Herald' Founder Member figure, out of production.

*1992    3.75in (12.5cm) high*

**£40-60**                          **PSA**

A Pendelfin 'Newsie' figure, membership piece.

*1996      4in (10cm) high*

**£25-35**                          **PSA**

A Pendelfin 'Deliah' figure, out of production.

*Model of the Year in 1996.*

*1996      5in (12.5cm) high*

**£30-50**                          **PSA**

A Pendelfin 'Woody' figure, Family Circle piece.

*1997        4in (10cm) high*

**£30-50**                          **PSA**

A Pendelfin 'Gran' figure, out of production.

*This was the Pendelfin Family Circle's Model of the Year 2000.*

*2000                      4.5in (11.5cm) high*

**£30-50**                          **PSA**

A Pendelfin 'Tidypatch' figure, Family Circle piece.

*1998      4in (10cm) high*

**£15-25**                          **PSA**

# HOT COLLECTING AREA

## POOLE POTTERY

The hand-thrown, hand-painted pottery produced by Carter, Stabler & Adams Ltd from 1921, now known as 'Poole Pottery' is hotly sought after. New interpretations of floral and foliate decoration, with bold, colourful and often abstract designs replaced more traditional styles.

*see p.87*  *see p.89*  *see p.88*

- ■ 1930s designs are among the most sought-after products. Created chiefly by Truda Carter, most designs are in soft yellows, bright blues and greens on a glazed white body. Similar to the work of their contemporaries Clarice Cliff and Susie Cooper, they tend to be stylised floral, foliate and geometrical patterns, often in an Art Deco style.

- ■ Prices have risen considerably over the past few years, making examples that show the company's trademark decoration and forms more valuable. As supplies of larger, more important pieces dry up, smaller pieces seem set to rise in value.

- ■ During the 1950s, after a post-war slump, the pottery was once again at the forefront of contemporary design due to designer Alfred Read. Inspired by Scandinavian ceramics, his modern 'Contemporary' and 'Freeform' ranges developed with thrower Guy Sydenham have become very desirable.

- ■ New, clean-lined and often asymmetric shapes were introduced. Patterns, many developed by Ruth Pavely, were linear or used repeated simple stylised motifs, often incorporating leaf shapes. Colour was hand painted on in stripes or bands.

- ■ In 1962 the factory became Poole Pottery Ltd and the following years saw an abundance of dramatic, abstract patterns in the oranges, yellows and browns that corresponded with the fashions of the 1960s and 70s. Increasing in popularity, this is an area to watch, particularly the studio wares by those such as Tony Morris.

# A CLOSER LOOK AT A POOLE POTTERY VASE

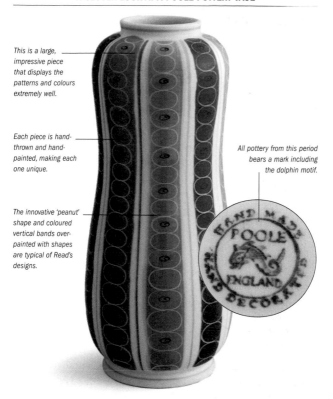

This is a large, impressive piece that displays the patterns and colours extremely well.

Each piece is hand-thrown and hand-painted, making each one unique.

The innovative 'peanut' shape and coloured vertical bands over-painted with shapes are typical of Read's designs.

All pottery from this period bears a mark including the dolphin motif.

A Poole Pottery 'PLC' pattern vase, designed by Alfred Read, painted by Gwen Haskins.

*c1953-54*

*13.25in (34cm) high*

**£700-900**

**GGRT**

## TOP TIPS

- All Poole Pottery pieces are marked on the base, with a factory name stamp, a painted symbol identifying the painter, and a number-and-letter combination signifying the pattern name and production period.

- Art Deco designs from the 1930s featuring geometric designs, birds or animals are particularly prized.

- The highest prices are paid for items with visual impact, such as large bowls, chargers or vases with typical, heavily stylised decoration.

- Look for pieces that exemplify the style of the relevant period in terms of form and decoration.

A 1930s Poole Pottery slender oviform vase, an unusual pattern probably designed by Truda Carter from the 'G' series and probably painted by Rene Hayes (Harvey).

*8.25in (21cm) high*

**£180-220** DN

A 1930s Poole Pottery Art Deco oviform vase, designed by Truda Carter and painted by Myrtle Bond.

*9.75in (25cm) high*

**£700-800** DN

A 1930s Poole Pottery broad oviform vase, designed by Truda Carter and possibly painted by Vera Wills.

*9.75in (25cm) high*

**£280-320** DN

A large 1930s Poole Pottery red-earthenware oviform vase, designed by Truda Carter and painted by Truda Rivers.

*14.25in (36cm) high*

**£800-900** DN

A rare 1930s Poole Pottery vase, designed by Truda Carter and painted by Ruth Pavely, impressed "Poole England" painter's mark and "203/KN".

*8in (20cm) high*

**£700-900** DN

A large 1930s Poole Pottery red earthenware dish, designed by Truda Carter and painted by Truda Rivers.

*15.25in (39cm) diam*

**£500-600** DN

An unusual 1930s Poole Pottery red earthenware dish, designed by Truda Carter and painted by Ann Hatchard, in Continental faïence manner.

*12in (30.5cm) diam*

**£300-400** DN

A large 1930s Poole Pottery red earthenware dish, designed by Truda Carter and painted by Ann Hatchard.

*14.75in (37.5cm) diam*

**£350-450** DN

A Poole Pottery 'Blue-bird' pattern jug, designed by Truda Carter, painted in vivid colours with two blue-birds in flight amid flowers and trellises, between formal bands, impressed "Carter Stabler & Adams Ltd" mark, "316/PN".

*4.5in (11cm) high*

**£150-200** **DN**

A Carter, Stabler & Adams Poole two-handled vase, painted with wild birds and stylized foliage in polychrome, impressed mark.

*c1925* *7in (18cm) high*

**£220-280** **GORL**

A Carter, Stabler and Adams Poole Pottery footed fruit bowl, incised "464", blue hand-painted "OT & H" in foot rim, small chip to foot rim, and with stained crazing.

*8in (20.5cm) diam*

**£100-150** **AS&S**

A Poole Pottery compressed round bowl, painted by Rita Curtis to a design by Truda Carter, impressed "Carter Stabler Adams Ltd. Poole England" with painter's mark and "0564/OT".

*9in (23cm) high*

**£250-350** **DN**

A Carter, Stabler & Adams square honey pot and cover, impressed mark and "TK" signature.

*5in (12.5cm) wide*

**£60-90** **AS&S**

A large 1920s Carter, Stabler and Adams Poole Pottery jug.

*8.5in (21.5cm) high*

**£100-150** **OACC**

A Poole Pottery vase, painted by Ruth Pavely to a Truda Carter design, of compressed globular shape with a broad frieze of stylized flowers and foliage, impressed "Carter Stabler Adams" and "Poole England" numbered "338/ZX".

*8.25in (21cm) high*

**£180-220** **DN**

A Poole Pottery shallow bowl, decorated with a geometric band.

*8in (20.5cm) diam*

**£60-80** **GORB**

A Poole Pottery water jug, impressed "Poole England".

*8in (20cm) h*

**£50-80** **AS&S**

A Poole Pottery 'PKT' pattern charger, designed by Alfred Read, painted by Diane Holloway.

*c1953-54 9.75in (24.5cm) diam*

**£280-350** GGRT

A Poole Pottery 'YAP' pattern vase, designed by Alfred Read, painted by Gwen Haskins.

*c1953-54 10in (25cm) high*

**£280-380** GGRT

A Poole Pottery 'YAP' pattern charger, designed by Alfred Read.

*c1953-54 12.75in (32.5cm) diam*

**£380-420** GGRT

A Poole Pottery 'PKC' pattern vase, designed by Alfred Read, painted by Gwen Haskins.

*c1953-54 10.75in (27.5cm) high*

**£380-480** GGRT

A Poole Pottery 'PLC' pattern lamp, designed by Alfred Read, painted by Gwen Haskins.

*c1953-54 7in (18cm) high*

**£220-280** GGRT

A Poole Pottery 'YAP' pattern vase, designed by Alfred Read, painted by Gwen Haskins.

*c1953-54 6in (15cm) high*

**£180-220** GGRT

A Poole Pottery 'PKC' pattern vase, designed by Alfred Read, painted by Gwen Haskins.

*c1953-54 10in (25.5cm) high*

**£450-500** GGRT

A Poole Pottery 'PKC' pattern vase, designed by Alfred Read, painted by Gwen Haskins.

*c1953-54 8.75in (22.5cm) diam*

**£150-200** GGRT

A Poole Pottery 'PRP' pattern charger, designed by Alfred Read, painted by Gwen Haskins.

*c1953-54 12.75in (32.5cm) diam*

**£400-450** GGRT

A Poole Pottery 'YFC' pattern vase, designed by Alfred Read, painted by Jean Cockram.

*c1953-54* 7in (18cm) high

**£400-450** GGRT

A Poole Pottery 'PGT' pattern vase, by Alfred Read.

*c1953-54* 7.5in (18.5cm) high

**£300-350** GGRT

A Poole Pottery 'GGU' Ravioli pattern vase, designed by Ruth Pavely, painted by Gwen Haskins.

*c1956-57* 8.75in (22.5cm) high

**£550-650** GGRT

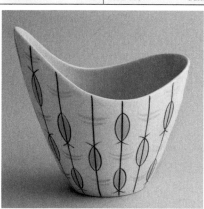

A Poole Pottery PY 'Totem' freeform pattern bowl, designed by Ruth Pavely, painted by Gwen Haskins.

*c1956-57* 7.5in (19cm) high

**£280-320** GGRT

A Poole Pottery HZT 'Scroll' vase, designed by Ruth Pavely, painted by Sylvia Davis.

*c1956-57* 4.25in (11cm) high

**£180-220** GGRT

A Poole Pottery PS 'Bamboo' pattern bowl, designed by Ann Read.

*c1956-57* 10in (25cm) wide

**£120-140** GGRT

A Poole Pottery GGU 'Ravioli' pattern vase, designed by Ruth Pavely, painted by Gladys Hallett.

*c1956-57* 4.25in (11cm) high

**£150-170** GGRT

A 1970s Poole Pottery vase, in orange, green and red with everted lip, the base with Poole Pottery mark, and incised 'CB' and '84' marks.

8.75in (22.5cm) high

**£80-120** AOY

A 1970s Poole Pottery leaf-shaped platter, with geometric green, yellow and red floral or foliate design, the base with Poole Pottery mark and incised 'R'.

12.25in (31cm) long

**£80-120** AOY

A Portmeirion Pottery 'Talisman' pattern vegetable dish, designed by Susan Williams-Ellis.

*c1962      6.5in (16.5cm) wide*

**£180-220**                    **GGRT**

A Portmeirion Pottery 'Tivoli' pattern, Seraph shape, coffee set, designed by Susan Williams-Ellis, including six cups and six saucers and a coffee pot.

*c1964      12.5in (31.5cm) high*

**£300-500 (SET)**              **GGRT**

A 1970s Portmeirion Pottery 'Talisman' pattern lidded jar, designed by Susan Williams-Ellis.

*7.5in (19cm) high*

**£30-40**                         **L**

A Portmeirion Pottery 'Talisman' pattern jug, in blue and green, designed by Susan Williams-Ellis.

*c1962      6.75in (17cm) high*

**£80-100**                     **GGRT**

A Portmeirion Pottery 'Tivoli' pattern medium store jar, in blue and green, designed by Susan Williams-Ellis.

*'Tivoli' was first produced in 1964, following her visit to the Tivoli Gardens in Copenhagen.*

*c1964      6in (15.5cm) high*

**£60-90**                     **GGRT**

A Portmeirion 'Magic Garden' pattern coffee set, designed by Susan Williams-Ellis, including six cups, six saucers and a coffee pot, of cylindrical shape.

*c1970      13.25in (33.5cm) high*

**£300-500 (SET)**             **GGRT**

A pair of Portmeirion Pottery 'Talisman' pattern oil and vinegar bottles, designed by Susan Williams-Ellis, in green and blue, some staining.

*c1962      8.75in (22.5cm) high*

**£60-90**                     **GGRT**

A 1970s Portmeirion Pottery 'Totem' pattern teapot, designed by Susan Williams-Ellis.

*6in (15cm) high*

**£20-30**                         **L**

A pair of Portmeirion Pottery 'Monte Sol' pattern oil and vinegar bottles, designed by Susan Williams-Ellis.

*c1965      9in (23cm) high*

**£100-120**                   **GGRT**

A Portmeirion Potteries 'Talisman' pattern mixing bowl, transfer-printed, designed by Susan Williams-Ellis.

*c1962*      11in (28cm) diam

**£20-35**      **FFM**

A Portmeirion Potteries 'Talisman' pattern cigarette box, transfer-printed, designed by Susan Williams-Ellis.

*c1962*    5.25in (13.5cm) wide

**£20-30**      **FFM**

A Portmeirion Potteries 'Talisman' pattern jug, transfer-printed, designed by Susan Williams-Ellis.

*c1962*    6.75in (17cm) high

**£20-35**      **FFM**

A set of three Portmeirion Potteries 'Talisman' pattern storage jars with lids, transfer-printed in three colourways, designed by Susan Williams-Ellis.

*c1962*      4.75in (12cm) high

**£40-60 (SET)**      **FFM**

Two Portmeirion Potteries 'Talisman' pattern storage jars, transfer-printed, designed by Susan Williams-Ellis.

*c1962*    6.25in (16cm) high

**£15-25 EACH**      **FFM**

Two Portmeirion Potteries 'Totem' pattern soup goblets, designed by Susan Williams-Ellis.

*1963*   Tallest 5in (12.5cm) high

**£15-25 EACH**      **FFM**

A Portmeirion Potteries cylinder shape 'Totem' pattern coffee pot, white glaze, designed by Susan Williams-Ellis.

*1963 (and produced until mid-1970s, and again from 2002)*

13in (33cm) high

**£40-60**      **FFM**

A Portmeirion Potteries Meridian shape 'Botanical Garden - Citron' pattern plate, transfer-printed, designed by Susan Williams-Ellis.

*1972 (made to present day)*
*7.25in (18.5cm) diam*

**£20-25** FFM

Two Portmeirion Potteries cylinder shape 'Greek Key' pattern coffee pots, transfer-printed on white and orange glazes, designed by Susan Williams-Ellis.

*1968 to 1970s* *13in (33cm) high*

**£25-35 EACH** FFM

A Portmeirion Potteries serif shape 'Cypher' pattern coffee pot, olive green glaze, designed by Susan Williams-Ellis.

*1963* *12in (30cm) high*

**£20-30** FFM

A Portmeirion Potteries serif shape 'Jupiter' pattern tureen with lid, designed by Susan Williams-Ellis.

*1963* *9in (23cm) wide*

**£20-30** FFM

A Portmeirion Potteries serif shape 'Magic City' pattern coffee cup and saucer, transfer-printed, designed by Susan Williams-Ellis.

*1966 to 1970s*
*Cup: 3.5in (8.5cm) high*

**£8-12** FFM

A Portmeirion Potteries 'Monte Sol' pattern storage jar, transfer-printed, designed by Susan Williams-Ellis.

*1966* *6.25in (16cm) high*

**£20-25** FFM

A Portmeirion Potteries 'Sailing Ships' pattern wall plate, transfer-printed, designed by Susan Williams-Ellis.

*c1966* *8in (20.5cm) diam*

**£12-18** FFM

A Portmeirion Potteries 'Tivoli' pattern herb jar, transfer-printed, designed by Susan Williams-Ellis.

*1964* *4.25in (10.5cm) high*

**£8-12** FFM

A Portmeirion Potteries cylinder shape 'Velocopedes' pattern plate, transfer-printed, designed by Susan Williams-Ellis.

*c1968* *7.25in (18.5cm) diam*

**£8-12** FFM

A Rye Pottery 'Cinque Ports Pottery' vase, with unusual pattern in blue, black and mauve, marked "38".

5.25in (13.5cm) high

**£120-180** **GGRT**

A Rye Pottery 'Mosaic' pattern mug, stamped date mark on red clay.

*The 'Mosaic' pattern was Walter Cole's favourite.*

1956 5.5in (14cm) high

**£150-200** **GGRT**

A Rye Pottery 'Mosaic' pattern jug, impressed "D" for David Sharp on white clay, with date mark.

c1957-71 8.5in (21.5cm) high

**£250-350** **GGRT**

A Rye Pottery 'Café Italian' pattern mug, by the Monastery Pottery, possibly designed by George Gray.

7.25in (18.5cm) high

**£50-120** **GGRT**

A Rye Pottery jug, thrown by David Sharp, marked "24".

c1957-71 4.5in (11.5cm) high

**£100-130** **GGRT**

A Rye Pottery 'Cinque Ports Pottery' butter-dish, designed by David Sharp, unmarked.

*The 1950s saw an enthusiasm for atomic and scientific subjects, which led to similar themes in design. The 'Festival Pattern Group' designed patterns based on molecular models or the crystalline design of materials – with bobble or tear shapes and connecting lines.*

4.75in (12cm) diam

**£10-20** **GGRT**

A Rye Pottery two-handled loving cup, inscribed "CHRISTMAS", impressed "J" for Jim Elliot on red clay.

1954 4.75in (12cm) high

**£200-250** **GGRT**

A Rye Pottery cockerel vase, mark for "1957-71" on white clay.

c1957-71 7in (17.75cm) high

**£150-200** **GGRT**

A Gustavsberg dish, by Stig Lindberg.

*c1940-50*     10in (25cm) wide

**£250-300**                    **GGRT**

A Gustavsberg oblong platter, by Stig Lindberg, with original trade labels.

*c1940-50*     13in (33cm) wide

**£350-400**                    **GGRT**

A Gustavsberg dish, by Stig Lindberg.

*c1940-50*   10.25in (26cm) wide

**£250-300**                    **GGRT**

A Gustavsberg oblong platter, by Stig Lindberg.

*c1940-50*  12.5in (31.5cm) wide

**£400-500**                    **GGRT**

A Gustavsberg freeform bowl, by Stig Lindberg, blue and white stripes, original trade labels.

*c1940-50*                              10.5in (26.5cm) wide

**£275-325**                                                    **GGRT**

A Gustavsberg dish, by Stig Lindberg.

*c1940-50*     8in (20.5cm) wide

**£150-200**                    **GGRT**

A Gustavsberg vase, by Stig Lindberg, painted on the inside of the mouth with wild flowers.

*c1942*     11.75in (30cm) high

**£185-245**                    **GGRT**

A Gustavsberg vase, by Stig Lindberg, of melon shape, with pink stripes and scalloped collar.

*c1940-50*   8.5in (21.5cm) high

**£325-400**                    **GGRT**

An Arabia white-glazed earthenware shell-shaped dish, by Kaj Franck, from the ARA series.

*1947-53*

**£30-40**                       **MHT**

Two Arabia porcelain matt-glazed teapots, by Ulla Procopé, with cane handles.

*c1953*

**£40-50 EACH**                                                 **MHT**

An Arabia porcelain bowl, by Friedl Bovesen Kjellberg with thin rice 'rice' design, signed "Arabia F H KI made in Finland", c1955     3.25in (8.5cm) high

**£80-120**     **MHT**

A 1950s Arabia ginger jar, by Franøøøøe Mazriw 1^ th, with pitted oxblood over green glaze.

**£80-100**     **MHT**

A Rorstrand 'Delikat' printed and handpainted vase, by Marianne Westmann.

*Many Scandinavian ceramics produced at this time had patterns that were interchangeable, so people could mix and match ranges and colourways.*

1954

**£40-60**     **MHT**

A 1960s Rorstrand leaf dish, stamped to base "Rorstrand".
    11in (28cm) wide

**£80-90**     **MHT**

A Soholm ceramic panel, modelled with bust of a girl, covered in a green-brown glaze, stamped "SOHOLM STENTOJ BORNHOLM DENMARK".
    17in (43cm) high

**£150-200**     **FRE**

A Soholm Pottery pitted stoneware vase, impressed marks to base "Solholm Bornholm Denmark Stentoj. handmade".

*Made on the Danish island of Bornholm.*

**£70-90**     **MHT**

A Rorstrand Studio/Atelje bowl, with moulded textured decoration, painted marks to base.
c1965     5in (12.5cm) high

**£80-120**     **MHT**

A Norwegian earthenware dish, unknown maker, highly decorated with abstract foliage, painted marks to base "806/414e handmade in Norway".
c1960

**£70-100**     **MHT**

# HOT COLLECTING AREA

## SYLVAC

Shaw & Copestake's 'SylvaC' name was coined in 1936 and is best known for its huge variety of coloured ceramic animal figures. Although modestly priced, they are no less prized by collectors than those from more prestigious factories.

see p.99    see p.100    see p.101

- Decorated in cheerful colours, they were produced from the 1920s until the 1980s, originally for the fairground and novelties market. A huge range of animals was produced, but rounded rabbits, pointy-eared hares and terrier dogs are the most popular.

- The all-over, single-colour matt glaze that typifies the SylvaC range was created in 1932. Some models were available both in this glaze and in the earlier cellulose-painted finish, which is damaged very easily. The later glossy finish called 'bright glaze' is currently less desirable amongst collectors unless the model is very rare, but prices are rising slowly.

- Every piece is stamped with a mould number, but this does not help to date a piece reliably as the dates relate to the date of the mould, not the piece itself. Also, mould numbers did not run consecutively. In general, earlier pieces have a more matt finish and a deeper colour than later ones.

- Values for SylvaC animals vary according to size, colour and rarity of form. Certain mould shapes are rare, such as one of a seated dog, numbered 1191. Many shapes were made in a variety of sizes within the range 5-30cm (2-12in).

- Colour is of great importance, with green and fawn being the most common. Pink is extremely rare, so highly collectable, and brown and blue are also uncommon and desirable. Traditionally less popular household objects, such as face pots and especially fruit-shaped pots, are rising slowly in desirability.

## A CLOSER LOOK AT A REPRODUCTION SYLVAC

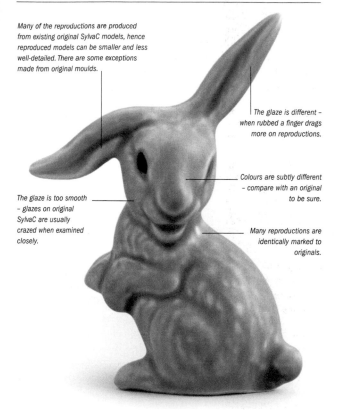

Many of the reproductions are produced from existing original SylvaC models, hence reproduced models can be smaller and less well-detailed. There are some exceptions made from original moulds.

The glaze is different – when rubbed a finger drags more on reproductions.

Colours are subtly different – compare with an original to be sure.

The glaze is too smooth – glazes on original SylvaC are usually crazed when examined closely.

Many reproductions are identically marked to originals.

A modern reproduction SylvaC fawn 'Rabbit'.

4.25in (10.5cm) high

£7-10                                    MCOL

## TOP TIPS

- Size is important and large models are generally worth more.

- Take care when handling SylvaC as it chips very easily, and this reduces value considerably.

- Modern reproductions are still being made from genuine moulds, and have little collectable value. Authentic glazes will show very fine 'crazing' and the modelling and detail are finer.

- Don't confuse fakes with period pieces imitating SylvaC made by firms such as Denby. These have some value, although are not as popular as genuine SylvaC.

A SylvaC green 'Terrier', stamped "1380".

*This is the largest of three sizes. This example is more matt and a darker green, indicating an early date.*

11.25in (28.5cm) high

**£100-150**                                              **MCOL**

A SylvaC green 'Mac Dog', stamped "1207".

*This is the middle in a series of five sizes. It is often copied.*

7.75in (19.5cm) high

**£50-80**                                              **MCOL**

A SylvaC green 'Spaniel Sammy', stamped "1247".

5.75in (14.5cm) high

**£40-60**                                              **MCOL**

A SylvaC blue 'Terrier', stamped "1378".

5in (13cm) high

**£30-50**                                              **MCOL**

A SylvaC green 'Spaniel Sammy', stamped "1461".

6in (16cm) high

**£40-60**                                              **MCOL**

A SylvaC green 'Howling Dog', stamped "2584".

6.25in (16cm) high

**£100-150**                                              **MCOL**

A SylvaC green 'Dog', stamped "1123".

*This shape was also made by a number of other factories, which used beads for eyes, unlike genuine SylvaC.*

7in (18cm) long

**£60-90**                                              **MCOL**

A SylvaC bright glaze 'Doberman', from the 'Supreme Dogs' range, stamped "5150".

7.5in (19cm) long

£30-50      MCOL

A SylvaC mongrel/dachshund, stamped "3320".

5in (12cm) high

£30-40      MCOL

A SylvaC stone-coloured 'Spaniel Sammy', stamped "1246".

4.5in (11.5cm) high

£20-30      MCOL

A SylvaC fawn rabbit, with painted eyes, moulded marks, bears paper label.

9.75in (24.5cm) high

£40-60      L&T

A SylvaC fawn 'Rabbit', stamped "MADE IN ENGLAND 1026" and printed "SYLVAC".

6.75in (17cm) high

£50-80      MCOL

A SylvaC fawn 'Rabbit', mould number 1400.

2in (5cm) high

£15-25      MCOL

A SylvaC green 'Rabbit', stamped "1028".

*This shows the largest and the smallest sized rabbits produced. All the smallest animals had the same mould number. Rumour has it that a two foot-high rabbit was produced for Boots the Chemist, but an example is yet to be found.*

9.75in (25cm) high

£100-150      MCOL

A SylvaC large pink 'Rabbit' cotton wool holder, stamped "1027 MADE IN ENGLAND".

*Pink is very rare and is one of the most sought-after colours.*

8.5in (21.5cm) high

£200-300      MCOL

A SylvaC vase, decorated in yellow glaze with two pixies peering into a mushroom.
*9in (23cm) high*

**£15-20** **D**

A SylvaC 'Lazy Pixie and Watering Can' posy holder, stamped "2277".
*3.25in (8cm) high*

**£20-30** **MCOL**

A SylvaC 'Leaping Dog' posy holder, mould number "3560".
*4.5in (11.5cm) long*

**£30-40** **MCOL**

A rare SylvaC jardinière, from the 'Lily' range, stamped "3285".
*10in (25.5cm) long*

**£60-90** **MCOL**

A SylvaC jardinière, from the 'Pebble' range, stamped "3419".
*6.75in (17cm) long*

**£10-15** **MCOL**

A rare SylvaC fawn posy holder, stamped "1336".
*7in (18cm) high*

**£80-120** **MCOL**

A SylvaC 'Gnome' posy ring.
*c1939   6.25in (16cm) diam*

**£30-40** **MCOL**

A 1940s SylvaC fawn and green ashtray, stamped "1532".
*5.5in (14cm) long*

**£30-40** **MCOL**

A very rare SylvaC 'Cactus', mould number 738.
*5in (12.5cm) high*

**£50-80** **MCOL**

A SylvaC 'Mr SylvaC' ashtray, stamped "3542".

*In 1964, 500 of these ashtrays, bearing the legend 'For Quality & Value', were produced for retailers. In 1989, a small number were reproduced by Crown Winsor for the launch of 'The SylvaC Story' publication, but bore no wording. Check that transfer letters have not been added to the front to make it look like the earlier, more collectable, version.*

*c1989* *8in (20.5cm) high*

**£100-150** **MCOL**

A SylvaC cellulose-painted 'Girl', stamped "880".
*8.75in (22cm) high*

**£80-120** MCOL

A SylvaC cellulose-painted '1930s Lady', stamped "881".
*9.5in (24cm) high*

**£80-120** MCOL

A SylvaC black 'Ukelele-playing' figure, stamped "1022".
*5.25in (13.5cm) high*

**£100-150** MCOL

A SylvaC cellulose-painted 'Sailor and Rum Keg' posy holder, produced for the florist George Monro Ltd., stamped "1258".
*8.75in (22cm) high*

**£70-100** MCOL

A SylvaC cellulose-painted 'Welsh Lady' character jug, stamped "1288".
*3.5in (9cm) high*

**£30-40** MCOL

A SylvaC cellulose-painted 'Cat', stamped "843".
*8.75in (22cm) high*

**£70-100** MCOL

A SylvaC cellulose-painted 'Cornflower Ware' vase, decorated with flowers, stamped "967".
*8.75in (22cm) high*

**£20-30** MCOL

A SylvaC cellulose-painted 'Harvest Poppy' vase, stamped "910".
*8.75in (22cm) high*

**£20-30** MCOL

A SylvaC cellulose-painted 'Bulldog', stamped "1043".

*This model was produced in four different sizes.*

*7.5in (19cm) high*

**£60-90** MCOL

# HOT COLLECTING AREA

## TROIKA

Troika was founded in 1963 when sculptor Lesley Illsley, architect Jan Thompson and potter Benny Sirota bought a pottery in St Ives, Cornwall. The past few years have seen interest in, and prices for, the production of this avant-garde pottery mushroom.

see p.106

see p.104

see p.105

- The first pieces were small domestic wares such as teapots, mugs and vases. Although many associate Troika with matt, textured pieces, most of these early pieces are glazed, giving a glossy or shiny finish.

- Early decoration included circle designs which were usually austere and sober in terms of both form and colour. Scandinavian ceramics of the time, with their muted decorative style, were a strong influence on the company, along with the work of artist Paul Klee and sculptor Constantin Brancusi.

- After their expansion and relocation to Newlyn in 1970, new shapes and designs were introduced – by 1974 the textured ware that is most recognisable today as Troika dominated the range.

- Shapes characteristic of Troika, such as wheel-shaped vases, 'anvil' or 'coffin' shaped vases are desirable. Patterns and colours should be typical and balanced.

- Much Troika can be dated to a period from the mark and the decorator's initials, both found on the base. The decorator affects the value considerably, so learn how to recognise decorator's monograms. Stella Benjamin is an early name from the 1960s, while Alison Brigden worked from 1976-1983.

- Fuelled mainly by tourism, Troika's popularity grew during the early 1970s. Pieces were also stocked by many fashionable retailers, including Selfridges, Heal's and Liberty. By the late 1970s its popularity began to decline. Due to a downturn in tourism and changing tastes, the pottery closed in 1983.

## A CLOSER LOOK AT A TROIKA MASK

The piece is signed with an "SK" monogram, signifying that it was decorated by Simone Kilburn, who worked at Troika from 1976-77.

Masks are much rarer than other, more functional, objects as they did not sell well at the time and would have been expensive.

Masks are large and visually impressive display pieces. They were introduced in the early 1970s and made until closure in 1983.

The design shows the influence of Paul Klee and Aztec designs and is in mint condition with no damage or wear.

A Troika Newlyn Pottery double-sided mask, by Simone Kilburn, one side with stylized Aztec design, the other depicting a Cycladic mask, blue and browns.

c1977                                                    10in (25.5cm) high

**£3,000-4,000**                                                    **B&H**

---

## TOP TIPS

- Look out for large or sculptural pieces and those dating from the first years of the pottery, especially if by the founders.

- Marks including 'St Ives' generally date from 1963-70, and a rare 'trident' in a square-shaped mark was used until 1967.

- If a piece is not marked 'St Ives', then it is likely to have been made at Newlyn after 1970, although 'Newlyn' never appears in any mark.

- Look out for utilitarian pieces by Troika, such as teapots, egg cups, dishes and tiles, as many are early and thus sought after.

A Troika Pottery 'wheel' vase, probably by Jane Fitzgerald, cast in low painted relief, painted "Troika LF" monogram, small chips.

*1977-83  7.75in (20cm) high*

**£400-500**                    **WW**

A Troika Pottery small 'wheel' vase, by Alison Brigden, with embossed stylized design depicting woman with a basket to one side and grid design to the other.

*1976-83  4.5in (11.5cm) high*

**£120-180**                    **B&H**

A Troika Pottery small 'wheel' vase, by Louise Jinks, in blues and browns with mottled blue ground and embossed geometric designs to both sides.

*1976-81  4.5in (11.5cm) high*

**£150-200**                    **B&H**

A late 1970s Troika Pottery 'wheel' vase, modelled in relief with face design, with painted marks for Tina Doubleday.

*7.75in (19.5cm) high*

**£450-550**                    **WW**

A Troika Pottery giant 'wheel' lamp base, with raised Aztec designs to one side and a fireplace to the opposing side, in blue greens and browns by Head Decorator Avril Bennett.

*Wheel vases were available in four sizes. The 'Giant' size was also available as a lamp base, as with this example.*

*1973-79  14.5in (37cm) high*

**£1,000-1,500**                 **B&H**

A Troika Pottery small 'wheel' vase, by Sue Bladen, with embossed domino and Aztec designs to either side.

*1975      4.75in (12cm) high*

**£80-120**                     **B&H**

A Troika Pottery small 'wheel' vase, monogrammed "C.H." and probably by Honor Curtis.

*1966-74  4.75in (12cm) high*

**£120-180**                    **B&H**

A late 1970s Troika Pottery 'wheel' lamp base, by Tina Doubleday, with textured green ground and embossed domino and arch designs.

*10.25in (26cm) high*

**£280-320**                    **B&H**

An early 1970s Troika Pottery medium 'cylinder' vase, by Linda Thomas, with painted disk design band.

*7.5in (19cm) high*

£120-180          B&H

A Troika Pottery large 'cylinder' vase, by Honor Curtis, with mottled blue ground and painted double band of geometric disks.

*14.5in (37cm) high*

£280-320          B&H

A late 1970s Troika Pottery large 'cylinder' vase, by Tina Doubleday, with textured green ground and geometric bands in high oranges and blues.

*14.5in (37cm) high*

£400-500          B&H

A Troika Pottery small 'cylinder' vase, by Ann Jones, with brown textured ground and painted disk design band.

*c1977   5.75in (14.5cm) high*

£100-150          B&H

A Troika Pottery 'cylinder' vase, in blues, with a band of linked diamond decoration.

*10in (25.5cm) high*

£80-120          WW

An early Troika St Ives Pottery medium 'cylinder' vase with neck, by Stella Benjamin, with mottled brown ground and a painted disk design band.

*7.75in (20cm) high*

£150-200          B&H

A Troika St Ives Pottery medium 'cylinder' vase with neck, by Stella Benjamin.

*7.75in (19.5cm) high*

£220-280          B&H

A late 1970s Troika Pottery 'anvil' vase, by Louise Jinks, with textured green ground and stylized embossed domino and mask designs to either side.

*Anvil vases were designed and produced after 1965. Louise Jinks worked at Troika from 1976-81 and as Head Decorator from 1979-81. The form, pattern and glazes work extremely well together on this example.*

8.5in (21.5cm) high

A 1970s Troika Pottery 'doublebased' vase, incised and painted with geometric devices, painted mark "Troika, Cornwall".

£550-650    **GORL**

£1,500-2,000    **B&H**

A rare early Troika St Ives Pottery 'urn' vase, with all-over white treacle glaze and bands of wax resist disks in matte black, trident mark to base.

10in (25.5cm) high

£450-550    **B&H**

A Troika Pottery 'urn' vase, by Penny Black, with mottled green ground and painted disk design band.

c1960-76   9.75in (25cm) h

£180-220    **B&H**

A Troika Pottery 'urn' vase, by Avril Bennett, with blue ground and brown painted disk design band.

1973-79   10in (25.5cm) high

£200-250    **B&H**

A 1970s Troika Pottery 'cube' vase, by Shirley Warf, with mottled blue ground and embossed geometric Aztec designs and hieroglyphics.

*The cube shape was produced in three sizes, ranging from No.1 at 3in (7.5cm) square to No.3 at 6in (15cm) square.*

3.5in (9cm) high

£100-150    **B&H**

A Troika Pottery plant holder, by Anne Lewis.

1967-72   5in (12.75cm) high

£350-450    **B&H**

A Troika Pottery 'coffin' vase, modelled in low relief, painted marks, chip to top rim, nicks to paintwork.

*6.75in (17cm) high*

£200-250    WW

A Troika Pottery 'coffin' vase, by Colin Carbis, embossed with stylized designs of a brick kiln and domino to either side.

*c1977*    *6.75in (17cm) high*

£200-250    B&H

A Troika 'coffin' vase, modelled in low relief, painted marks, nicks to paintwork.

*6.75in (17cm) high*

£200-250    WW

A late 1970s Troika Pottery 'coffin' vase, by Tina Doubleday, with textured blue ground and embossed domino and brick kiln designs to either side.

*The 'coffin' vase was introduced in 1970 when the pottery moved to Newlyn, and was immensely popular during that decade. It is one of the most common shapes found by collectors today.*

*6.5in (16.5cm) high*

£100-150    B&H

A Troika Pottery 'rectangle' vase, with unidentified monogram "E.W".

*8.5in (21.5cm) high*

£220-280    B&H

A rare early Troika St Ives Pottery lidded vessel, in blues and purples, with painted geometric designs, retailer's price "16/-" on base.

*5.5in (14cm) high*

£600-700    B&H

A Troika Pottery 'rectangle' vase, by Marilyn Pascoe, with embossed abstract helmet and arrow designs, blues and browns.

*1970-74 8.5in (12.5cm) high*

£250-350    B&H

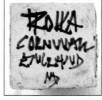

An early Troika St Ives D-plate, of rounded square form, having embossed geometric flower head and leaf designs, in blues and greens, with impressed trident mark to base.

*7.25in (18.5cm) diam*

**£350-450**                    **B&H**

A rare early Troika St Ives Pottery shallow dish, with mottled blue ground and stylized hieroglyphic designed centre panel, with impressed trident mark to the base.

*1963-7*                    *11.75in (30cm) wide*

**£1,500-2,000**                    **B&H**

A rare Troika St Ives Pottery floor tile, with blue painted Aztec sun design, marked on reverse.

*Floor tiles were amongst the earliest objects produced and were discontinued not long after the pottery was founded.*

*5.75in (14.5cm) diam*

**£450-550**                    **B&H**

A Troika Newlyn Pottery pocket vase, by Louise Jinks, with embossed geometric stylized designs in greens and browns.

*1976-81*          *8in (20cm) high*

**£700-800**                    **B&H**

A Troika St Ives Pottery double eggcup, with plain high white ground and blue painted geometric designs to base.

*Double egg-cups were introduced in 1965. Although expensive, a great many were made and sold.*

*c1965*          *3.5in (9cm) high*

**£100-150**                    **B&H**

A rare Troika St Ives Pottery teapot, of cylindrical form decorated with black-glazed shoulders, a painted disk design band in browns and blues, with original bent cane handle.

*Teapots and coffee pots ceased to be produced just after 1967, having been made for around four years.*

*1963-67*                    *7in (18cm) diam*

**£400-500**                    **B&H**

A Troika Pottery tin mine lamp base, by Alison Brigden, in the form of a stone building and chimney, in browns and greens.

*1976-83  8.5in (21.5cm) high*

**£600-700**                    **B&H**

A miniature Goldscheider
wall mask.
*c1925-8 4.5in (11.5cm) high*

**£300-450** SCG

A Goldscheider wall mask.

*1925-8        11in (28cm) high*

**£800-900** SCG

A Goldscheider wall mask.

*c1925-8        10in (25cm) h*

**£800-900** SCG

A Goldscheider 'Tragedy' wall
mask.
*c1925-8        (34.5cm) long*

**£900-1,200** SCG

A miniature Goldscheider wall
mask.
*c1925-8 4.5in (11.5cm) high*

**£300-450** SCG

A C. & Co. wall mask, by Copes.

*c1934        7in (18cm) high*

**£100-150** BEV

A C. & Co. wall mask, by Copes.

*c1934        8in (20cm) high*

**£120-180** PC

A C. & Co. wall mask, by Copes.
*c1934                  6.5in (16.5cm) high*

**£100-150** BEV

An Austrian Goebel wall mask.
*1928-34        8in (20cm) high*

**£150-200** BEV

# GLASS

Glass is one of the most clicked-on collectable categories on eBay, and the glass of the 20th century has become a growing area of fascination.

Whitefriars, from its 1920s and 30s Art Deco forms to the textured glass of the 1960s and 70s, has featured large in the past few years and this interest is likely to continue with work available within so many price brackets. Scandinavian glass, too, with the clean lines and varied colours that complement our modern interiors so well, is another fashionable area. Ranging from highly textured pieces to geometric, ultra-modern shapes, look out for the work of prominent designers such as Nanny Still at Riihimaki and Tapio Wirkkala at Iittala.

Colourful forms from Murano continue to be popular, particularly those dating from the 1950s and 60s when pieces were produced in diverse styles and huge numbers. Many of these forms are easily affordable today, although prices scale up considerably in association with a prominent or notable designer. Lalique also maintains its popularity in the market, but if you're looking for more price flexibility keep an eye out for examples by smaller companies such as Sabino or Etling. Factories such as Mdina on Malta and Isle of Wight studio glass, King's Lynn and Wedgwood in England continue to grow in desirability.

A 'Magpie' pattern dark amethyst carnival glass bowl.

*Edges on these dishes can be serrated or smooth. The bird is probably a New Zealand Parson bird, not a magpie.*

5.5in (14cm) diam

£60-70 **BA**

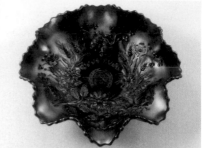

A Northwood 'Good Luck' pattern amethyst carnival glass bowl.

8.5in (21.5cm) diam

£150-200 **BA**

A 'Kingfisher' pattern deep amethyst carnival glass bowl.

*This pattern was first made in 1923.*

9.5in (24cm) wide

£100-150 **BA**

A Dugan Diamond 'Grape Delight' pattern amethyst carnival glass bowl.

7in (18cm) diam

£45-55 **BA**

A pair of Northwood 'Acorn Burrs' amethyst carnival glass bowls.

c1911    4.75in (12cm) high

£60-70 (PAIR) **BA**

A Fenton 'Wild Blackberry' pattern amethyst carnival glass bowl.

6.5in (16.5cm) diam

£60-70 **BA**

A Northwood 'Three Fruits' pattern amethyst carnival glass bowl.

8.75in (22cm) diam

£55-65 **BA**

A 'Windmill' pattern amethyst carnival glass bowl.

7.25in (18.5cm) diam

£80-120 **BA**

An Imperial 'Heavy Grape' pattern amethyst carnival glass nappy.

*A nappy is a shallow bowl or dish.*

5.25in (13.5cm) diam

£60-70 **BA**

A pair of Northwood 'Peacocks on a Fence' pattern amethyst carnival glass bowls.

*This pattern was produced in large numbers in many different colours.*

*9in (23cm) diam*

**£450-550** BA

An Imperial 'Pansy' pattern amethyst carnival glass nappy.

*6.5in (16.5cm) diam*

**£60-70** BA

A Diamond 'Stork and Rushes' pattern amethyst carnival glass punch cup.

*2.75in (7cm) high*

**£25-30** BA

A 'Lotus and Dragon' pattern amethyst carnival glass bowl.

*8.5in (21.5cm) wide*

**£55-65** BA

A Fenton 'Peacock and Grape' pattern amethyst carnival glass bowl.

*8.75in (22cm) diam*

**£50-60** BA

A 'Peacock's Tail' pattern amethyst carnival glass bowl.

*5.5in (14cm) diam*

**£35-45** BA

A Dugan Diamond 'Question Marks' pattern amethyst carnival glass two-handled compote.

*1910-20 6.5in (16.5cm) wide*

**£45-55** BA

An Imperial 'Ripple' pattern amethyst carnival glass vase.

*10.5in (26.5cm) high*

**£80-90** BA

One of a pair of Fenton 'April Showers' pattern carnival glass vases.

*14in (35.5cm) high*

**£300-400 PAIR** AOY

A Fenton 'Horses' Head Medallion' pattern marigold carnival glass bowl.

*c1912*   *7.5in (19cm) diam*

£55-65 · BA

A Northwood 'Wishbone' pattern marigold carnival glass bowl.

*7.5in (19cm) diam*

£50-60 · BA

A rare Fenton 'Little Fishes' pattern marigold carnival glass bowl, model no. 1607.

*c1914-18*   *6in (15cm) diam*

£75-85 · BA

A rare Fenton 'Panther' pattern marigold carnival glass bowl.

*5in (12.5cm) diam*

£70-100 · BA

A Diamond Glass 'Pony' pattern marigold carnival glass bowl.

*8.25in (21cm) diam*

£45-55 · BA

A 'Kangaroo' pattern marigold carnival glass bowl.

*c1924*   *5in (12.5cm) diam*

£65-75 · BA

A 'Hobnail and Button' pattern marigold carnival glass bowl.

*6.5in (16.5cm) diam*

£40-50 · BA

A rare 1920s 'Golden Harvest' pattern marigold carnival glass decanter, possibly by the Diamond Glass Company.

*These decanters, often accompanied by sets of goblets, were less expensive than similar cut glass examples and were sold at a time when bright colours and iridescent finishes were very popular.*

*12in (30.5cm) high*

£60-80 · BA

A pair of Brockwitz 'Triands' pattern marigold carnival glass vases.

*Brockwitz of Germany was opened in 1903 and was the largest European carnival glass producer by the late 1920s.*

*c1930*   *8in (20cm) high*

£35-45 · BA

A Fenton 'Butterflies' pattern green carnival glass two-handled compote.

*Note the difference in the pattern on this example, despite the similarity in names to the previous example. This pattern has eight butterflies on the rim and one in the centre.*

7in (18cm) diam

**£50-60**                          **BA**

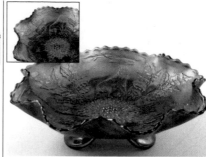

A Fenton 'Stag and Holly' pattern green carnival glass bowl. c1912

8.5in (21.5cm) diam

**£80-90**                          **BA**

An Imperial 'Lustre Rose' pattern Helios carnival glass bowl.

7.75in (20cm) diam

**£55-65**                          **CA**

A Northwood 'Wild Rose' pattern green carnival glass bowl.

7.5in (19cm) diam

**£65-75**                          **BA**

A Fenton 'Wild Blackberry' pattern green carnival glass footed compote.

6.25in (16cm) diam

**£60-70**                          **BA**

A Fenton 'Dragon and Lotus' pattern blue carnival glass bowl.

*Plates in this pattern are rare.*

8.5in (21.5cm) diam

**£80-120**                         **BA**

A Northwood 'Grape and Cable' pattern green carnival glass milk jug.

*This was one of Northwood's most prolific patterns, being produced in over 40 different shapes from 1910 onwards. There are also a number of variations to the pattern.*

An Imperial 'Ripple' pattern green carnival glass vase.

9in (23cm) high

**£30-40**                          **BA**

3in (7.5cm) high

**£50-60**                          **BA**

A small blue Caithness Glass vase, designed by Domhnall O'Broin.

c1967    5in (12.5cm) high

**£15-25**                          **GC**

A heavy-cased blue Caithness Glass vase.

c1965    4.5in (11.5cm) high

**£30-40**                          **MHT**

A small blue Caithness Glass vase, with flared rim.

c1965    5in (12.5cm) high

**£30-40**                          **MHT**

A heather (purple) Caithness Glass vase, designed by Domhnall O'Broin.

c1967    6.5in (16.5cm) high

**£30-50**                          **GC**

A heather (purple) Caithness Glass lamp base, designed by Domhnall O'Broin, with original factory label.

c1967    10in (25.5cm) high

**£50-70**                          **GC**

A large sage green Caithness Glass lamp base.

c1965    10in (25.5cm) high

**£60-70**                          **MHT**

A wide green Caithness Glass lamp base, with original label.

*Designed by Domhnall O'Broin and featured in 'Modern Glass' by Geoffrey Beard (Studio Vista 1968) as being the most modern glass design, first produced in 1967.*

7.25in (18.5cm) high

**£50-70**                          **GC**

A smoked Caithness Glass vase, designed by Domhnall O'Broin.

c1967    8.75in (22cm) high

**£50-70**                          **GC**

An amber Caithness Glass fruit bowl, designed by Domhnall O'Broin.

c1967    7in (17.5cm) high

**£40-60**                          **GC**

A grey Caithness Glass decanter, designed by Domhnall O'Broin, with hollow stopper.

c1967 11.25in (28.5cm) high

**£30-50**                          **GC**

A No. 1 vase or parfait in Amber Cloud Glass.

*5.5in (14cm) high*

**£20-30** **BAD**

A pair of tall No. 283 candlesticks in Amber Cloud Glass.

*7.25in (18.5cm) high*

**£60-100** **BAD**

An Amber Cloud Glass powder bowl from a No. 283 trinket set.

*5in (13cm) high*

**£15-25** **BAD**

A Purple Cloud Glass No. 1910BD flower set.

*Purple is a more desirable colour than amber.*

*9in (22.5cm) high*

**£30-50** **BAD**

A Purple Cloud Glass No. 279 vase.

*These were made in three sizes: 6, 8 and 10 inches.*

*8in (20.5cm) high*

**£50-70** **BAD**

A Green Cloud Glass No. 712 vase.

*The colouring on this example is unusual, increasing its value.*

*9.75in (24.5cm) high*

**£150-200** **BAD**

A Blue Cloud Glass No. 50 vase.

*Blue is a very popular colour at the moment.*

*8.5in (21.5cm) high*

**£60-80** **BAD**

Two Ronald Stennett-Willson for King's Lynn Glass vases.

*1967  Taller 15in (38cm) high*

**£80-100 (EACH)**　　　**GC**

Two Ronald Stennett-Willson for King's Lynn Glass 'Rustic Range' vases, in speckled blue.

*1967 Taller 9.5in (24cm) high*

**£80-100 (EACH)**　　　**GC**

A Ronald Stennett-Willson for Wedgwood vase and bowl.

*c1970  Vase 8.25in (21cm) h*

**£60-80 (EACH)**　　　**GC**

Two Ronald Stennett-Willson for King's Lynn Glass orange vases.

*Taller 7.5in (19cm) high*

**£80-120 (EACH)**　　　**GC**

Two Ronald Stennett-Willson for King's Lynn Glass vases, made to commemorate the landing on the moon.

*The uneven, crater like surface of these vases recall the moon's surface. They also have similarities to the uneven surfaces of the stylish 'Nailhead' finish vases designed by Geoffrey Baxter for Whitefriars during the same period.*

*1967  Taller 10in (26cm) high*

**£80-100 (EACH)**　　　**GC**

Two Ronald Stennett-Willson for Wedgwood vases.

*Taller 10.75in (27.5cm) high*

**£80-120 (EACH)**　　　**GC**

Three Ronald Stennett-Willson for Wedgwood 'Studio Range' rose-coloured glass pieces, including two vases and a bowl.

*The bowl is rarer and commands a higher price than the vases.*

*1970*

**BOWL £300-350, VASES £150-250 (EACH)**　　　**GC**

A Ronald Stennett-Willson for Wedgwood vase.

*5in (13cm) high*

**£60-80**　　　**GC**

A Ronald Stennett-Willson for Wedgwood 'Studio Range' bowl.

*7in (18cm) high*

**£200-350**　　　**GC**

A Ronald Stennett-Willson
candle holder.

10.25in (26cm) high

**£120-150** GC

Two Frank Thrower for
Dartington candle holders.

*Frank Thrower previously
worked with Ronald Stennett-
Willson at Wuidart in the
1950s. He became associated
with Wedgwood Glass when it
acquired a stake in Dartington
Glass, the company he worked
for, in 1982.*

*1969*

*Tallest 7.25in (18.5cm) high*

**£25-30 EACH** GC

Three Ronald Stennett-Willson
for Wedgwood candle holders.
*1967 Tallest 7in (18cm) high*

**S £35, M £65, L £90** GC

Five Ronald Stennett Willson for Wedgwood 'Sheringham'
candle holders.
*1967* *Tallest 14in (36cm) high*

**£200-300 (EACH)** GC

A Ronald Stennett-Willson for
Wedgwood fruit bowl.
*9in (23cm) high*

**£80-100** GC

A Ronald Stennett-Willson for
Wedgwood fruit bowl.
*5in (13cm) high*

**£160-180** GC

Three sculptural glass pieces,
made to commemorate the
landing on the moon.

*The moon landing and interest
in outer space during the
1960s spawned a huge interest
in futuristic themes that was
expressed in popular fashion
as well as decorative styles.*

*1969 14.5in (37cm) high*

**£200-300 (EACH)** GC

Three Ronald Stennett-Willson
for King's Lynn Glass
paperweights.

*1967 Tallest 5in (13cm) high*

**£80-150** GC

# HOT COLLECTING AREA

## LALIQUE

René Lalique (1860-1945) trained as a jeweller and began working with glass in 1893. His first perfume-bottle designs for Coty in 1908 began his real interest in glass and from the 1920s until 1945, he designed hundreds of forms that are much sought after by collectors today.

see p.123

see p.123

see p.125

- In the 1920s, he had three factories making an ever-growing range of pressed and moulded glass items, including perfume bottles, vases, bowls, ashtrays and statuettes. They typically used frosted, opalescent, milky or clear glass. The glass was also often gently stained with colour to highlight moulded elements.

- The majority of Lalique's designs were modern and stylised, most being representative of the Art Deco era. Repeated decorative motifs, often geometric or inspired by nature, are typical, as are friezes of animals or figures.

- Car mascots in the form of figures or animals, female statuettes and large, strongly stylised pieces fetch the highest values. Always aim to buy pieces that show forms and motifs typical of his designs rather than plain forms with little decoration.

- Lalique marks can be both etched and moulded and will help in roughly dating a piece. After his death in 1945, no genuine pieces were marked with his initial 'R' before his surname. Pieces with a small 'registered mark' of an 'R' in a circle were manufactured recently, as the company still exists producing new and old designs.

- Because of Lalique's popularity, many competitors at the time copied him. Finer quality copies such as those by French makers Sabino, Etling and Genet are also collected, but values are not as high as for similar objects by Lalique.

# A CLOSER LOOK AT A LALIQUE VASE

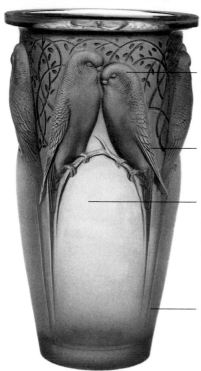

Animals are a typical form of imagery used by Lalique. As well as birds, he used fish, reptiles and insects.

The designs are formed by pressing molten glass into a mould.

Opalescent glass was produced by adding phosphates, fluorides and aluminium oxide. This was followed by carefully controlled amounts of pigment to give very subtle hints of colour.

As in this example, colours are typically delicate, becoming part of the design.

A Lalique 'Ceylan' pattern frosted and opalescent vase, of tapering cylindrical form with broad rim, moulded with a frieze of budgerigars, blue staining, wheel-etched marks.

*c1925*                                              *9.75in (25cm) high*

**£3,000-4,000**                                              **L&T**

## *TOP TIPS*

- Lalique's coloured glass is keenly collected. Green and blue are two desirable examples, but red is particularly hard to find.

- Handle as much authentic Lalique as possible to help you recognise the many fakes. Look for crude production, odd colours or sizes, thick rims and examples that are lighter in weight.

- Pieces marked with the words 'Paris', 'Rene' and 'Made in France' should be viewed with suspicion, although the latter is used on some very modern pieces.

A Lalique opalescent bowl, designed by Cremieu, moulded mark "R. LALIQUE FRANCE" with inscribed "No. 400", small scratches to the well and two bruises to the lip, one appears to have been ground.

*1928     12in (30.5cm) diam*

**£650-750**                    **JDJ**

A Lalique 'Ondines' pattern opalescent bowl, moulded on the exterior with a group of six mermaids swimming amid bubbles, signed "R. Lalique France" and numbered "380".

*8.25in (21cm) diam*

**£900-1,000**                    **DN**

A Lalique 'Actina' pattern opalescent shallow bowl, signed "R.Lalique, France".

*10in (25.5cm) diam*

**£450-550**                    **GORL**

A mid-20thC Lalique opalescent bowl.

*8in (20.5cm) diam*

**£200-300**                    **BONS**

A Lalique 'Vaguest No.1' pattern clear glass bowl, signed "Lalique, France".

*9.5in (24cm) diam*

**£220-280**                    **GORL**

A mid-20thC Lalique bowl, tapered towards the foot and cut with a design of thistle heads divided by thorned canes, engraved script "Lalique France" mark.

*10.25in (26cm) diam*

**£250-350**                    **BONS**

A small Lalique clear glass bowl.

**£80-120** GORL

A Lalique dish, with green petal and cut decoration, signed "Lalique, France".

*12in (30.5cm) diam*

**£450-550** GORL

An R. Lalique 'Fauvettes' pattern clear glass ashtray.

*7in (18cm) diam*

**£80-120** GORL

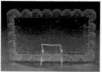

A Lalique moulded glass 'Oeillets' pattern tray, the rim moulded with stylized blossoms, stamped "R. LALIQUE/FRANCE".

*1936  15.75in (40cm) wide*

**£450-550** SL

A Lalique ashtray, decorated with a galleon, signed "Lalique".

*7in (18cm) diam*

**£70-90** GORL

An octagonal Lalique bowl, with petalled rim, signed "Lalique, France".

*8.5in (21.5cm) diam*

**£120-180** GORL

A frosted Lalique fan-moulded ovoid bowl, signed "Lalique, France".

*8.5in (21.5cm) diam*

**£150-200** GORL

A Lalique clear glass ashtray, decorated with impressed frosted flowerheads.

**£80-120** GORL

A mid-20thC cylindrical Lalique vase, moulded with long leaves and berries towards the rim, stained in blue, moulded "R. Lalique France" mark to side of vase.

*7in (17.5cm) high*

**£500-600** BONS

A Lalique 'Rampillon' pattern frosted and clear glass vase, engraved "R. LALIQUE".

*5.25in (13cm) high*

**£250-350** GORL

A Lalique 'Poisson' clear glass dish, signed "Lalique, France".

*14in (35.5cm) diam*

**£500-600** GORL

A square Lalique 'Roses' pattern bowl, signed "Lalique, France".
*9.5in (24cm) wide*

£280-320 **GORL**

A Lalique 'Bagatelle' pattern frosted glass vase, the sides with birds in foliate compartments, inscribed with "Lalique, France".
*6.75in (15.5cm) high*

£250-350 **SL**

An R. Lalique 'Ronces' pattern opalescent vase, with moulded thorny vines, engraved "R. Lalique France" retailer's label.
*9.25in (23.5cm) high*

£1,800-2,200 **FRE**

An R. Lalique 'Archer' vase, frosted amber glass with a blown-out moulded decoration of ten archers and ten birds, signed in block letters on the underside as well as in script.
*10.5in (26.5cm) high*

£8,500-9,500 **JDJ**

A green coloured R. Lalique vase, with moulded design of leaves, signed on base "R. Lalique FRANCE H984".
*6.5in (16.5cm) high*

£3,000-4,000 **JDJ**

An R. Lalique 'Ornis' pattern opalescent vase, with two applied bird handles, signed "R. Lalique, FRANCE".
*7.5in (19cm) high*

£150-200 **JDJ**

An R. Lalique frosted glass 'Thais' figure, signed "R. LALIQUE".
*8.5in (21.5cm) high*

£6,000-7,000 **JDJ**

A Lalique frosted glass 'Chrysis' figure, signed on base "LALIQUE FRANCE".
*6.25in (16cm) long*

£1,000-1,500 **JDJ**

An R. Lalique 'Grape' pattern decanter set, with six matching tumblers and tray, all signed in block letters "R LALIQUE", slight damage to tray and tumblers.

*Decanter 10.5in (26.5cm) high*

£650-750 **JDJ**

A Lalique 'Eventail' pattern moulded glass ice cream cup.
*1928* *3in (7.5cm) diam*

£60-80 **SL**

A Lalique 'Copellia' pattern clear and frosted glass box, the hinged cover with gilt metal mounts, engraved "Lalique, France".

*6.75in (17cm) long*

**£300-350**      **DRA**

A Lalique 'Hirondelles' pattern clear and frosted glass cigarette box.

*4in (10cm) wide*

**£400-500**      **DRA**

A Lalique 'Sirenes' pattern frosted glass perfume burner, of cylindrical form moulded with a frieze of mermaids, lacking stopper, moulded mark "R. Lalique".

*9in (22.5cm) high*

**£350-450**      **L&T**

A modern Lalique cigarette lighter, holder and ashtray, with heavy lion bosses, "Lalique France" inscribed in script.

**£350-550**      **CW**

A Lalique 'Sainte-Christophe' pattern clear and frosted glass car mascot, with amethyst tint, moulded "R. LALIQUE FRANCE".

*5in (13cm) high*

**£500-600**      **DRA**

A Lalique 'Feuilles D'Artichaut' pattern clear and frosted glass rocker blotter, with sepia patina, original metal, moulded "R. Lalique".

*6.25in (16cm) long*

**£700-1,000**      **DRA**

A Lalique-style lime green frosted glass night light, in the form of a nude with feather shawl, original electrification, two small surface mould lines.

*11in (28cm) high*

**£650-750**      **JDJ**

A Mdina blue, white and yellow cased 'Lollipop' vase.

*The colours and thick glass are typical Mdina features.*

7.5in (19cm) high

£60-80                                    GC

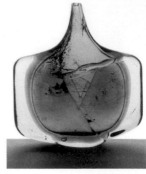

A 1970s massive Mdina clear and blue glass 'Fish' vase, with applied clear casing and trails, designed by Michael Harris.

*This piece is worth more than others as large pieces are less common and this is a hallmark Harris design.*

10.75in (27cm) high

£180-220                                  GC

An unusual, mould blown textured Mdina blue glass vase.

*The neck is made separately and dropped in. This vase is often mistaken for Whitefriars due to the similarity of the texturing.*

8.75in (22.5cm) high

£80-120                                   GC

A Mdina blue cased sand and aqua hammer head-shaped bottle.

8.25in (21cm) high

£60-70                                    PC

A Mdina clear, blue, brown and blue trailed glass vase, designed by Michael Harris.

8.75in (22cm) high

£70-90                                    GC

A Mdina faceted blue and brown clear-cased vase, signed and dated "Mdina 1978" on the base.

1978    6.75in (17.5cm) high

£70-100                                   TGM

A 1970s Mdina three-sided sculptural Mdina vase, unsigned.

10.75in (27cm) high

£40-60                                    PC

An Isle of Wight 'Blue Aurene' glass vase, with 'flame' pontil mark and early sticker.

*1974-82*    *3.75in (9.5cm) h*

**£50-80**                          **TGM**

An Isle of Wight large 'Blue Aurene' glass vase, with 'flame' pontil mark.

*Although the vase does not appear blue, it is. The glass is blown very thinly and the colour is less dense.*

*1974-82*                  *8.75in (22cm) high*

**£150-250**                          **PC**

An Isle of Wight 'Blue Aurene' glass attenuated bottle, with unmarked broken pontil.

*1973*        *15in (38cm) high*

**£150-250**                          **PC**

An Isle of Wight 'Tortoiseshell' attenuated bottle, with unmarked broken pontil.

*1973*        *15in (38cm) high*

**£150-250**                          **PC**

An Isle of Wight 'Tortoiseshell' vase, with 'flame' pontil mark.

*1974-82*        *9.5in (24cm) high*

**£60-90**                          **PC**

An Isle of Wight large 'Black Azurene' glass vase, with 22ct gold and silver leaf decoration, broken, unmarked pontil and triangular Isle of Wight label.

*The gold and silver leaf in earlier pieces of Azurene, first introduced in 1978, are often duller and have less contrast, perhaps due to the hot glass affecting the colour.*

*c1979*        *9.5in (24cm) high*

**£150-200**                          **PC**

A 1980s Isle of Wight 'Fish' clear cased, multilayered 'Black Azurene' vase, decorated with silver and gold leaf.

*7.5in (19cm) high*

**£150-250**                          **PC**

A Monart glass vase, the mottled body with bubble inclusions.

*6.75in (17cm) high*

**£200-300**    **L&T**

A Monart glass vase, the mottled body with band of multicoloured swirls, pale mottled band to rim.

*7.75in (20cm) high*

**£120-180**    **L&T**

A Monart glass vase with green mottling and pulled threads from shoulders to rim, small bruise.

*10.5in (27cm) high*

**£150-200**    **DN**

A Monart glass vase, the mottled body with amethyst and aventurine inclusions to the rim.

*9in (23cm) high*

**£100-150**    **L&T**

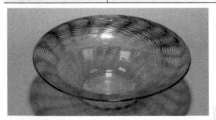

A near pair of Monart vases, the mottled bodies with amethyst inclusions to the rim.

*9in (23cm) high*

**£400-600**    **L&T**

A Monart flared glass bowl, 'UB' shape, with horizontal webbing in milky-orange tones, shading through amethyst to black with areas further decorated with aventurine.

*13in (33cm) diam*

**£100-150**    **DN**

A Vasart glass vase, the green body with amethyst inclusions to the rim; and another Vasart vase, the pale blue body with turquoise rim, etched mark.

*7.75in (20cm) high*

**£50-75 (EACH)**    **L&T**

A Vasart glass vase, the pink body with a band of blue swirls and with green to the rim; and a Strathearn glass vase, the green body with amethyst and aventurine inclusions to the rim.

*Taller 7.75in (20cm) high*

**£40-60 (EACH)**    **L&T**

A Vasart tapered cylindrical glass vase, the mottled body with red swirling band, etched mark; also another Vasart glass vase similar design, etched mark.

*7.5in (19.5cm) high*

**£40-60 (EACH)**    **L&T**

A Vasart glass table lamp, with pale mottled blue glass and mottled rust glass to the rim, etched mark.

**£300-500**      **L&T**

A Vasart glass bowl, the mottled body with orange inclusions to the rim and all-over swirl design, etched mark.

*8.75in (22cm) diam*

**£70-100**      **L&T**

A Vasart vase, the base of the rim decorated with swirled inclusions, pontil mark to base.

*7.25in (18.5cm) high*

**£80-120**      **AOY**

A Vasart hat-shaped bowl, with mottled base and rim, pontil mark and signed on base.

*2.25in (6cm) high*

**£30-50**      **AOY**

A Vasart glass posy basket, mottled glass, with pontil mark and signature to base.

*4in (10cm) high*

**£30-40**      **AOY**

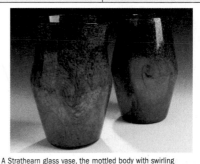

A Strathearn glass vase, the mottled body with swirling inclusions and moulded marks; and another Strathearn glass vase with aventurine inclusions and moulded marks.

*10in (25cm) high*

**£50-75 (EACH)**      **L&T**

A Strathearn glass vase, with ring of coloured swirls to waist, the pontil mark impressed with the leaping salmon motif.

*8.25in (21cm) high*

**£60-90**      **AOY**

A Venini honey-coloured glass bowl, by Vittorio Zecchin.

*c1925  5.75in (21.5cm) high*

| £400-450 | QU |

A Venini flaring pillow vase, with bubbles and gold foil on a red sommerso ground, unmarked.

*6.75in (17cm) wide*

| £220-280 | DRA |

A 1950s A.V.E.M. Murano glass toothpick holder, with red interior and red foil sticker.

*2.5in (6.5cm) high*

| £30-50 | MHC |

A Barbini oversized flaring ribbed bowl, the exterior of clear purple glass lined in lattimo, with Barbini label.

*18in (45.5cm) diam*

| £180-220 | CR |

A Venini marquetry turtle figure, with amber head, legs and tail with amber shell and marquetry inlay of turquoise blue iridescent squares, signed on the bottom "VENINI ITALIA".

*5in (12.5cm) long*

| £450-550 | JDJ |

A Cenedese block form aquarium glass sculpture, a few scratches and a nick to one corner, unmarked.

*5.5in (14cm) wide*

| £120-180 | DRA |

A 1950s A.V.E.M. Murano oval glass dish, with red base.

*A.V.E.M. stands for 'Arte Vetreria Muranese', a company which was founded c1932 and flourished during the 1950s under the guidance of Giorgio Ferro in the early 1950s and Ansolo Fuga from 1955-1968*

*12.75in (32.5cm) wide*

| £120-150 | TGM |

A Cenedese charcoal smoked glass bull figure, unmarked.

*Founded in 1946, the Gino Cenedese factory employed the renowned Alfredo Barbini as artistic director between 1947-50.*

*7.5in (19cm) high*

| £300-350 | DRA |

A Venini & Co. glass bottle vase, marked "Venini Murano ITALIA", of cylindrical form with thin pulled-in neck, dark green with white and dark red overlay, etched on three lines, lacks stopper.

*1946-50  11.5in (29cm) high*

**£280-320**                    **HERR**

A Venini glass bottle vase, by Fulvio Bianconi, of tall cylindrical form with dark green overlay and one light blue and two red melted-on glass stripes, the spherical stopper with partial overlay in cornflower blue, marked "Venini Murano ITALIA", etched on three lines.
*c1951-5*
                    *16.25in (41cm) high*

**£750-850**                    **HERR**

A Venini glass bottle vase, by Fulvio Bianconi, the slender oviform vessel with tall cylindrical neck, in deep emerald green with primrose-yellow band around the lower section, the drop-in ovoid stopper also in primrose-yellow, indistinct marks on base.

*14.25in (36cm) high*

**£180-220**                    **DN**

A Venini bottle vase, by Paolo Venini, of hexagonal form, smoke-coloured, decorated with red spiral threads, the colourless glass stopper with red overlay, marked "Venini Murano Italia" etched on three lines.

*8.5in (21.5cm) high*

**£650-750**                    **HERR**

A Venini cased hankerchief vase, with red exterior and white interior, acid etched mark.

*7.75in (19.5cm) high*

**£350-400**                    **DN**

A small Venini handkerchief vase, internally decorated with alternating bands of lemon and amethyst latticino threading.

*2.75in (7cm) high*

**£80-120**                    **DN**

A Venini tessuto vase, of heavily bulbous form with thick, vertically melted-on glass bands in white, yellow and purple, etched mark "Venini Italia 81" and two labels.

*1981  12.75in (32.5cm) high*

**£500-600**                    **HERR**

A 1960s Fratelli Ferro opaline glass vase, with foil labels.

8.25in (21cm) high

**£30-40** MHC

A Seguso Vetri d'Arte sommerso vase, by Flavio Poli, tear-drop shaped with cased amber glass.

c1955    10.5in (26cm) high

**£400-450** QU

A 1950s Seguso Vetri D'Arte Archimede opaline glass vase, the body sprinkled in pink with gold foil overlay, unmarked.

6.75in (17cm) high

**£220-280** HERR

A Seguso Vetri d'Arte sommerso vase, by Flavio Poli, of funnel form with clear cased cobalt blue body and green base.

c1958    9.75in (24cm) high

**£750-850** QU

A Seguso for Oggetti tall cylindrical vase, with orange and black stripes on clear glass, etched "Seguso A.V. por Oggetti".

*Oggetti is a luxury retailer of decorative home accessories founded in 1975 by Robert & Nancy Frehling. Originally, all their items were selected from Italian makers, but since the 1980s they have looked further afield. The word 'oggetti' is Italian for 'objects'.*

15.75in (40cm) high

**£150-200** CR

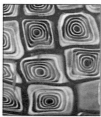

A Fratelli Toso murrine two-handled vase.

*Murrines are small, flat squares of glass, which are heated and then stuck to a clear glass body making them appear like the tesserae of a mosaic.*

c1910    4in (10cm) high

**£320-380** QU

A 1950s Murano sommerso glass vase, triple cased green, amber and red, in the form of an owl.

*10.5in (27cm) high*

**£80-120** TGM

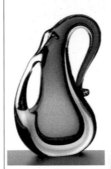

A 1950s Murano triple cased sommerso freeform vase.

*Glass using techniques such as 'sommerso' is popular and remains surprisingly inexpensive.*

*11in (28cm) high*

**£120-150** PC

A 1950s Murano triple-cased sommerso freeform vase.

*9in (23cm) high*

**£60-70** PC

A 1950s Murano triple cased sommerso swan figure, in clear green and amber.

*The sommerso technique involves encasing strongly coloured glass in a layer of contrasting coloured glass before the whole is encased in a heavy layer of clear glass. The clear glass exterior casing can be carved with strong facets, or pulled into extended shapes, creating interesting and complex optical effects.*

*14.5in (37cm) high*

**£120-150** PC

A 1950s Murano triple cased sommerso freeform vase.

*6.75in (24.5cm) high*

**£80-90** PC

A 1950s Murano triple cased sommerso duck figure, with green foil sticker with curling edges.

*6.25in (16cm) high*

**£25-35** TGM

A Murano tall frosted yellow glass vase, with clear frosted foot.

*17.5in (44.5cm) high*

**£50-60** GC

A fine Murano glass stoppered vessel, with controlled bubbles and gold foil against an orange ground, some small chips and gold foil Murano label.

*9.5in (24cm) high*

**£180-220**     **DRA**

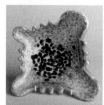

A 1980s VeArt Murano honey-coloured glass vase, with company label, boxed.

*18in (46cm) high*

**£200-250**     **HERR**

A pair of Murano sommerso glass pheasants, with Murano glass labels.

*Largest 13.75in (35cm) high*

**£60-70**     **CR**

A contemporary Italian glass sculpture, by Silvio Vigliaturo.

*16.5in (42cm) high*

**£700-1,000**     **FM**

A 1960s Murano glass bowl, with random red spots, and gold aventurine, with an outer layer of white glass to the base.

*8.25in (21cm) wide*

**£30-40**     **AOY**

A contemporary glass piece 'Fussvogel', by R Z Sperl.

*13.5in (34cm) high*

**£1,200-1,800**     **FM**

A contemporary glass piece, by Zanfiriro.

*21.5in (55cm) high*

**£1,000-1,500**     **FM**

An Aureliano Toso glass fish, by Dino Martens, of clear glass with white trails with pierced bubbles and azure blue, cobalt blue, dark violet and orange/yellow powder enamel.

*c1960*     *9.75in (24.5cm) long*

**£500-600**     **QU**

A Royal Bohemia lined and graduated red, orange and yellow glass vase.

*c1960s*      6.25in (16cm) high

**£35-45**                    GC

A Royal Bohemia vase, made by the Rudolfova Glassworks to a Rudolf Jurnikl design.

*1964+*      5in (12.5cm) high

**£20-30**                    GC

A Royal Bohemia graduated red, orange and yellow glass vase.

*c1960s*      13.5in (34cm) high

**£50-70**                    GC

A Royal Bohemia vase, made by the Rudolfova Glassworks to a Rudolf Jurnikl design.

*1964+*                7.5cm) high

**£30-40**                    GC

A Royal Bohemia small clear glass vase, by the Rosice Glassworks to a Vladislav Urban design.

*1967+*      8in (20cm) high

**£15-25**                    GC

A Royal Bohemia amber glass vase, with geometric patterns.

*1960s/70s*  7in (17.5cm) high

**£30-40**                    GC

A Royal Bohemia vase, by the Hermanova Glassworks to a Frantisek Vizner design.

*1965+*      9.75in (25cm) high

**£25-35**                    GC

A Royal Bohemia large vase, by the Rosice Glassworks to a Vladislav Urban design.

*Made from pressed glass in a number of Czech factories, most of these high quality pieces were made for many years. Information is beginning to surface, increasing interest.*

*1967+*      9.75in (25cm) high

**£35-45**                    GC

A Royal Bohemia clear glass vase, with vertical textured wavy pattern.

*1960s/70s*  9in (23cm) high

**£30-40**                    GC

# HOT COLLECTING AREA

## SCANDINAVIAN GLASS

In the 1930s, Scandinavian glassmakers began a drive to bring hand-crafted quality to factory-produced designs, developing pieces that were both aesthetically pleasing and affordable. Their success has led to the establishment of one of the fastest-growing and varied collecting areas in modern glass today.

see p.138          see p.141          see p.143

- Many styles were modern, with geometric, angular shapes in jewel-like colours. Popular factories included Finland's Riihimaen Lasi Oy (Riihimaki) who employed noted designers such as Nanny Still, Helena Tynell and Tamara Aladin. Clear, cased bases help 'lift' and strengthen the strong colours.

- Pieces were blown into moulds, allowing consistency and large production numbers. These styles became very popular at the time and can be readily found at affordable prices today. As interior decorators and collectors turn their attention to these examples, prices will rise.

- Nature and the Scandinavian landscape were also important inspirations. Examples are found with textured surfaces recalling ice and bark. Look out for the work of Tapio Wirkkala and Timo Sarpaneva at Iittala as these are very popular with collectors.

- Organic, asymmetric forms, almost based on bud-like forms, were designed by Per Lutken at Denmark's Holmegaard Glassworks. Many of his pieces are signed on the base with a monogram and date. Colours tended to be clear or cool and classical.

- Optical effects were also popular. Vicke Lindstrand is a notable designer for Kosta who incorporated spiralling threads of colour into his designs. Internal ribs or waves are also common. Engraved glass was also produced, with complex Art Deco designs being much in demand, especially those produced by Orrefors.

The mould interior is rough wood, giving the texture to the glass. This idea was used later by Baxter at Whitefriars.

Each time the mould is used, the molten glass burns it, changing it, and making each piece effectively unique.

Designed in 1964, 'Finlandia' is a key range.

Nature often inspired Scandinavian glass designers – here, the inspiration is tree bark.

An Iittala bark pattern 'Finlandia' vase, designed by Timo Sarpaneva, signed 'TIMO SARPANEVA 3331' on the base.

*c1965*

*6.75in (17cm) high*

**£100-150**

**TGM**

## *TOP TIPS*

- The striking purity of coloured Swedish glass and its texture are highly desirable factors, so avoid scratched, chipped or scuffed examples.

- Artist-signed pieces are usually more valuable, as are those from notable factories such as Kosta and Orrefors as they have larger followings. Look for pieces typical of famous designers, such as Per Lutken or Tapio Wirkkala.

- Look out for pieces designed by currently less well-known names and companies such as Eric Hoglund and Strombergshyttan as interest is growing.

A Nanny Still cased vase, for Riihimaën Lasi Oy, pattern no. 1339 and acid stamp "Riihimaën Lasi Oy" with polar bear on base.

*7.75in (21.5cm) high*

**£50-60**                 **MHT**

Two Nanny Still 'Tiimalasi' vases, for Riihimaën Lasi Oy.

*1970s*        *7in (18cm) high*

**£50-70 EACH**            **MHT**

A Nanny Still cased vase, for Riihimaën Lasi Oy, pattern no. 1436 and acid stamp "Riihimaën Lasi Oy" with polar bear on base.

*6in (15cm) high*

**£50-60**                 **MHT**

Two Tamara Aladin large undulating vases, for Riihimaën Lasi Oy.

*1960s*        *11in (28cm) high*

**£50-80 EACH**            **MHT**

A Tamara Aladin large undulating vase, for Riihimaën Lasi Oy.

*1960s*        *11in (28cm) high*

**£50-70**                 **MHT**

Two Tamara Aladin vases, for Riihimaën Lasi Oy.

*c1970s*     *7.75in (20cm) high*

**£30-50 EACH**            **MHT**

A Tamara Aladin undulating vase, for Riihimaën Lasi Oy.

*1960s*      *7.75in (20cm) high*

**£40-60**                 **MHT**

A Tamara Aladin 'Tuulikki' vase, for Riihimaën Lasi Oy.

*c1976*      *7.75in (20cm) high*

**£30-50**                 **MHT**

A Tamara Aladin undulating vase, for Riihimaën Lasi Oy.

*1960s*       *9.75in (25cm) high*

**£60-80**                 **MHT**

A Riihimaën Lasi Oy Fossil range aqua blue glass vase, by Helena Tynell.

*The 'Fossil' range has become harder to find over the past few years, and as a result prices have risen.*

6.25in (16cm) high

£70-100      GC

A Riihimaën Lasi Oy 'Pironki' vase, by Helena Tynell.

c1974     8.25in (21cm) high

£120-180      MHT

A Riihimaën Lasi Oy mould-blown 'Venturi' vase, by Helena Tynell.

c1974    8.25in (21cm) high

£120-180      MHT

A Riihimaën Lasi Oy large 'Pompadour' vase, by Nanny Still, with export label for "Finncristal".

c1968    11in (28cm) high

£120-180      MHT

A Riihimaën Lasi Oy small 'Pompadour' vase, by Nanny Still.

c1968    8.75in (22cm) high

£80-120      MHT

Two Riihimaën Lasi Oy 'Pompadour' vases, with turned rims, by Nanny Still.

c1968   Tallest 11in (28cm) h

S £100-150 L £140-180   MHT

Three Riihimaën Lasi Oy vases, by Nanny Still.

1969-70 Tallest 12in (30cm) h

£50-80 (EACH)      GC

Three Riihimaën Lasi Oy vases, by Iamara Aladln.

1969-70 Tallest 11in (28cm) h

£50-80 (EACH)      GC

A Holmegaard brown glass tapering vase, by Per Lütken, signed with his monogram on the base.

*8.75in (22cm) high*

**£30-50**                        **GC**

A Holmegaard green vase, by Per Lütken.

*1959-60   11.5in (29cm) high*

**£90-100**                       **GC**

A Holmegaard cylindrical blue glass vase, by Per Lütken, signed with his monogram on the base.

*12in (30.5cm) high*

**£60-90**                        **GC**

A Holmegaard purple tri-form section vase, by Per Lütken, dated and inscribed "HOLMEGAARD" on the base.

*1955    10.25in (26cm) high*

**£100-150**                      **GC**

A Holmegaard white bowl, by Michael Bang, from the Atlantis range.

*c1980        3in (7.5cm) high*

**£20-30**                       **MHT**

A Kosta oviform vase, by Vicke Lindstrand, marked "Lindstrand Kosta" and signed "LH 1260".

*2.75in (7cm) high*

**£80-120**                       **DN**

A Boda large bottle vase, by Eric Hoglund.

*Hoglund's designs are characterised by thickly rendered glass, often in orange, blue and ruby glass, with impressed or moulded primitively formed figures or animals as decoration.*

*c1965     14.5in (37cm) high*

**£120-160**                     **MHT**

A 1930s Kosta large, internally ribbed, optic blue vase, by Ellis Berg, signed to base "B473".

*10.5in (26.5cm) high*

**£100-120**                     **MHT**

A Helena Tynell 'Pala' vase, for Riihimaën Lasi Oy.

A Helena Tynell 'Sun' juice carafe, for Riihimaën Lasi Oy.

*'Sun' bottles were available in four different sizes.*

A 1930s Alvar Aalto-style 'Savoy' vase, for Iittala.

*The Finnish designer Alvar Aalto (1898-1976) is better known for his architectural, interior and furniture designs. As well as glass, he also worked in lighting and textiles.*

c1969-76  4.5in (11.5cm) high

c1964-74  9in (23cm) high

1990s  4in (10cm) high

**£30-50**  MHT

**£70-100**  MHT

**£50-70**  MHT

An Otto Brauer "Gul" white cased vase, for Kastrap/Holmegaard.

*1960s*

**£80-90**  MHT

A selection of Otto Brauer "Gul" vases, for Kastrap/Holmegaard.

*1960s*

**£50-120 (EACH)**  MHT

A Boda Sun Catcher, by Eric Hoglund, with impressed abstract animals, signed "H866/F".

11.75in (30cm) wide

A Paul Kedelv still-mould blown vase, for Reijmyre.

c1965  8.25in (21cm) high

A Holmegaard ice bucket, by Per Lutken, signed "Holmegaard 8715".

6in (15cm) high

**£80-120**  MHT

**£40-60**  MHT

**£40-50**  MHT

A Nuutajärvi Notsjö chestnut dish, by Kaj Franck, signed "Nuutajärvi Notsjö".

*Kaj Franck worked for Nuutajärvi Notsjö between 1950 and 1976.*

2.5in (6.5cm) wide

£40-60  MHT

A Nuutajärvi Notsjö bowl, model no. kf233, by Kaj Franck.

*1962*  3.5in (9cm) wide

£70-100  MHT

A Nuutajärvi Notsjö bowl, model no. kf245, by Kaj Franck, signed "K Franck Nuutajärvi Notsjö 64".

*1964*  7in (18cm) wide

£80-120  MHT

A Nuutajärvi Notsjö candlestick, by Oiva Toikka, signed "Nuutajärvi Notsjö".

9in (23cm) high

£100-150  MHT

A Flygfors low green glass vase, by Paul Kedelv.

3.5in (9cm) high

£40-60  GC

A Hadeland vase, by Willy Johansson, signed "Hadeland 60 WJ".

*1960*  6.5in (16.5cm) high

£80-100  MHT

A Nuutajärvi Notsjö glass vase, by Gunnel Nyman, the slender oviform having an internal cavity of 'rose' colour, cased in clear glass and surrounded by a web of bubbles, signed on base "G.Nyman", "Notsjö" and dated "1947".

12.5in (31.5cm) high

£180-220  DN

An Afors glass vase, by Ernest Gordon, of flattened oviform, internally decorated with a ruby-coloured cavity and applied with an extra clear glass 'skin' set at an angle on the lower part of the vessel, signed on base "Afors", "GH391" and "Ernest Gordon".

8in (20cm) high

£80-120  DN

A Kastrup tall tapering vase, by E. Bang, with 'knop' form.

17.75in (45cm) high

£60-90  GC

A late 1950s Aimo Okkolin Free Form vase, for Riihimaën Lasi Oy, with air-bubbled decoration around the base, signed "AIMO OKKOLIN Riihimaën LASI OY" on base.

*9.25in (23.5cm) high*

**£80-100**    **MHT**

A Bengt Orup vase, for Johansfors, graduated colour, signed to base "J Fors Orup".

*16.6in (42cm)*

**£120-140**    **MHT**

A Bengt Orup olive green tail glass, for Johansfors, signed "Johansfors Orup".

*16.5in (42cm) high*

**£120-140**    **MHT**

An Orrefors 'Selena' dish, by Sven Palmqvist, signed "Orrefors Pu 3092/31".

*6in (15.5cm) wide*

**£50-60**    **MHT**

An Orrefors vase, by Sven Palmqvist.

*6.75in (17.5cm) high*

**£70-90**    **MHT**

One of a set of four Timo Sarpaneva 'Klinka' whiskey glasses, for Iittala, with box.

*3.5in (8.5cm) high*

**£50-70 (SET)**    **MHT**

A Boda vase, with abstract celestial motifs, signed "Boda Artist B Vallien 48330".

*5.75in (14.5cm) high*

**£65-75**    **MHT**

A Finnish ruby red carafe and a turn-mould blown tumbler, for Nuutajatui Notsjo.

*1962-63*    *7.5in (19cm) h*

**£80-90**    **MHT**

A Mona-Morales-Schildt vase, for Kosta, signed "Kosta".

*4.5in (11.5cm) high*

**£50-60**    **MHT**

## WHITEFRIARS

Although founded in London in the 17th century, the great period for Whitefriars was the 20th century, from the simple forms and cool colours of the Art Deco period to the textured shapes in the dramatic yet fashionable colours of the 1960s.

see p.147          see p.146          see p.149

- From 1834 until 1962, the factory was known as 'Powell & Sons'. The early 20th century saw the company become known for its fashionable art glass, producing subtly coloured and clear glass often decorated with internal streaks or waves and applied external 'trails' of glass.

- Scandinavian glass, with its organic forms and varying subtle or strong colours, was a strong influence. In 1954 the talented designer Geoffrey Baxter was employed and took this aesthetic further, introducing new colours, asymmetrically shaped cased glass, pulled lips and more fluid forms.

- His 'Textured' range was released in 1967 and is a focus for many collectors today. Glass was blown into moulds with differently textured interiors to give a strongly textured surface to the end product. Bark is a common texture, as are abstract, linear patterns created by wire or nail heads in the mould.

- Diverse and immensely popular then and now, it was produced in the fashionable bright colours of the time. Some colours, such as 'meadow green', are scarcer than other more common colours, such as 'tangerine'. Shapes were modern, ranging from the simple cylinder to abstracted shapes such as the 'Banjo' and 'Drunken Bricklayer'.

- Despite this success, problems with the British economy resulted in the closure of the factory in 1980. Collecting interest has been strong for over ten years causing some prices to plateau, yet Whitefriars glass still looks to have future potential, particularly for rare, large and characteristic pieces.

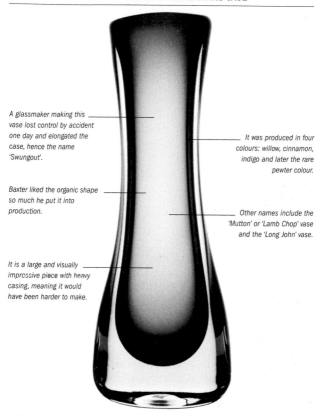

A glassmaker making this vase lost control by accident one day and elongated the case, hence the name 'Swungout'.

Baxter liked the organic shape so much he put it into production.

It is a large and visually impressive piece with heavy casing, meaning it would have been harder to make.

It was produced in four colours: willow, cinnamon, indigo and later the rare pewter colour.

Other names include the 'Mutton' or 'Lamb Chop' vase and the 'Long John' vase.

A Whitefriars 'Swungout' willow-coloured glass vase, by Geoffrey Baxter.
*c1962*

15.75in (40cm) high

**£600-800**

**GC**

## TOP TIPS

- Pieces tend to be unmarked, but auction catalogues and reference books can be used to identify them from the shape and size.

- Look out for iconic shapes such as the 'Drunken Bricklayer' and 'Banjo', which have risen the most in value and remain desirable.

- With textured examples, look for a good and varied range of texture on the exterior, as each time the mould was used it was burnt. Pieces made in heavily used moulds have less variation in the texture and are therefore less collectable.

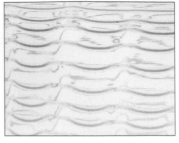

A 1930s Whitefriars threaded blue vase.

£200-300          GC

A Whitefriars/Powell sea green vase, from the 'Wealdstone' range, with applied prunts.
c1938     6in (15cm) high

£50-70       MHT

A Whitefriars/Powell sea green lidded jar.
c1940     6.25in (16cm) high

£30-50       MHT

A Whitefriars/Powell golden amber ribbed vase.

c1940     6.75in (17cm) high

£35-40       MHT

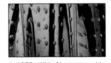

A 1950s Whitefriars vase, with air bubbles.
         5in (12.5cm) high

£25-35       JH

A Whitefriars/Powell golden amber souvenir tankard, from the "Britain Can Make It" exhibition.
1945     4.5in (11.5cm) high

£35-45       MHT

A 1950s Whitefriars ruby glass vase, 1930s shape.

        7.25in (18.5cm) high

£70-90       JH

A Whitefriars red cased in clear glass vase.

1954-7    7.5in (10.5cm) high

£60-80       JH

Above left: A Geoffrey Baxter for Whitefriars "Drunken Bricklayer" glass vase, of rectangular section formed as three blocks with the central portion dislodged and in "pewter" toned glass.

*13in (33cm) high*

**£1,000-1,500**　　　**DN**

Above right: A Whitefriars "ribbon-trailed" glass lamp base, designed by Barnaby Powell, the body of pale green tone and decorated with a horizontal spiralling band.

*8.25in (21cm) high*

**£180-220**　　　**DN**

A large ruby Geoffrey Baxter for Whitefriars vase, with bulbous pinched form.

*10.5in (27cm) high*

**£60-80**　　　**MHT**

A Geoffrey Baxter 'Kingfisher' blue bud vase.

*c1960s　8.5in (21.5cm) high*

**£25-30**　　　**MHT**

A pair of Geoffrey Baxter for Whitefriars ruby bud vases.

*c1960s　7.85in (20cm) high*

**£20-25 EACH**　　　**MHT**

A Geoffrey Baxter for Whitefriars textured 'Nailhead' vase, pattern 9683.

*c1967　6.75in (17cm) high*

**£30-40**　　　**MHT**

A Geoffrey Baxter for Whitefriars, amethyst soda glass vase.

*1962-64　4in (10cm) high*

**£40-60**　　　**MHT**

Two Geoffrey Baxter for Whitefriars small shadow green soda glass vases, pattern no.9548.

*4in (10cm) high*

**£30-50 EACH**　　　**MHT**

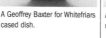

A Geoffrey Baxter for Whitefriars willow cased bowl, pattern no "9660".

*c1965　11.5in (29.5cm) wide*

**£60-80**　　　**MHT**

A Geoffrey Baxter for Whitefriars cased dish.

*c1960s 5.25in (13.5cm) high*

**£25-30**　　　**MHT**

A Geoffrey Baxter for Whitefriars ruby dish, with splayed rim.

*c1960s　6.25in (16cm) high*

**£25-30**　　　**MHT**

A Whitefriars 'Cow Parsley' vase, by Geoffrey Baxter.

*c1955*    8.75in (22cm) high

**£300-400**    **GC**

Two Whitefriars 'Bat Wing' vases, by Geoffrey Baxter. *c1957*    9.5in (24.5cm) high

**£200-250**    **GC**

Two Whitefriars 'Beak' vases, by Geoffrey Baxter.

*c1957*    12.25in (31cm) high

**£800-1,200**    **GC**

A rare Whitefriars 'Aquamarine' vase, by Geoffrey Baxter.

*This vase is made from two different coloured glasses – blue and green. They were incompatible in the furnace and always broke down leading to the work being discarded. Only around five successful examples have ever been found by collectors.*

*c1957*    3.75in (9.5cm) high

**£900-1,200**    **GC**

A rare Whitefriars 'Evening Sky' vase, by Geoffrey Baxter.

*Like 'Aquamarine', this vase is made from two different coloured glasses – blue and pink. Again, they were incompatible in the furnace. These were the only two colourways to have such problems. Only around ten successful examples are known.*

*c1957*    10in (25.5cm) high

**£900-1,000**    **GC**

A late 1960s Whitefriars vase.

6.25in (16cm) high

**£25-30**    **JH**

A Whitefriars special commission large red dish, by Geoffrey Baxter.

*c1958*

**£130-160**    **MHT**

A large Whitefriars clear glass duck, with applied beak and foot and internal repeated rings of bubbles decoration.

6.5in (16.5cm) high

**£35-45**    **GC**

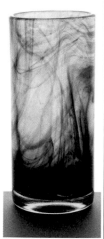

A Whitefriars 'New Studio' range ruby colour glass vase, by Geoffrey Baxter, with applied silver chloride decoration.

*The addition of silver chloride gives the glass this particular coloured and streaked effect.*

*c1974*      7in (18cm) high

**£250-300**      GC

A Whitefriars 'Streaky Green' glass vase, by Geoffrey Baxter.

*The Streaky range came in two colourways, Streaky Green and Streaky Purple.*

*c1972*      7in (17.5cm) high

**£60-80**      GC

A Whitefriars aubergine colour 'Stitched Square' glass vase, Geoffrey Baxter.

6in (15cm) high

**£180-220**      GC

A Whitefriars 'Banjo' vase, by Geoffrey Baxter.

*c1967*      12.5in (32cm) high

**£1,500-2,000**      GC

A Whitefriars cinnamon colour 'Totem Pole' glass vase, by Geoffrey Baxter.

*The pattern was made by nailing a curled thick wire to the inside of the mould. The nail head shapes can be seen at some of the corners. From the Textured range designed in 1966 and sold from 1967.*

10.25in (26cm) high

**£180-220**      GC

A Whitefriars Ruby Red 'Late Textured' range vase, by Geoffrey Baxter.

*c1972*      8in (20cm) high

**£60-80**      GC

A Whitefriars pewter colour 'Pineapple' glass bottle, by Geoffrey Baxter, from the 'Late Textured' range.

*c1972*      8in (20.5cm) high

**£80-90**      GC

A Whitefriars tangerine colour 'Pineapple' glass vase, by Geoffrey Baxter, from the 'Late Textured' range.

*c1972*      7in (17.5cm) high

**£80-90**      GC

A Whitefriars orange TV vase, designed in 1966.

*c1967-73*      6.75in (17cm) high

**£100-120**      JH

# AROUND THE HOUSE

The appeal of household objects hinges on their period style and novelty value. Tins were commonly produced until the 1940s, and for strong collectables look for those in excellent condition from notable brands such as Huntley & Palmer and those featuring bright colours, complex designs or novelty shapes.

Plastic and Bakelite household items, which were developed in the early 20th century and are very much of their time, have a wide market. Finds with a strong future will be those that show superb period design, particularly Art Deco styling, and bright and fun colours.

The 1950s and 60s looks have great fashionable sway with collectors, with the 'retro' look of this time now well established in our modern consciousness. Appealing both to young collectors wanting the latest trends as well as those to whom the period has nostalgic appeal, this area of interest looks set to continue. A popular icon of the 1930s and 50s, Scottie-dog memorabilia could once be found in many homes and today is becoming rapidly sought after.

Because household items were produced in large quantities, always scrutinise your prospective purchases for damage or wear and only consider pieces in the very best condition showing strong hallmarks of period design.

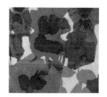

# HOT COLLECTING AREA

## TINS

The 'golden age' of the tin was between the 1860s and the 1940s, peaking in interest from around 1900 onwards. Varied in use, shape and decoration, they provide a record of graphic advertising during the early decades of the 20th century.

see p.155    see p.159                    see p.156

- Tins provided air-tight packaging in a decorative form for perishable goods including biscuits, sweets and tobacco. These three areas are the most popular amongst collectors.

- Other examples of tins designed for individual products are tea, cocoa, mustard and record needles. Many of these provide a more accessible collecting theme for those with a more limited budget.

- Collectors look particularly for bright colours and intricate, printed designs. Designs that show hallmarks of the style of the period are also very desirable. Novelty shapes such as books, vehicles and figurative shapes are especially popular today, more so if they have moving parts.

- Production of shaped tins peaked from the early 1900s to the 1930s. Many were kept after the contents had been used and were displayed if very decorative, or played with as toys. Due to this many show signs of wear, so mint-condition examples command a sizeable premium.

- Because they were made as disposable items, early items in good condition can fetch high prices. Many of these early tins have highly complex and well-detailed printed designs, which makes them particularly desirable today.

- Some brand names have more collecting caché than others – Huntley & Palmer had an impressive range of shapes and styles and are much sought after by today's collectors. Other names to look out for are Crawford's, Jacob's and Peek Frean. After the 1940s, the development of cheaper packaging saw the gradual demise of tin.

Novelty-shape tins are always more desirable amongst collectors, particularly vehicle shapes. This is also a rare tin.

The condition of this tin is excellent, which is surprising since many were played with and damaged.

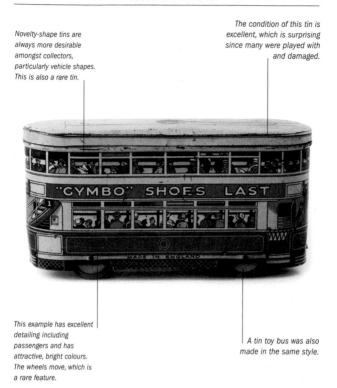

This example has excellent detailing including passengers and has attractive, bright colours. The wheels move, which is a rare feature.

A tin toy bus was also made in the same style.

A 1920s Carrs London Bus-shaped biscuit tin, advertising Gymbo Shoes.

8.5in (21.5cm) wide

£800-1,200

DH

## TOP TIPS

- Artwork featuring sporting scenes or aviation- or car-related themes will often fetch higher prices due to extra interest from cross-market appeal.

- Do not immerse a tin in water to clean it as this can cause rust and will often damage the printing.

- Keep tins away from bright sunlight, which will bleach colours, and do not varnish tins to protect the designs.

- Only buy post-war tins if in absolutely mint condition, as more will have survived.

A Huntley & Palmers 'Maplewood Casket' biscuit tin, in the form of an octagonal veneered wood casket with inlaid stringing around edges, the hinged lid with a central oval hunting scene, with an inscription on the base including "No.4813".

*1926-27*

**£40-60** DN

A pair of Huntley & Palmers 'Worcester Vase' biscuit tins, of tapered octagonal shape with removable necks forming the lids, marked "H.B. and S. Ltd. Reading" beneath the bases.

*c1934*

**£100-150** DN

A Macfarlane Lang 'Wonderland Cottage' tin money box.

*c1930*  *5.25in (13.5cm) high*

**£40-80** DH

A Huntley & Palmers 'Ginger Nuts' tin.

*c1930*  *1.5in (4cm) wide*

**£20-40** DH

A. J. Lyons biscuit tin, to commemorate the silver jubilee of King George V and Queen Mary.

*c1935*  *10in (25.5cm) wide*

**£20-30** DH

A W. & R. Jacob & Co Ltd 'Coronation Coach' biscuit tin, in the form of the royal coach with tinplate wheels, the removable roof with crown-shaped knop.

*c1936*

**£100-150** DN

A Carr & Company Ltd biscuit tin, to commemorate the coronation of Queen Elizabeth II.

*1953*  *11.35in (29cm) high*

**£14-18** DH

A Cadbury's Dairy Milk Chocolate money box tin, in the shape of a milk churn with removable lid, the coin slot near the top of one side.

**£20-30** DN

A Huntley & Palmers "The Shell" biscuit tin.

*c1912*                                    *7in (18cm) long*

**£400-450**                                          **DH**

A Huntley & Palmers 'Library' biscuit tin, in the form of eight red-leather bound books, titled on the spines: "History of Reading"; "Biscuits"; "Poetry"; "Essays"; "Travels"; "Science"; "Cakes"; and "Modern Reading"; bound together with a simulated leather strap and buckle, a bookmark acting as pull-tab to open the lid. *c1900*

**£150-200**                                          **DN**

A 1950s Huntley & Palmers soldier-shaped biscuit tin.

                                *8in (20cm) high*

**£120-180**                                          **DH**

A Huntley & Palmers "The Black and White Minstrel Show" biscuit tin, dated.

*1963*        *8.5in (21.5cm) wide*

**£20-30**                          **DH**

A Huntley & Palmers 'Rude' biscuit tin.

*Designed by a disgruntled employee, the picture includes couples engaged in explicit acts concealed within the artwork.*

*1980*        *8in (20cm) diam*

**£25-35**                          **DH**

A William Crawford's biscuit tin, formed to resemble an inlaid walnut stationery box, the domed hinged cover printed with a pictorial panel depicting an interior scene.

                                *7in (18cm) high*

**£25-35**                             **F**

A 1950s Chad Valley Carrs Biscuits tin.

                                *10in (25.5cm) wide*

**£400-450**                                          **DH**

A William Crawford's biscuit tin, formed to resemble an inlaid Georgian knife box.

                                *9.25in (23.5cm) high*

**£45-55**                             **F**

A Tours biscuit tin basket.

*c1910*        *7in (18cm) wide*

**£100-150**                          **DH**

A Lèfevre-Utile tin biscuit barrel, with Art Nouveau artwork by Alphonse Mucha.

*Alphonse Mucha (1860-1939) was one of the most famous illustrators and designers working in the Art Nouveau style. He is best known for his poster designs. A similar tin can be found in the Mucha Museum in Prague, Czech Republic.*

c1905                          6.5in (16.5cm) high

**£1,000-1,500**                                    **DH**

A 1930s Normandie biscuit tin.

9in (23cm) wide

**£80-120**                    **DH**

A 1930s French biscuit tin, with spin-the-pointer game on the lid.

9in (23cm) diam

**£80-120**                    **DH**

A Peak Freens Biscuits "The Winner" biscuit tin, with horse racing game.

c1940        6in (15cm) high

**£150-200**              **DH**

A Elkes gas mask biscuit tin.

c1940    8.5in (21.5cm) high

**£20-30**                **DH**

A Prince Charles and Lady Diana commemorative biscuit tin.

1981        5in (13cm) diam

**£4-6**                  **DH**

A 1920s Sharp's Super-Kreem Toffee miniature oval toffee tin.

1.5in (4cm) high

**£35-45**                **DH**

A 1920s Sharp's Super-Kreem Toffee miniature drum toffee tin, featuring Sir Kreemy Knut and Kreemy the Parrot.

1.5in (4cm) high

**£15-25**                **DH**

A 1920s Sharp's Super-Kreem Toffee miniature toffee tin.

3.25in (8.5cm) high

**£20-30**                **DH**

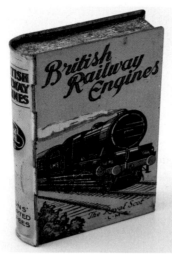

A Lyons Assorted Toffee book shaped tin, entitled "British Railway Engines" and featuring the "Royal Scot LMS".

*This was one of six railway "books" produced.*

c1929                                                5.5in (14cm) high

**£200-250**                                                      DH

A 1920s Edmondson's Red Seal Toffee sample tin.

1.5in (4cm) high

**£25-35**                                                        DH

A Clarnico London, Eng. golf club-shaped cachou tin.

c1905   5.75in (14.5cm) long

**£80-120**                                                       DH

A John Buchanan & Bros. confectionery tin, formed to resemble an inlaid wooden salt box.

11in (28cm) high

**£35-45**                                                        F

A Rowntree's Cachous cricket bat-shaped sweet tin.

c1910    4.5in (11.5cm) long

**£55-65**                                                        DH

A Hudson Scott & Son sentry box-shaped sweet tin.

c1910    6.5in (16.5cm) high

**£180-220**                                                      DH

A 1920s sweet cigarette vending machine tin money box, probably German.

6in (15cm) high

**£180-220**                                                      DH

A 1930s French Midy cough pastille tin.

2.25in (5.5cm) wide

**£25-30**                                                        DH

A 1930s French Radio BonBon sweet tin.

8in (20cm) high

**£120-180**                                                      DH

A 'Tatjana Needles' record needles tin.

c1910          1.5in (4cm) wide

**£50-70**          DH

A 'Herald Tango' record needles tin.

c1910          1.5in (4cm) wide

**£50-80**          DH

A 1920s HMV 'His Masters Voice, Loud Tone' record needles tin.

1.5in (4cm) wide

**£5-10**          DH

A rare Art Nouveau olive oil tin, with inscription "A. Bennasser, Marcca registrada Mallorca".

c1905          6in (15cm) high

**£150-200**          DH

A Sem record needles tin.

1.5in (4cm) wide

**£50-80**          DH

A 'Three British Queens' tin, in the form of a brass-bound carved wood casket, the surfaces embossed with Queen Mary's royal initials "R" and "M.I."

**£20-30**          DN

A Rowntree & Co Ltd tin, to commemorate the coronation of King George V and Queen Mary.

1902          5in (12.5cm) wide

**£14-18**          DH

A J. S. Fry & Sons tin, to commemorate the silver jubilee of King George V and Queen Mary.

1935          7.5in (19cm) wide

**£20-25**          DH

A Queen Mary's Troops Christmas tin.

1914          5in (13cm) wide

**£20-30**          MB

A Disk Talking Machine needles tin, manufactured at Redditch, England.

*This is a relatively early needle tin - note that gramophones, popularized just after the turn of the century, were still called 'Disc Talking Machines'.*

*c1910* 1.75in (4.5cm) wide

**£50-70** DH

A 1920s Sem Needles Fortissimo record needles tin.

1.75in (4.5cm) wide

**£20-30** DH

A 1920s Salon Tanz Nadeln record needles tin.

**£40-60** DH

A 1920s Sem record needles tin.

1.75in (4.5cm) wide

**£20-30** DH

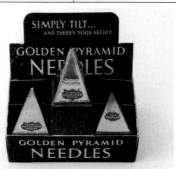

A 1940s Golden Pyramid Needles display box.

5in (12.5cm) wide

**£100-150** DH

An Embassy Gramophone record needles tin.

*c1930* 1.5in (4cm) wide

**£5-10** DH

A Black Cat cigarettes advertising vesta case, with security lock.

*You have to spin the case before opening it to release the secret security lock.*

*c1905* 2.5in (6.5cm) wide

**£150-200** DH

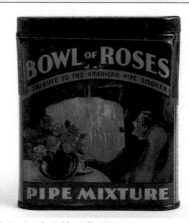

An American Bowl of Roses Pipe Mixture tobacco pocket tin.

*'Pocket' tobacco tins are currently extremely desirable to collectors in America. They date from the late 19thC until the early 20thC when cardboard took over. Collectors should look for intricate and detailed coloured lithographs, such as this example, as well as those that cross collecting areas.*

3.5in (9cm) high

**£300-350** TRA

A 1930s Jester Towel Soap box.

6in (15cm) wide

£10-15     DH

A wartime Clozone Concentrated Patent soap box, by J. Bibby & Sons.

5.5in (14cm) high

£6-12     DH

A 1930s Bell & Sons bottle of Chillexine for the Udder.

8in (20cm) high

£22-26     DH

A wartime pure dried whole eggs tin.

4in (10cm) high

£10-15     DH

A World War II Ovaltine tin.

5in (12.5cm) high

£15-25     DH

A 1940s Lever box of Wisk washing powder, with inscription 'For the Whole Family Wash'.

6in (15.5cm) high

£6-12     DH

A 1940s box of Rinso washing powder, with inscription 'Washes Whites Whiter than New'.

7in (18cm) high

£12-14     DH

A wartime C. Kunzle Ltd Mello chocolate bar.

*6in (15cm) wide*

**£10-15**      **DH**

A 1940s bottle of Evening in Paris, by Bourjois.

*5.75in (14.5cm) high*

**£10-15**      **DH**

A Vim tin, with inscription 'For Safe Smooth Cleaning for Pots, Pans and Cookers'.

*c1950  8.75in (22.5cm) high*

**£10-14**      **DH**

A box of Oxydol washing powder, with inscription 'Super Soapy for Extra Whiteness'.

*1950  5in (13cm) high*

**£8-12**      **DH**

A Puritan soap box, with inscription 'The Gentle Green Soap'.

*6.25in (16cm) wide*

**£12-14**      **DH**

A 1950s box of White Tide washing powder.

*7.75in (20cm) high*

**£8-12**      **DH**

A Dr. Whites compressed sanitary towel box.

*c1955  2.75in (7cm) wide*

**£2-4**      **DH**

A Boots Regaid compressed sanitary towel.

*c1955  2.25in (6cm) wide*

**£2-4**      **DH**

A 1960s Bassetts dummy double-sided packaging, for Jelly Babies.

*4in (10cm) wide*

**£5-10** DH

A 1960s Bassetts dummy double-sided packaging, for Liquorice Allsorts.

*4in (10cm) wide*

**£5-10** DH

A 1960s Kane's Pocket Pack sweet cigarette box, for ATV, with a cut-out cigarette card for "The Scarlet Pimpernel".

*3in (7.5cm) high*

**£10-15** DH

A wartime Bird's Custard Powder sachet, with powder.

*4.25in (11cm) high*

**£4-6** DH

A 1950s Birds dummy double-sided packaging, for chicken/turkey pie.

*6in (15cm) wide*

**£10-15** DH

A 1950s Nicholas Products Swan Lake bath cubes display box, containing six cubes.

*4.25in (11cm) wide*

**£4-6** DH

A 1950s bottle of Zac brilliantine hair cream, by Hough, Heseasen & Co.

*25.5in (10cm) high*

**£10-13** DH

A bottle of 'Saturday Night' lotion.

*c1930* *5in (13cm) high*

**£10-15** DH

A 1930s large Watermans ink bottle, unused.

*11.25in (28.5cm) high*

**£30-40** REN

A 1960s French Gitanes cigarette box, in the shape of a Thomson Transistor radio, with cigarettes.

*3.5in (9cm) wide*

**£25-30** DH

A clear glass shell X-100 motor oil bottle.

*c1955*  *11in (28cm) high*

**£15-20**  **DH**

A clear glass Castrol bottle.

*c1955*  *0.5in (27cm) high*

**£18-22**  **DH**

A clear glass premium grade Staminol Motor Oil bottle.

*c1955*  *13.5in (34cm) high*

**£25-30**  **DH**

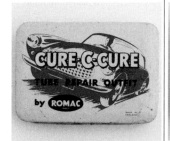

A Cure-C-Cure tape repair outfit tin for car tyres, by Romac.

*c1960*  *5in (13cm) wide*

**£6-12**  **DH**

A Cure-C-Cure repair pack for motorbike tyres, by Romac.

*c1960*  *3.25in (8.5cm) wide*

**£6-12**  **DH**

A pot of Silvikrin hair cream.

*c1960*  *3in (7.5cm) high*

**£12-14**  **DH**

A box of Bibby Best soap.

*c1935*  *6in (15.5cm) wide*

**£14-16**  **DH**

A box of Robin starch.

*c1960*  *2in (5.5cm) high*

**£4-6**  **DH**

# HOT COLLECTING AREA

## EARLY PLASTICS

Plastics and Bakelite allowed for the cost-effective mass production of many products. In all their coloured variations and imaginative styling, they broke away from the staid styles of previous centuries and ushered in a new age of colour and style.

see p.166    see p.167    see p.168

- Bakelite, the first synthetic plastic tagged as 'the material of 1,000 uses', was developed in 1907 and can be identified by the strong carbolic smell it gives off when rubbed. It was made in mottled and plain browns, black, cream, green, red and blue.

- Other early plastics that are keenly collected include cast phenolic resins, such as Catalin. These plastics are typically very brightly coloured. Also look out for Lucite, which is usually clear or translucent and often carved with a design. Both were commonly used for jewellery.

- Colours other than brown or black make any piece more desirable. The brighter the better, especially if it has marbled or speckled effects. Pieces that reflect the Art Deco style of the 1930s, with stepped forms, streamlining and clean lines are hotly sought after. Look out for brand names such as 'Beetleware', 'Bandalasta' and 'Carvacraft'.

- Many plastic objects were aimed at the domestic market, most notably the radio, but also kitchenalia and desk accessories. Plastic also had office and even industrial uses, such as for switches and insulators, but these tend to be less popular being in dull colours with little styling.

- Plastics from the 1950s onwards tend to be less desirable as styling is often not as strong and quality is generally poorer. Later plastics also tend to be lighter and less robust. The post-war invention of cheaper injection-moulded plastic saw the end of the plastic age.

This ink stand features period Art Deco styling with stepped sides. The form is also 'streamlined' following the popular designs of the period.

The item is well made and bears the maker's stamp depicting a hammer on the underside.

This item is in amber, one of the three colours used for Carvacraft. Green is the rarest. The third colour used was yellow.

Carvacraft objects were manufactured by the English company Dickinson in the late 1940s from a cast phenolic resin. The range also included blotters and notepad holders.

An amber Carvacraft double ink stand.
*c1948*

*10.5in (27cm) wide*

**£80-120**

**MHC**

## TOP TIPS

- Avoid chipped or cracked objects, unless they are extremely rare.

- Look for large objects made of Bakelite, as these are rare and often valuable.

- Bakelite and plastic radios are very collectable and, if colourful and stylish, valuable.

- Look for bright colours and deep-cut or moulded designs typical of the Art Deco period.

A brown mottled Bakelite Kodak Hawkette No.2 folding camera.

*This camera was given away as a free gift with selected products such as Cadbury's chocolates and was designed by E.K. Cole.*

1927                                    7in (18cm) high

**£30-40**                                    MHC

A Plastalite desk lamp, designed by Wells Coates and manufactured by E.K. Cole Ltd.

*E.K.Cole Ltd is better known as manufacturer of the famous round 'EKCO' Bakelite radios.*

1930s              14.5in (37cm) high

**£150-200**                                    MHC

A Dunlop promotional ashtray, by Roanoid Ltd.

*These came in a variety of colours but cracks affect the value considerably. The three black cigarette rests fold inwards into the ball over the ashtray to complete the sphere.*

c1930            5in (12cm) diam

**£100-150**                                    MHC

A blue Bakelite wall mirror.

*These popular mirrors were made in a variety of colours, brown was the most common.*

1930s            9in (23cm) wide

**£20-30**                                    MHC

A marbled Bandalastaware plate, cup and saucer.

*Bandalastaware was used extensively in 1930s picnic sets. Manufactured by Brookes & Adams, it was made from urea formaldehyde under the tradename 'Beatl'. In 1929 a shop called the Beatl shop opened in London's Regent Street.*

1930s            Saucer 5in (13cm) diam

**£20-30**                                    MHC

Three novelty animal-shaped cast-phenolic napkin rings.

*These were made in a variety of animal shapes and bright colours, some being mounted on small wheels.*

1930s   Hen 3in (7.5cm) high

**£15-20**                                    MHC

Four novelty animal-shaped cast-phenolic napkin rings.

1930s      squirrel 3in (7cm) h

**£15-20**                                    JBC

A blue urea formaldehyde lemon squeezer.

1930s 5.25in (13.5cm) diam

**£20-30**                                    JBC

An Art Deco cream and brown swirl urea formaldehyde Hurricane cigarette box, made by Nutt Products Ltd.

c.1930　　　　8.75 in (22cm) wide

**£50-70**　　　　JBC

A 1930s pale blue and copper marbled celluloid dressing table set, boxed.

comb 7.5in (19cm) long

**£40-60**　　　　JBC

A multi-coloured urea formaldehyde six-person tea service.

1940s　　　　plate 6in (15cm) diam

**£40-60**　　　　JBC

A Parker brown Bakelite "Baccy Flap" tobacco holder.

1930s　　　　3.5in (9cm) diam

**£15-20**　　　　JBC

An Art Deco carved blue acrylic horse brooch.

1930s　　　　4.25in (10.5cm) long

**£20-30**　　　　JBC

A rare pale green urea formaldehyde chandelier.

1930s　　　　21in (53cm) wide

**£80-120**　　　　JBC

A Lingalonga Ware muffin dish, in orange marbled urea formaldehyde.

1930s　　　　6in (15cm) diam

**£40-60**　　　　JBC

A marbled Bandalasta tea cup and biscuit tray.

1930s cup 3.25in (8cm) diam

**£30-40**　　　　JBC

A set of four egg cups, in marbled urea formaldehyde.

1930s　　　　1.75in (4.5cm) diam

**£20-30**　　　　JBC

A salt and pepper set, in blue and white marbled urea formaldehyde.

1930s　　　　2.75in (7cm) high

**£25-35**　　　　JBC

A brown Bakelite and cream urea formaldehyde bird cigarette dispenser.

*1930s*     *7.5in (19cm) long*

**£50-70**     **JBC**

A rare brown mottled Bakelite 'Eloware' desk stand and double inkwell manufactured by Birkby's of Liversedge, England.

*c1936*     *9in (23cm) wide*

**£120-180**     **MHC**

A green Carvacraft stamp sponge holder.

*These holders were often used as ashtrays and burns inside the well reduce the value considerably.*

*1940s*     *3in (8cm) wide*

**£60-80**     **MHC**

A Kodak Bullet camera, black Bakelite with box.

*1940s*     *4.75in (12cm) wide*

**£5-10**     **JBC**

A rare green acrylic and black Bakelite ink stand.

*1940s*     *6.5in (16.5cm) wide*

**£100-150**     **MHC**

A brown mottled Bakelite desk telephone directory.

*1940s*     *8in (20cm) high*

**£10-15**     **MHC**

A maroon mottled Bakelite torch.

*1940s*     *4.75in (12cm) long*

**£10-15**     **JBC**

A pink urea formaldehyde floral flask, marked "The British Vacuum Flask Co Ltd."

*1940s*     *10.5in (27cm) high*

**£30-40**     **JBC**

A red and yellow urea formaldehyde egg cup.

*1940s*     *1.75in (4.5cm) diam*

**£3-5**     **JBC**

Three 1930s maroon mottled Bakelite egg cups.

*1.75in (4.5cm) diam*

**£2-3 (EACH)**    **JBC**

Two 1930s multicoloured urea-formaldehyde bowls.

*4in (10cm) diam*

**£5-10 (EACH)**    **JBC**

A 1920s circular trivet, in brown mottled Bakelite.

*5.5in (14cm) diam*

**£10-15**    **JBC**

A 1920s circular Linsden ware trivet, in dark brown and biscuit Bakelite.

*6.25in (16cm) diam*

**£15-20**    **JBC**

A 1940s multi-coloured urea-formaldehyde cruet set.

*Pepper pot 2in (5cm) high*

**£15-20**    **JBC**

A 1930s urea-formaldehyde collapsible picnic cup.

*2.5in (6.5cm) diam*

**£10-15**    **MHC**

A 1930s boxed set of six knives, with dark blue and yellow mottled urea-formaldehyde handles.

*Knife 7.25in (18.5cm) long*

**£20-30**    **JBC**

A 1940s Bel cream maker, in blue urea-formaldehyde and glass, boxed.

*This cream maker is common and made in many different colours, but to find one in the original box is rare.*

*7.75in (19.5cm) high*

**£25-30**    **JBC**

A 1950s ceramic teapot, modelled as a Scottie dog, with paw raised to form the spout.

*6.75in (17cm) high*

**£30-40** ROX

A 1950s set of colour-printed metal drinks coasters.

*3.25in (8cm) diam*

**£20-30** ROX

A 1930s linen cloth, with woven design showing Scottie dogs outside a barn.

*20in (51cm) wide*

**£12-18** ROX

A 1930s carved wood seated Scottie dog egg timer, lacks tail.

*5in (12cm) high*

**£40-60** DCC

A 1930s pair of American K&O Co. painted brass bookends, in the form of a little cowboy climbing a book, with a Scottie dog.

*6.75in (17cm) high*

**£100-150** ROX

A 1930s novelty Scottie dog table mirror, possibly a travelling mirror, with gilt metal frame, the reverse inset with a colour lithograph of a Scottie.

*3.25in (8cm) high*

**£20-30** DCC

A 1950s Swank wall-mounted belt-rack, of carved wood-effect and painted composition.

*Swank were an American manufacturer of gentlemen's accessories and are known to have used the Scottie motif regularly.*

*11in (28cm) wide*

**£30-40** ROX

A rare 1930s Scottie dog dice, with weighted revolving wooden dice and two metal dogs on a wooden base.

*Base 5in (13cm) wide*

**£80-120** DCC

A 1930s American Art Deco styled Bakelite and painted metal box.

*3.5in (9cm) wide*

£30-40     **ROX**

A 1930s American Hershey chrome paper knife, mounted with black painted cast Scottie dog.

*8.5in (21.5cm) long*

£15-20     **ROX**

A 1930s cast metal and painted 'Flush the Scotty dog' desk pencil holder, with mechanical pencil.

*Probably by L.G. Balfour Company, Attleboro, Mass., USA.*

*2in (5cm) high*

£15-20     **DCC**

A 1930s wooden Scottie dog desk calendar, with a black dog and wooden holder with paper calendar.

*4.5in (11.5cm) high*

£30-40     **DCC**

A pressed glass Scottie dog inkwell, with silver-plated mounts.

*Becomes black when filled.*

*c1900*     *3.5in (9cm) high*

£100-150     **DCC**

A 1930s cast and painted metal novelty desk thermometer, with seated Scottie dog.

*2.75in (7cm) wide*

£20-30     **DCC**

A 1930s painted cast metal match holder, formed as a Scottie dog sitting on a book.

*2.5in (6.5cm) wide*

£50-80     **DCC**

A 1930s carved wood Scottie dog ashtray, with glass liner.

*6.25in (16cm) wide*

£50-80     **DCC**

A 1960s ceramic ashtray commemorating John F. Kennedy's visit to Berlin.

*5.5in (14cm) wide*

**£80-120**　　　　　　**CW**

A 1950s French red tin advertising ashtray, with sultry semi-nude lady.

*The desirability and value of these advertising ashtrays rests on the appearance of the naked lady. Naked and shapely blondes in revealing, teasing poses are particularly sought after! This ashtray is a good example.*

*4.75in (12cm) wide*

**£40-60**　　　　　　**CW**

A 1950s American advertising ashtray, with naked lady wearing a chef's hat.

*4.75in (12cm) wide*

**£15-25**　　　　　　**CW**

A 1950s Made in Japan ceramic naked lady double-sided ashtray, a souvenir from Florida.

*6.25in (16cm) high*

**£30-40**　　　　　　**CW**

A 1950s Made in Japan erotic dancer ceramic ashtray.

*3.75in (9.5cm) wide*

**£15-25**　　　　　　**CW**

A 1960s ceramic lady in a bathtub ashtray, "Cool Your Butt In My Old Tub".

*5.25in (13.5cm) high*

**£40-60**　　　　　　**CW**

A 1960s ceramic lady ashtray, with moving legs.

*5.25in (13.5cm) wide*

**£70-100**　　　　　　**CW**

A 1930s French Aladdin ceramic ashtray.

*Aladdin ashtrays are rare, they are better known for their inkwells, bottles and powder jars.*

4.25in (10.5cm) high

**£300-400** **CW**

A 1920s French ROB J ceramic ashtray, with black saxophone player.

*The design, subject matter and the good maker make this ashtray very desirable. It is also in mint condition with no damage or wear.*

5.5in (14cm) high

**£300-500** **CW**

A Schafer and Vader ceramic match holder and ashtray.

*The character's head and toes have holes to hold matches and ash is flicked into his mouth.*

c1930s 3.25in (8cm) high

**£150-200** **CW**

An early 20thC Fancies Fayre character head ashtray.

*When ash is flicked into the tray in the mouth, smoke comes out of his ears!*

4.75in (12cm) high

**£40-60** **CW**

A novelty ceramic sailor's head ashtray, marked "FOREIGN", with moving bottom jaw.

c1920s 4.25in (11cm) high

**£50-80** **CW**

A 1930s German ceramic Fakir's character head ashtray.

4in (10cm) wide

**£50-80** **CW**

A 1950s Davar Originals scared lady character ashtray.

5.5in (14cm) high

**£70-100** **CW**

A Japanese NAPCO 'Lady in Dress' ashtray, with floral parasol.

*NAPCO also made lady head vases.*

c1956 6in (15cm) high

**£70-100** **CW**

A 1950s Nippon ceramic 'Black Americana' ashtray.

6in (15cm) wide

**£100-150** **CW**

A 1960s Old Hall stainless steel tall 2 pint 'Connaught' coffee pot.

*6.75in (17.5cm) high*

£20-30       GC

A 1960s Old Hall stainless steel coffee pot or teapot.

*Note the differently shaped finials on some of these tea or coffee pots, which may have indicated the contents.*

*6in (15.5cm) high*

£25-35       GC

An Old Hall stainless steel sugar sifter.

*3in (8cm) high*

£15-25       GC

A 1960s Old Hall stainless steel half-pint milk jug.

*2.5in (6.5cm) high*

£15-20       GC

A 1960s Old Hall stainless steel 8oz sugar bowl.

*2in (5cm) high*

£15-20       GC

An Old Hall stainless steel conical salt and pepper shakers with black plastic bases.

*3in (7.5cm) high*

£15-25       GC

A pair of 1960s Old Hall stainless steel salt and pepper shakers, marked "PAT 607716".

*2.75in (7cm) high*

£15-20       GC

An Old Hall stainless steel toast rack, with rectangular section bars and rivetted base, designed by Robert Welch

*1961*    *6.5in (16.5cm) long*

£20-30       GC

An Old Hall 'Campden' stainless steel toast rack, designed by Robert Welch.

*With its pagoda-esque lines and extreme simplicity, this award-winning toast rack was made in two- and six-section versions.*

*c1958*      *7.25in (18.5cm) long*

£20-30       GC

A pair of 1960s Old Hall stainless steel candlesticks, designed by Robert Welch.

*11.75in (30cm) high*

**£150-200** GC

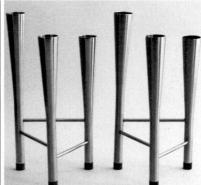

A pair of Old Hall stainless steel triple candlesticks, with wooden feet, designed by Robert Welch.

*9in (23cm) high*

**£100-150** GC

A 1960s Viners stainless steel and gold-plated wine goblet, designed by Stuart Devlin.

*7in (17.5cm) high*

**£25-35** GC

An Old Hall set of six 'Alveston' tablespoons, designed by Robert Welch, in original box.

*c1962* *6in (15cm) long*

**£80-90** GC

A 1960s set of six Viners stainless steel 'Studio' pattern grapefruit forks, designed by Gerald Benney, in original box.

*5.75in (14.5cm) long*

**£80-90** GC

A Viners 'Sable' dessert set, designed by Gerald Benny, with textured handles.

*c1970* *5in (13cm) high*

**£35-45** MHT

A 1930s Art Deco chrome and black enamelled metal table lamp, with original shade and chroming.

*18in (46cm) high*

**£400-500** DETC

A 1930s pair of tiered copper Art Deco tabletop torchères, with wooden bases.

*10.25in (26cm) high*

**£450-500** DETC

A 1930s copper and chrome 'Machine Age' pivoting desk lamp.

*The shade swivels and pivots.*

*13.75in (35cm) high*

**£250-300** DETC

A 1930s pair of Art Deco table lamps, with frosted glass stepped shades, chromed gazelles and black vitrolite glass bases.

*The stepped bases, figures and frosted shades that mimic the work of Rene Lalique are typical hallmarks of the Art Deco period.*

*8.75in (22cm) high*

**£300-350** DETC

A 1940s painted plaster, wood and brass 'carousel horse' table lamp, with original fabric shade.

*27.5in (70cm) high*

**£150-200** DETC

A 1930s Art Deco painted wood table lamp, with original paint.

*15.25in (29cm) high*

**£150-200** DETC

A rare 1930s enamelled metal penguin night light, the catalin beak being the switch.

*10.25in (26cm) high*

**£300-350** DETC

A 1930s hollow painted metal 'elephant' boudoir lamp, bookend and ashtray set, by Jennings Brothers, Brooklyn NY.

*It is hard to find a complete set as they were often split up.*

*13in (33cm) high*

**£250-300** DETC

A frosted glass 'Saturn' lamp, with internally painted stars and planets.

*These lamps were produced to commemorate the 1939 New York World's Fair, which celebrated technology and the future. This theme is shown in the 'planet' shaped shade with stars and planets on it.*

1939     12in (30.5cm) high

**£250-300**     **DETC**

A Walter Dorwin Teague for Polaroid Corp. executive desk lamp, with brown Bakelite base and hooded shade, on a conical brushed aluminum shaft, unmarked.

*Designer and typographer Walter Dorwin Teague (1883-1960) was influenced by Le Corbusier after visiting Paris. On his return to New York, he founded one of the first industrial design consultancies and designed cameras for Kodak, pens for Scripto and glass for Steuben, as well as others. His streamlined and functional designs arose from his interest in symmetry and proportion.*

c1939     12.75in (33cm) high

**£550-650**     **DRA**

A rare brown Bakelite, wood and chrome 'airplane' lamp with clock, by Sessions.

*Later versions have rubber, not wooden wheels. The propellers on this example are replaced - they were originally chrome.*

c1948     20.5in (52cm) wide

**£300-350**     **DETC**

A pair of 1950s painted plaster 'fairy' lamps, with original shades.

33.75in (86cm) high

**£500-600**     **DETC**

A pair of 1950s Modernist painted and textured plaster table lamps, with original parchment shades.

32.75in (83cm) high

**£250-300**     **DETC**

A very rare 1950s painted chalk and fabric lady dancer table lamp, the dress as a shade.

37in (94cm) high

**£750-850**     **DETC**

A 1950s brass-coloured glazed ceramic parrot table lamp, the parrot illuminates.

17in (43cm) high

**£150-200**     **DETC**

# HOT COLLECTING AREA

## THE 1950S

The 1950s saw the overriding post-war optimism being reflected in the enthusiastic adoption of exciting new products, materials and styles. Nostalgia and today's vogue for 'retro' styling has caused the market to mushroom.

see p.177          see p.180          see p.183

- After 1950, when technological know-how was redirected away from the war towards the domestic and commercial sphere, new materials such as formica, glass fibre and nylon, alongside labour-saving electric household appliances such as kitchen mixers, started to make their appearance.

- Newly available materials and constructions allowed the development of products that were more efficient and maximised available space, with many examples of items such as trolleys, sofa beds, stacking furniture and flat-packed furniture. Man-made materials, such as plastic, vinyl and Dralon were very popular.

- The 1950s hailed the emergence of Pop music, the birth of the teenager and a rejection of the austerity of the post-war years. Items related to these themes are fun, cheerful and particularly hotly collected. Many were not made to last or were thrown away once fashions changed. This makes certain pieces rare.

- Hallmarks of this new, modern decade were colour, frivolous motifs and a preoccupation with glamour, worlds away from the austerity of wartime. Typical motifs include scantily clad ladies, gambling and drinking images as well as glamorous personalities and heart throbs from the big screen or from the music world. Cats, often with elongated necks, were also popular.

- Many notable designers, such as Charles and Ray Eames and Terence Conran, are associated with this period. Pieces designed by them often command a substantial premium, although there are plenty of other objects available to suit all pockets that represent the era perfectly.

## A CLOSER LOOK AT A LADY HEAD VASE

Condition is very important. Clean interiors attract a premium, as do examples with no chips to the rim or base and paint that has not crazed or flaked. Colours should be bright and not faded.

This example has delicately rouged cheeks and a good hairstyle. Collectors look for features such as well-modelled and well-painted hair and good-quality painting, especially on the 'made-up' face. Also look for applied eyelashes.

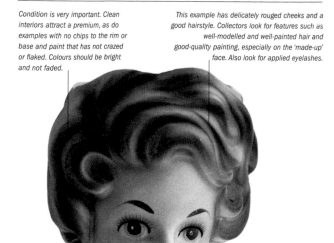

The way the head is modelled is also important, with many having an attractive tilt to the head.

The applied flowers that stand out from the body of the vase are another feature that makes this example desirable. They are easily damaged, but the flowers on this example are not. The earrings and 'pearl' necklace are also original and intact.

A 1950s Lady Head Vase.
**£60-80**

PC

## *TOP TIPS*

- Look for typical shapes of the period such as kidney tables, artist palettes, and asymmetric forms. Strong angled spindle legs with ball feet are also typical.

- Examine patterns closely – stylised, 'modern' designs incorporating motifs of the period such as pin-up girls, atomic patterns, playing-card motifs, pop music and contemporary living in pastel colours are especially popular.

- Because many of these items were mass-produced for a domestic market, condition is vital. Sets should be complete and individual items undamaged.

A Ridgways 'Homemaker' series plate, transfer-printed, designed by Enid Seeney.

*The 'Homemaker' series of tableware is perhaps one of the most recognisable objects from the 1950s. Sold in vast numbers through 'Woolworths', they gave any home an inexpensive, but very fashionable, table setting. As so many were made, they are commonly found now, but are now worth much more than they sold for during the period, if in excellent condition. Both the simple forms and the highly characteristic motifs used sum up the essence of 1950s styling.*

c1957 (made to early 1970s)          10in (25.5cm) diam

**£12-18**                                    **FFM**

A Ridgways 'Homemaker' series cereal bowl, transfer-printed, designed by Enid Seeney.

1957-1970s  6in (16cm) diam

**£10-15**                                    **FFM**

A Ridgways 'Parisienne' pattern plate, transfer-printed.
c1957     9.75in (25cm) diam

**£10-15**                                    **FFM**

A Ridgways 'Homemaker' series side-plate, transfer-printed, designed by Enid Seeney.

1957-1970s  7in (18cm) diam

**£8-10**                                     **FFM**

A Ridgways 'Homemaker' series trio, transfer-printed, designed by Enid Seeney.

*This range was only available with black cups with white interiors.*

1957-1970s  7in (18cm) diam

**£20-25**                                    **FFM**

A Ridgways 'Barbeque' pattern meat plate, print and enamel, unnamed designer.

1958          11in (28cm) diam

**£15-18**                                    **FFM**

Four 1950s playing card glasses.

*Playing card symbols were highly popular motifs during the 1950s.*

4.5in (11.5cm) high

**£40-50**                            **MA**

A 1950s pin-up girl glass, decorated on both sides with transfers.

4.25in (11cm) high

**£18-22**                                    **CVS**

A 1950s Vacwonder 'Olympia' vacuum flask, with scenes of various field sports.

An English 14-piece coffee service, comprising six cups and saucers, coffee pot and sugar bowl, marked "British Anchor".

A Japanese 15-piece tea service, by Lucky, comprising six cups and saucers, teapot, sugar and milk jug, with crown backstamp.

*10.25in (26cm) high*

*1958 Pot 7.75in (20cm) high*

**£40-50**     **MA** | **£120-180**     **MA** | **£80-120 (SET)**     **MA**

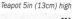

A Carlton ware-style coffee pot, unmarked, with vegetable decoration.

A Kosy Kraft 'Ever-Hot' three-piece tea service, chrome over pink ceramic, mint and boxed.

*This is one of at least five colourways. Without the original box this set would be worth under £30.*

*11.5in (29cm) wide*

*Teapot 5in (13cm) high*

**£12-18**     **MA** | **£50-80**     **MA**

A 1950s Czechoslovakian or German porcelain cup and saucer.

An unmarked English plate, with dancing couple motif.

A Royal Tudor 'Fiesta' pattern plate, by Barker Bros.

*Saucer 4.5in (11.5cm) wide*

*9.5in (24.5cm) diam*

*6.5in (16.5cm) diam*

**£15-25**     **AOY** | **£15-20**     **MA** | **£4-6**     **L**

A Crown Devon 'Oceania' pattern three-section dish.

*15in (38.5cm) wide*

£20-25　　　　　　　　　　**MA**

A 1950s Beswick 'Zebrette' bowl, marked "1354".

*Note the similarities to Midwinter's Zambezi range, designed by Jessie Tate, which was highly imitated.*

*9in (23cm) long*

£80-120　　　　　　　　　**BAD**

A 1950s black lady vase, with yellow and white abstract patterns.

*5.5in (14cm) high*

£20-30　　　　　　　　　　**AOY**

A 1950s cream Bakelite Goblin Teasmaid.

*The 1950s saw a boom in electronic household products that were aimed to make life easier and more luxurious, such as this coffee maker. The majority were aimed at the hardworking housewife.*

*10.5in (26.5cm) wide*

£80-120　　　　　　　　　　　　**L**

A 1950s Italian Brevetta coffee maker, with rare pink finished aluminium and Bakelite handle.

£8-12　　　　　　　　　　**PC**

A 1950s EKCO transistor radio, in cream with red trim.

*9.5in (24cm) wide*

£25-35　　　　　　　　　　**MA**

A 1950s pair of novelty 'A Few Too Many' cocktail glasses.

*5.75in (14.5cm) high*

£30-50　　　　　　　　　**CVS**

A 1960s/70s cream and tan plastic Bush radio.

*This radio was designed in 1959 and was made until the mid-1970s.*

*13in (33cm) wide*

£50-70　　　　　　　　　　　**L**

A set of Venus salt and pepper shakers.

c1950                                              4in (10cm) high

**£50-80**                                                      **SM**

An electrical mixer, by Excelsior.

1955

**£80-120**                                                     **ATK**

A set of six 1930s Australian pale blue Bakelite kitchen canisters.

*A full set of these canisters in blue is extremely rare, although separate pieces are found. Blue is a very sought after colour for Bakelite.*

Largest 9.5in (24cm) high

**£120-180**                                                    **MA**

A 1950s Prince Pineapple string holder, some damage.

**£80-120**                                                     **DAC**

A Dutch boy laundry sprinkler.

**£120-180**                                                    **DAC**

A 1950s picnic set, with four settings.

19in (48.5cm) wide

**£50-80**                                                      **MA**

Two 1950s ceramic cat vases and matching fan vase, made in Western Germany.

**FAN £30-35, CATS £20-30 EACH** MA

A 1950s Pilkingtons ceramic free-form bowl, designed by Mitzi Cunliffe.

*10.5in (26.5cm) diam*

A 1960s ceramic Siamese cat.
*14.5in (36.5cm) high*

**£30-40** MA

**£100-150** REN

A 1950s 'bridge' cigarette lighter and ashtray, made in China.
*3.5in (9cm) high*

**£30-40** MA

A 1950s alabaster vase, with musical theme design.
*9.75in (25cm) high*

**£100-150** V

A Robert Welch candlestick, made from vitreous cast iron at Chipping Campden.
*c1964   5.75in (14.5cm) high*

**£45-50** MHT

A Poul Henningsen PH5 hanging lamp, produced by Louis Poulsen, Denmark, designed 1958, tiered, enamelled metal shade with red and blue interior.
*c1958*                                   *19in (48cm) diam*

**£350-450** FRE

A 1960s bronze and Baccarat crystal chandelier, with nickelled bronze dome over an illuminated interior with stepped rows of 80 crystal teardrop pendants, stamped "BACCARAT Bronze".

*16in (40.5cm) diam*

**£1,800-2,200** **FRE**

A 1950s Lightolier table lamp, with plastic shade, enamelled metal shaft and base.

*19in (48cm) high*

**£250-350** **FRE**

A 1950s table lamp, with plastic shade.

*39in (99cm) high*

**£50-80** **MA**

A pair of Dralon-upholstered and wire constructed dressing table chairs.

*31.5in (80cm) high*

**£40-60** **CA**

A 1950s artist's easel table, by Dennis & Robin Portslade SX D&R products.

*This table is rare. The legs are detachable and can be clipped to the base and whole hung from the wall to resemble an artists easel with 'brushes'. This also acts as a useful 'space-saving' device, which was another popular theme during this period.*

*19.75in (50cm) high*

**£80-120** **MA**

A 1940s Hoover.

**£25-35** **MA**

A Photoplay magazine, featuring Elvis Presley on the cover, November edition.

*1962* *11.5in (29cm) high*

**£20-25** **CVS**

A Picture Goer magazine, featuring Sal Mineo on the cover, March edition.

*1960* *11.75in (30cm) high*

**£5-8** **CVS**

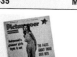

A Picture Goer magazine, featuring Valerie Alan, March edition.

*1957* *11.75in (30cm) high*

**£5-8** **CVS**

A Tit Bits magazine, featuring Zsa Zsa Gabor, January edition.

*1954* *12.5in (31.5cm) high*

**£3-5** **CVS**

A 1950s Decca portable record player, decorated with nursery rhyme scenes after Dora Roderick.

*13.5in (34.5cm) wide*

**£80-120**                          **MA**

A 1950s gold-plated hanging Aristocrat pencil on a sprung chain, the pencil engraved with two colour floral and foliate design, in original box.

*Pencil 4in (10cm) high*

**£40-50**                          **TAB**

A late 1950s lipstick vending machine, by Priscilla Azden Cosmetics Inc, Clifton New Jersey, retains original lipsticks to interior, with the exception of 'Coral Twist'.

*14in (36.5cm) wide*

**£250-350**                          **MA**

A 1959 Playboy 'Playmate' calendar, including Jane Mansfield as Miss July.

*Hugh Heffner launched Playboy magazine in December 1953, the first issue having a nude centrefold of Marilyn Monroe. Retailing at 50cts, over 54,000 copies were sold. The desirability and values of early magazines and items such as this calendar are usually discerned from the subject of the cover and centrefold, any other content relating to notable names and the condition.*

*1959*                          *12.5in (32cm) high*

**£80-120**                          **CVS**

A 1960s set of six plastic Playboy cocktail swizzle sticks.

*8.25in (21cm) long*

**£30-40**                          **CVS**

A late 1950s/early 1960s hot-water bottle, modelled after Jane Mansfield, by Combex of England.

*20in (51cm) high*

**£80-120**                          **MA**

A 1960s gold-plated Playboy bunny pin.

*The 'Playboy' pin was designed by Art Paul.*

*1in (3cm) high*

**£15-25**                          **CVS**

A 1960s gold and black decorated cocktail shaker, with bands of stylized violins and musical notes.

*Chrome coloured versions of this cocktail shaker were also made and are more common and less collectable.*

*9.25in (23.5cm) high*

**£50-70**                          **CVS**

A 1950s 45rmp record case.

The 1950s saw both the explosion of the pop music movement and the emergence of the 'teenager'. For the first time, young people had music aimed specifically at them that was different to other popular music. With freedom growing, teenagers were able to work in their spare time to earn money with which they bought 'singles'. These inexpensively produced, brightly coloured bags were produced to store collections, but as they were heavily used and not made to last, many have not survived.

*9.5in (24cm) high*

**£20-25** MA

A 1950s 45rmp case, with a jiving couple.

**£20-25** MA

A 1960s 45rmp record case.
*7.5in (19cm) high*

**£15-30** MA

A 1950s pin-up girl lighter.

**£8-10** CVS

A 1950s pin-up girl lighter, with box.

**£40-60** CVS

An English toffee tin.
*c1960      4.25in (11cm) diam*

**£10-15** DH

A 1960s tin money box, with outer space scene.

*4.5in (11.5cm) high*

**£10-15** DH

A 1950s battery-powered Moon Rocket toy.

*The 1960s saw a growing fascination with outer space, which reached its high point with the first man landing on the moon in 1969.*

*9.5in (24cm) wide*

**£220-280** DH

A 1960s novelty cigarette holder, in the form of a globe on stand, with telescopic top above fitted interior.

*6.25in (16cm) high*

**£80-100**  **CVS**

A 1960s German ceramic bowl.

*4in (10cm) high*

**£12-18**  **L**

A 1960s German vase, marked "249/30".

*12in (30.5cm) high*

**£50-60**  **L**

A piece of 1960s 'Sea Holly' fabric, by David Whitehead.

*David Whitehead Fabrics were manufactured in Lancashire, during the 1950s and 1960s. The company employed many leading artists and designers including Terence Conran, John Piper, Henry Moore and Eduardo Paolozzi.*

**£15-20 (PER METRE)**  **L**

A piece of 1970s fabric, by Kendex International.

**£15-25 (PER METRE)**  **L**

A piece of 1970s unmarked fabric.

**£10-15 (PER METRE)**  **L**

A piece of 1970s Heals 'Poppies' pattern fabric, designed by Howard Carter.

**£18-22 (PER METRE)**  **L**

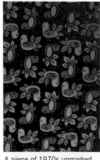

A piece of 1970s unmarked fabric.

**£15-20 (PER METRE)**  **L**

A 1970s West German vase, marked "202-22".

*9in (23cm) high*

**£15-18**  **L**

A 1970s West German vase, marked "205-32".

*12.75in (32.5cm) high*

**£25-35**  **L**

A 1970s matt brown glazed German vase, with incised decoration.
*8.5in (21.5cm) high*

£25-35     L

A 1970s matt white porcelain Bavarian vase.
*7.5in (19cm) high*

£40-50     L

A 1970s Carlton ware guardsman moneybank.
*5.5in (14cm) high*

£30-50     L

A 1970s Carlton ware coffee set, comprising coffee pot, milk jug and sugar.
*Pot 12.5in (31.5cm) high*

£50-60     L

A 1960s/70s Pac-A-Pic picnic set for four people, by Preci-Ware Syston, Leicester, the four trays complete with beakers and cutlery, with registered design mark.
*14in (36cm) wide*

£40-60     CVS

A 1970s Heinz ice bucket, made by Insulex-Isslex.
*7.75in (20cm) high*

£10-15     MA

A 1970s Pifco Warmasphere floor heater.
*12.75in (32.5cm) diam*

£35-45     L

A 1970s Italian 'Penny' 45rmp 'handbag' record player.

£70-100     MA

A 1970s Peerless Transistor Six globe radio.
*8.5in (21.5cm) high*

£80-120     L

A 1970s cream plastic Braun AG desk fan.
*6in (15cm) high*

£50-60     L

CŒUR A CŒUR.

# BOOKS & EPHEMERA

If books appeal to you, the collecting themes are endless. Much of the fascination for book collectors comes from the historical and literary context of each title, often reflected in the jacket artworks with styles inevitably changing with the times as a book is reprinted.

There are a few important rules to follow – mint-condition books will always be worth more, classics will reach higher prices than other titles and first editions of sought-after titles are hotly collected. To stamp covetable appeal on your collection, look for prize-winning authors or books have been made as films or TV series, such as Evelyn Waugh or Agatha Christie titles. Children's books follow the same rules, with classics and much-loved characters being the most desirable.

Ephemera, meaning advertising and promotional pieces, is another sizeable area, but to simplify the theme a little it is the big names that count to collectors, such as Guinness and Coca Cola – who both produced an astonishing range of pieces, from trays to advertising standees in every imaginable form throughout the 20th century. Beware, though, of fakes and later reproductions, because as with any popular collecting area, they're always there to test every buyer's knowledge of the market.

# HOT COLLECTING AREA

## FIRST-EDITION BOOKS

The first edition of a book is the closest version to the author's original and is produced in varying, but limited numbers. Many are bought, read and then left forgotten on a shelf or given away, leaving them to be found by an ever-growing number of enthusiasts.

see p.194    see p.195    see p.200

- Within a first edition, you will also find a number of printings – again the first print of a first edition is worth more than a second or later printing. To identify a true first edition, look for the number '1' in the series of numbers on the copyright page, or a statement that it is a first edition. Also compare the publishing date to the year that the title was first published in.

- First editions of popular books that captured the public's imagination will generally be highly desirable. Good examples include Agatha Christie's detective stories, Roald Dahl's fantasy tales and J. K. Rowling's 'Harry Potter' stories.

- Books with a cult following such as Brett Easton Ellis' "Less Than Zero" can also fetch high prices as can those that summed up an age or decade such as Tom Wolfe's 1980s satire 'Bonfire of the Vanities'. Fashion also dictates desirability and hence value too, with some authors like Ian Fleming being constantly popular.

- A classic title written at the height of an author's career will often be worth less than an early and less well-received piece, as these earlier titles are usually produced in much smaller numbers making them rarer.

- Speculate and buy books by writers that are likely to capture the public's imagination over the long term, or may be made into a successful film. Also look for early works by today's popular writers such as Martin Amis, Salman Rushdie, Nick Hornby and Fay Weldon.

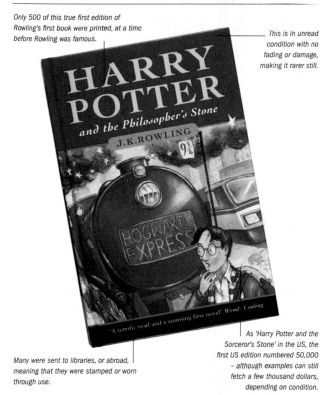

*Only 500 of this true first edition of Rowling's first book were printed, at a time before Rowling was famous.*

*This is in unread condition with no fading or damage, making it rarer still.*

*Many were sent to libraries, or abroad, meaning that they were stamped or worn through use.*

*As 'Harry Potter and the Sorceror's Stone' in the US, the first US edition numbered 50,000 – although examples can still fetch a few thousand dollars, depending on condition.*

J. K. Rowling, 'Harry Potter and the Philosopher's Stone', first edition, with original pictorial boards.

*1997*

**£15,000–20000**                                    **BLO**

## TOP TIPS

- As well as the general condition of the book, the presence and condition of the original dust cover is highly important and will make a significant difference to the market value.

- Seek out first editions signed by the author – these will have extra collecting interest. Dedications or inscriptions will usually devalue a book unless the inscription relates to a notable person.

- If you buy (preferably) signed copies of first editions nominated for major prizes like the Booker before the winner is announced and the book wins, values can soar.

De Bernières, Louis, "Captain Corelli's Mandolin", first edition, published by Secker & Warburg, London, signed by the author on the title page, first issue white boards, usual tanning to edges, vertical crease to inner rear flap.
*1994*

**£600-650** PB

De Bernières, Louis, "The Troublesome Offspring of Cardinal Guzman", first edition, published by Secker & Warburg, London, signed and dated by the author on the title page, usual faint browning to page edges.
*1992*

**£200-250** PB

Burton, Miles (John Rhode), "The Cat Jumps", first edition, published by Collins Crime Club, light vertical crease to front free endpaper, spine slightly bumped, spine slightly darkened, slight wear to top edge.
*1946*

**£100-150** PB

Christie, Agatha, "Destination Unknown", first edition, published by Collins Crime Club, London, margins of pages slightly browned, spine slightly rubbed, back panel dusty and faintly browning, price clipped.
*1954*

**£40-50** PB

Christie, Agatha, "4.50 from Paddington", first edition, published by Collins Crime Club, London, top edge slightly browned, some internal foxing, spine slightly darkened and one small closed tear at spine.
*1957*

**£40-50** PB

Cornwell, Bernard, "Sharpe's Gold", first edition, published by Collins, London, signed by the author on the title page, edges slightly dusty, head of spine very slightly rubbed, inner flaps very faintly spotted.
*1981*

**£200-250** PB

Cumberland, Marten, "The Man Who Covered Mirrors", first edition, published by Doubleday Crime Club, Garden City, NY, pages browned, spine and edges very slightly rubbed.
*1949*

**£30-40** PB

Dexter, Colin, "The Secret Annexe 3", first edition, published by Macmillan, London, signed by the author on the title page, edges of pages sunning slightly, with minimal sunning to top edge.
*1986*

**£300-350** PB

Dexter, Colin, "Last Seen Wearing", first edition, published by Macmillan, London, the second Inspector Morse novel, usual faint tanning to pages.
*1976*

**£850-950** PB

Ellis, Bret Easton, "Less Than Zero", first American edition, published by Simon and Schuster, New York.

*1985*

**£150-200**     **BRB**

Fleming, Ian, "Moonraker", first edition, published by Jonathan Cape, London, extremely scarce, particularly with dust jacket.

*1955*

**£3,500-4,500**     **BIB**

Fleming, Ian, "Diamonds Are Forever", first edition, published by Jonathan Cape, London.

*1956*

**£1,500-2,000**     **BIB**

Fleming, Ian, "Dr. No", first edition, published by Jonathan Cape, London.

*1958*

**£1,200-1,800**     **BIB**

Fleming, Ian, "Goldfinger", first edition, published by Jonathan Cape, London.

*1959*

**£70-90**     **BIB**

Fleming, Ian, "For Your Eyes Only", first edition, published by Jonathan Cape, London.

*1960*

**£500-700**     **BIB**

Fleming, Ian, "You Only Live Twice", first edition, published by Jonathan Cape, London.

*1964*

**£80-120**     **BIB**

Fleming, Ian, "The Man With the Golden Gun", first edition, published by Jonathan Cape, London.

*An alternative first edition without the gold-blocked revolver on the front cover was also produced, but is worth considerably less.*

*1965*

**£3,000-3,500**     **BIB**

Freeman, R. Austin. "John Thorndyke's Cases", first edition, published by Chatto & Windus, London.

*1909*

**£450-550** PB

Greene, Graham, "Loser Takes All", first edition, published by Heinemann, London.

*1955*

**£80-120** BIB

Greene, Graham, "In Search of a Character: Two African Journals", first edition, published by Bodley Head, London.

*1961*

**£20-40** BIB

Greene, Graham, "May We Borrow Your Husband?", first edition, published by Bodley Head, London.

*1967*

**£30-50** BIB

Greene, Graham, "Travels with my Aunt", first edition, published by Bodley Head, London.

*1969*

**£25-35** BIB

Harris, Thomas, "Red Dragon", first American edition, published by G.P. Putman's Sons, New York.

*1981*

**£120-180** BRB

Harris, Thomas, "The Silence of the Lambs", first American edition, published by St Martin's Press, New York.

*1988*

**£100-150** BRB

Hemingway, Ernest, "To Have and Have Not", first American edition, published by Charles Scribner's Sons, New York.

*1937*

**£1,000-1,500** BRB

Herbert, Frank, "Dune", first American edition, published by Chilton Books, Philadelphia and New York.

*"Dune" won the first Nebula award for best science fiction novel in 1965.*

*1965*

**£5,200-5,800** BRB

Irish, William (Woolrich, Cornell), "The Dancing Detective", first edition, published by Lippincott, Philadelphia, spine slightly bumped, tanning to edges of pages, extremities worn, head and foot of spine chipped with slight creases to front panel.

*1946*

**£180-220**  PB

Irish, William (Woolrich, Cornell), "Somebody on the Phone", first edition, published by Lippincott, New York, top edge very faintly tanned and head of spine very slightly bumped, back panel slightly dusty with faint foxing on the outer edge, a scarce title.

*1940*

**£600-700**  PB

James, P.D., "The Skull Beneath the Skin", first edition, published by Faber & Faber, London, signed by the author on the title page.

*1982*

**£70-80**  PB

Leon, Donna, "Death in a Strange Country" first edition, published by Chapmans, London, the author's second novel.

*1993*

**£100-130**  PB

Marsh, Ngaio, "Died in the Wool", first edition, published by Collins Crime Club, London, owner's tiny inscription on front free endpaper, edges tanned, back panel darned.

*1945*

**£80-120**  PB

Mortimer, John, "Charade", first edition, published by Bodley Head, London, the first book from the creator of Rumpole of the Bailey, a review copy with the publisher's slip laid in, top edge very slightly darkened and rubbed.

*1947*

**£100-160**  PB

Murdoch, Iris, "The Italian Girl", first edition, published by Chatto & Windus, London, back panel dusty.

*1964*

**£40-60**  PB

O'Brian, Patrick, "The Fortune of War", first edition, published by Collins, London, the sixth Jack Aubrey novel, spine very slightly faded.

*1979*

**£280-320**  PB

O'Brian, Patrick, "H.M.S. Surprise", first edition, published by Collins, London, the third book in the Jack Aubrey series, very slight browning to top edge and spine slightly faded with one very small closed tear.

*1973*

**£450-500**  PB

Seymour, Gerald, "Harry's Game", first edition, published by Collins, London, the author's first book.

*1975*

**£100-125** PB

Smith, Zadie, "White Teeth" first edition, published by Hamish Hamilton, London, signed by the author on the title page, as new.

*2000*

**£100-125** PB

Steinbeck, John, "Winter of our Discontent", first edition, published by Viking, New York, lightly sunned.

*1961*

**£100-140** PB

Walters, Minette, "The Ice House", first edition, published by Macmillan, London, the author's first novel.

*1992*

**£550-650** PB

Walters, Minette, "The Sculptress", first edition, published by Macmillan, London, signed and dated by the author on the title page, the author's second book, very faint tanning to edges of pages.

*1993*

**£70-90** PB

Waugh, Evelyn, "Brideshead Revisited", first edition, published by Chapman & Hall, London, boards slightly faded, spine and corners bumped and edges foxed, rather soiled, worn and chipped at the corners and spine but reinforced and presentable.

*1945*

**£400-450** PB

Waugh, Evelyn, "Black Mischief", first edition, published by Chapman & Hall, London, slight stain to fore-edge, chipped and creased at head of spine but without loss to title, slight soiling and spine darkened, scarce in the dust jacket.

*1932*

**£400-500** PB

Wingfield, R.D., "Night Frost", first edition, published by Constable, London, as new.

*1992*

**£300-400** PB

Winterson, Jeanette, "Sexing the Cherry", first edition, published by Bloomsbury, London, presentation copy signed by the author on the title page, as new.

*1989*

**£80-120** PB

Attwell, Mabel Lucie, "Lucie Atwell's A B C Pop-up Book", Dean, illustrated glazed boards with simple pop-ups, colour illustrations throughout, very good condition.
*1960*

**£30-40** | BIB

Awdry, The Rev. W., "The Little Old Engine – Railway Series No. 14", Edmund Ward, illustrations by John T. Kenney.
*1959*

**£60-80** | BIB

Barker, C.M., "Flower Fairies of the Summer", Blackie, with dust jacket, clean with little loss to head and tail of spine.
*c1940*

**£55-65** | BIB

Blyton, Enid, "You Funny Little Noddy", Sampson Low, Marston & Co., first edition.
*1955*

**£20-30** | BIB

Briggs, Raymond, "Father Christmas Goes on Holiday", Sir Joseph Causton & Sons, first edition.
*1975*

**£40-60** | BIB

Blake, Quentin, "Words and Pictures", Chris Beetles Ltd, features pictures from 20 years of publication, signed, with very slight bumped spine, colour illustrations, large format.
*2000*

**£35-45** | BB

Blyton, Enid, "The Secret Seven", The Brockhampton Press Ltd, first edition with illustrations by George Brook.
*1949*

**£80-120** | BIB

Johns, Captain W.E., "Biggles Sets a Trap", Hodder and Stoughton, first edition with black and white illustrations by Stead, bumped at top and bottom, very good condition.
*1962*

**£50-70** | **BIB**

Potter, Beatrix, "The Tailor of Gloucester", Warne & Co., first edition.
*1903*

**£300-350** | **BIB**

Ransome, Arthur, "Swallows and Amazons", Jonathan Cape.
*1953*

**£180-220** | **BIB**

Potter, Beatrix, "The Tale of Piggling Bland", Warne & Co., first edition with paper-covered boards, lettered in maroon, with pictorial onlay to upper cover, pictorial noticeboard endpapers, 15 colour plates and many line drawings, ownership inscription on half title and front blank, with modern protective box.
*1913*

**£300-350** | **BIB**

Seuss, Dr., "How The Grinch Stole Christmas", NY Random House, first edition, a scarce book with illustrations by the author.
*1957*

**£800-1,200** | **BIB**

Tourtel, Mary, "Rupert, Little Bear, More Stories", Sampson Low, Marston & Co.
*1939*

**£750-850** | **BIB**

Uttley, Alison, "Moldy Warp The Mole", Collins, first edition with illustrations by Margaret Tempest.
*1940*

**£35-45** | **BIB**

Tolkien, J.R.R., "The Hobbit," Allen & Unwin, third edition, seventh impression, illustrations by the author.
*1972*

**£120-180** | **BIB**

Lisbeth Stone, "1.2.3", Book No. 206, colour-printed illustrated numbers book.
*c1918      8.75in (22cm) high*
**£40-60**                    **BONC**

F.M. Barton, "A.B.C", Book No. 3, colour-printed illustrated ABC book.
*1903            6in (15cm) high*
**£15-20**                    **BONC**

M. Morris, "The Animals went in 2 by 2", Book No. 200, colour-printed 'Fluffidown' illustrated verse book.
*c1917      8.25in (21cm) high*
**£15-25**                    **BONC**

R. James Williams, "A to Z in the Puff Puff", Book No. 211, colour-printed illustrated A to Z of the railways.
*c1921                7in (18cm) high*
**£50-80**                    **BONC**

A.E. Kennedy, "Big Animal Rag Book", Book No. 344, colour-printed illustrated book.
*c1939      14.5in (37cm) wide*
**£15-25**                    **BONC**

M. Morris, "Fluffy Chick Farm", Book No. 173, colour-printed illustrated book.
*c1916      8.25in (22cm) wide*
**£30-50**                    **BONC**

André Helle, "Dutchie Dolls' Doings", Book No. 192, colour-printed illustrated storybook.
*c1917    11in (28cm) high*
**£50-80**                    **BONC**

Dutchie Dolls Doings

E. Larcombe, "Mother Goose", Book No. 187, colour-printed illustrated nursery rhyme book.
*c1916      8.25in (21cm) wide*
**£10-15**                    **BONC**

Sybil Stuart, "Peter and Pam at Play", Book No. 292, colour-printed illustrated storybook.
*c1932      8.25in (21cm) high*
**£15-18**                    **BONC**

J.A. Walker, "Friends from the Farm", Book No. 35, colour-printed illustrated animal book.
*c1905      8.76in (22cm) wide*
**£15-25**                    **BONC**

# HOT COLLECTING AREA

## ADVERTISING

The enormous growth in advertising during the 20th century has left us with a diverse and often desirable legacy, from posters to pamphlets and tin trays to signs. Representing changing tastes in design, they also strongly evoke nostalgia.

see p.210

see p.204

see p.212

- As the range is so large, collectors often focus on one brand, a single period or a type of object. Essential considerations that dictate value include age, condition, quality of production and materials, the brand and market availability.

- Brands with long and diverse histories such as Guinness, who have advertised from the 1920s, and Coca-Cola, who have advertised since 1902, are among the most varied and desirable names among collectors. Material from lesser-known brands is likely to be less expensive and still provides great scope for a collection.

- Aim to collect items that reflect the colours and style of the period or that are quirky, eye-catching and fun. An appealing or highly typical image will make a piece much more desirable and often more valuable.

- Much is printed on card or paper and although produced in large numbers, most would have been discarded or destroyed. Paper and card items should be clean and with bright colours and intact edges. Examples of complex printing will add value. Tin signs are sought after and valuable, as are many advertising figurines.

- Visit museums and read books to learn about the styles, trends and brands associated with a period. The style of lettering can often be a good clue to dating a piece, as can the hairstyles and clothing of any people featured. Advertising material is also a fascinating document of the lifestyle and outlook of society at the time.

The famous animal series of posters was designed by John Gilroy in 1935 after a visit to London Zoo.

The campaign launched Guinness' legendary icon, the toucan, here seen taking centre stage.

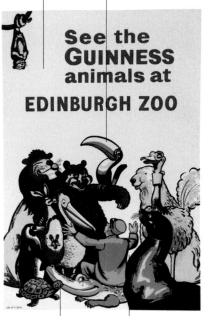

The campaign was very successful during the 1930s and was re-introduced in the 1950s, ending around 1961.

The colourful animals are always depicted on a white background. They typically outwit the zookeeper to obtain the pint – just like the ostrich here.

A Guinness "See the Animals at Edinburgh Zoo" poster, designed by J. Gilroy.

c1955                                   30in (76cm) high

**£300-350**                              **DO**

## TOP TIPS

- Look for objects that display the brand name and known slogans or characters associated with the brand, such as Guinness' toucan.

- Posters can be expensive, so consider smaller advertisements, calendars and display cards that often use the same or similar artwork. These are also easier to display and store.

- Examine the surface of a supposedly old item closely. If it is too clean and with no signs of wear, or if it is worn where it shouldn't be, it is probably a reproduction.

A very rare 1930s card Coca-Cola advertising standee showing Lupe Velez, printed by the Niagara Litho Ltd of Buffalo & New York.

*Lupe Velez was a beauty and film star during the 1920s, 1930s and 1940s, and starred in 'The Mexican Spitfire' in 1939. This example has been restored. If it was in excellent and unrestored condition, its value would be nearer £1,700.*

20.5in (52cm) high

£700-1,000 ATA

An American Coca-Cola tin advertising sign, with thermometer.
*c1941 15.75in (40cm) high*

£200-300 ATA

A 1950s Coca-Cola advertising porcelain push plate.

£200-300 SOTT

A plastic and card Coca-Cola miniature novelty billboard store display.
*6in (15.5cm) wide*

£40-60 ATA

A Coca-Cola advertising miniature card six-pack, with glass bottles.

£40-60 SOTT

A rare 1940s box of Coca-Cola advertising straws.
*8.75in (22cm) high*

£100-150 SOTT

A Coca-Cola amber glass, straight-sided bottle, marked "Norfolk, Virginia".
*c1910*

£60-80 SOTT

A 1950s Coca-Cola advertising Christmas carton stuffer, with cut-out Santa Claus doll.
*7.25in (18.5cm) high*

£50-70 SOTT

A 1950s Coca-Cola free sample cup.

*2.75in (7cm) high*

**£5-7** SOTT

A 1950s/60s Starr X bottle opener, complete in box.

*These would have been fitted to dispensing machines or to a bar.*

*8in (20cm) wide*

**£10-20** SOTT

A 1930s Coca-Cola promotional "Refresh Yourself" coupon.

*3.75in (9.5cm) wide*

**£20-30** SOTT

A rare 1950s complete set of Coca-Cola promotional nature study cards.

**£40-60** SOTT

A 1940s/50s Coca-Cola advertising metal pencil sharpener.

*1.75in (4.5cm) long*

**£40-60** SOTT

A Coca-Cola advertising 'Juanita' celluloid pocket mirror.

*c1906* *2.75in (7cm) long*

**£100-150** SOTT

A late 1950s Matchbox No. 37 Karrier Bantam Coca-Cola advertising lorry, with 'uneven' load, lacks box.

**£50-70** SOTT

A Dinky No. 402 Bedford Coca Cola advertising truck.

*1966-69 4.5in (11.5cm) wide*

**£40-60** SOTT

A 1950s Coca-Cola tie tack, set with rubies and diamonds.

*0.75in (2cm) wide*

**£80-120** SOTT

A Carlton Ware Guinness man with joey advertising figure.

*4in (10cm) high*

£120-180 **BEV**

A pair of ceramic Guinness canisters.

£50-70 **D**

A 1960s Guinness advertising plastic cruet set.

*5in (12.5cm) high*

£15-20 **DH**

A blue Guinness tankard.

£30-40 **D**

A 1950s Guinness advertising wooden brush.

*8in (20cm) high*

£15-20 **DH**

A card Guinness beer mat, probably 1950s.

*4in (10cm) wide*

£3-4 **LG**

A 1930s card Guinness beer mat.

*4in (10cm) wide*

£3-4 **LG**

A card Guinness menu.

*9.75in (25cm) high*

£7-10 **LG**

A 1990s set of Guinness playing cards, the major cards with reproductions of 1930s Guinness advertising.

£7-10 **LG**

A wooden Guinness advertising cribbage board.

*c1913*        *10.75in (27.5cm) wide*

**£20-30**        **DH**

A 1930s Ashtead Potters Guinness ashtray, "Guinness is Good for You".

*4.25in (11cm) diam*

**£40-50**        **DH**

A late 1940s Guinness blue and white plate, "My Goodness My Guinness".

*6.75in (17.5cm) diam*

**£30-50**        **DH**

A 1950s Guinness paper cup, "Guinness is good for you".

*4.5in (11.5cm) high*

**£5-10**        **DH**

A pair of 20thC novelty Guinness pottery salt and pepper shakers, each in the form of a pint of Guinness.

*2in (5cm) high*

**£70-100**        **J&H**

A Guinness rubber toucan advertising figure.

*1950s 6.75in (17cm) high*

**£100-150**        **DH**

A Guinness pocket calendar, "My Goodness My Guinness".

*1959*        *3.5in (9cm) high*

**£20-30**        **DH**

A Carlton Ware Guinness penguin table lamp, holding a plaque inscribed "Draught Guinness", the figure with original fitting and shade.

*6.75in (17cm) high*

**£500-600**        **BAR**

A South African Oranges 'The Only Empire Summer Orange' poster.

*20in (51cm) high*

**£180-220** DO

A Kodavox 'Pour Votre Magniphone, Produit Kodak' poster.

*23.5in (60cm) high*

**£80-120** DO

A Daily Express 'A Help Your Neighbour...' poster.

*23in (58cm) high*

**£60-80** DO

A Ministry of Food 'The Vegetabull' double crown poster, designed by Jan Lewitt and George Him.

*c1941* *30in (76cm) high*

**£600-800** REN

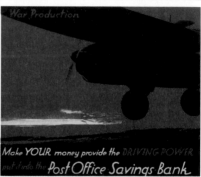

A Post Office Savings Bank 'War Production' quad crown poster, designed by Auben Cooper.

*c1944* *40in (101.5cm) long*

**£1,000-1,500** REN

A General Post Office 'Helps the Export Drive' quad crown poster, designed by Tom Eckersley of the Eckersley Studio.

*1948* *40in (101.5cm) wide*

**£1,500-2,000** REN

A 'Dick Whittington' David Allen & Sons poster.

*27in (69cm) high*

**£200-300** DO

'A La Francaise Diamant' poster.

*23.5in (60cm) high*

**£150-200** DO

An 'Exposition Internationale Mai-Novembre, Ministre du Commerce et de l'industrie' poster.

*1937      12in (35.5cm) high*

**£120-180      DO**

A 'La Houppa' colour lithographic advertising poster, by R. Faye, of woman in top hat in bright polychrome, mounted on linen, unframed, some creases and folds, signed upper right in print.

*c1930      62in (157.5cm) high*

**£250-300      DRA**

A French Renault tractors advertising poster, signed "Coulon".

*62.75in (159cm) wide*

**£50-60      ATK**

An early hand-painted Mutascope poster for "What the Moon Saw".

*A Mutascope was an early optical toy. A metal box with a viewing aperture contained a reel of photographs. By putting a coin in a slot and turning a handle, the reel revolved at speed and the viewer saw a 'moving' picture.*

*c1920      21.75in (55cm) high*

**£180-220      ATK**

A French 'Foire De Paris' advertising poster, artwork by Azebel.

*1918      43in (109cm) high*

**£450-550      P**

A Belgian 'Maëstro' cigars lithographed advertising poster.

**£70-100      ATK**

A WPA lithographed advertising poster, for skating in New York City Building, Flushing Meadow Park, framed under glass, a few short folds with accompanying loss of ink and light rippling.

*13in (33cm) wide*

**£170-200      DRA**

A Berlin Film Festival A1 poster.

*1960      32in (81.5cm) high*

**£300-350      P**

A Dubonnet card sign, 'Donne de l'appetit pour deux'.

*14.5in (36.5cm) high*

£40-60     **DO**

A Salamander Brandy card sign.

*15.75in (40cm) high*

£100-150     **DO**

An Ovaltine card sign, 'Drink Delicious Ovaltine & Face the Winter with a Smile'.

*14.5in (37cm) high*

£50-70     **DO**

A Symons Devonshire Cider card sign.

*13in (33cm) wide*

£40-50     **DO**

An Edmondson's Toffee card sign.

*18in (45.5cm) high*

£40-50     **DO**

A Marquise Slumber & Setting Net card sign, 'In all Hair Pastel Shades, Made in England'.

*12.5in (32cm) high*

£35-45     **DO**

A Crème Mouson card sign, 'Agissant en Profondeur.'

*12in (30.5cm) high*

£50-70     **DO**

A Drocourt card sign, 'Desserts de la favorite desserts du roi'.

*15.75in (40cm) high*

£20-30     **DO**

A Pitralon card sign.

*16.5in (42cm) high*

£25-35     **DO**

A Radiator Glace de Lingue card sign.

*15.75in (40cm) high*

**£50-80**     **DO**

A Maëstro card sign.

*17.25in (43.5cm) high*

**£50-70**     **DO**

A Charles Roberson & Co. card sign.

*17.75in (45cm) high*

**£40-60**     **DO**

A Nuit à l'Arlequin card sign, Paris.

*14in (35.5cm) high*

**£40-60**     **DO**

An Anggoer Obat Serravallo card sign.

*11.5in (29.5cm) high*

**£30-50**     **DO**

An Anggoer Obat Serravallo card sign.

*16.25in (41cm) high*

**£30-50**     **DO**

A Players embossed tin advertising sign.

*c1910   15.25in (39cm) diam*

**£500-550**                    DH

A Craven A cigarettes enamel sign, with some rusting and other damage.

*35.75in (91cm) wide*

**£150-200**                    DN

A 1950s Middlemass Forfar Scotch Shortbread advertising sign, with artwork by Mabel Lucie Attwell.

*12in (30.5cm) high*

**£200-250**                    DH

A 1930s OXO double-sided tin advertising sign.

*13in (33cm) high*

**£80-100**                    DH

A double-sided Pratt's Motor Oil enamel sign, with serial number "B 9/30" on one side.

*26in (66cm) diam*

**£150-200**                    DN

A 1960s Skol suntan lotion advertising standee.

*22in (56cm) high*

**£25-35**                    DH

A Double Diamond advertising figure, by Beswick.

*8in (20.5cm) high*

**£250-300**                    BEV

A 1970s Home Pride Flour Man plastic container.

*8.75in (22cm) high*

**£15-20**                    FFM

A Johnny Walker whisky ashtray, with inscription 'Born 1820 Still Going Strong', by Magnier Blangy.

c1960          4in (10cm) wide

**£8-10**                          **DH**

A Woodbine Virginia Cigarettes ashtray.

c1960     4.5in (11.5cm) wide

**£4-6**                          **DH**

A 1960s Trumans advertising figure, with inscription 'Brewers of Good Beer'.

8in (20cm) high

**£40-50**                          **DH**

A 1960s Carlsberg advertising figure, depicting a woman seated on a rock.

7in (18cm) high

**£15-25**                          **DH**

A 1960s Tia Maria plastic advertising figure.

10.5in (27cm) high

**£40-50**                          **DH**

A box of ten commemorative boxes of matches, to commemorate the wedding of HRH Princess Anne and Captain Mark Philips.

3.25in (8.5cm) wide

**£4-6**                          **DH**

A set of three Biba cosmetics containers.

c1970     Bottle 4.25in (11cm) high

**£10-15 EACH**                   **DH**

A plastic Nairn elephant, by Eduardo Paolozzi, designed for Nairn Floors Ltd, no. 911 of 3000.

1972          11.75in (30cm) high

**£600-700**                      **L&T**

A propaganda postcard, with "The Kaiser When The War Is Over" cartoon.

*5.5in (13.5cm) wide*

£4-5  LG

A propaganda postcard, with "What Is A Fine Sight?" British army cartoon.

*5.5in (13.5cm) high*

£1-2  LG

A propaganda postcard, with "You've not said how I've grown, Daddy" cartoon, by the Hostel for Blind Women.

*5.5in (13.5cm) high*

£4-5  LG

A propaganda postcard, with "I'm going to wipe them out" cartoon.

*5.5in (13.5cm) high*

£7-9  LG

A propaganda postcard, with Lloyd George cartoon on Land Tax.

*5.5in (13.5cm) high*

£3-5  LG

A postcard, with Lloyd George political cartoon.

*5.5in (13.5cm) high*

£5-6  LG

A 1910s 'The Holiday Season' saucy seaside postcard, with canoodling couples.

*5.25in (13.5cm) wide*

50P-£1  LG

A seaside postcard, 'I take the first opportunity', cartoon by E Parkinson, S Hildeheimer & Co London & Manchester.

*5.25in (13.5cm) wide*

£3-4  LG

An unused Belgian 'Coeur A Coeur' saucy seaside postcard.

*5.25in (13.5cm) wide*

£1-1.50  LG

A 1910s Bognor seaside souvenir postcard.

*5.25in (13.5cm) high*

**£1-1.50** LG

A location postcard of the Hovis shop in West Ham, London.

*c1910-15 5.5in (13.5cm) high*

**£20-25** LG

A 1900s 'The Good Old Summertime' saucy seaside postcard, with boaters ogling a lady in bathing costume.

*5.25in (13.5cm) high*

**£1-1.50** LG

A 1920s humorous seaside postcard for Margate.

*5in (13cm) high*

**£2-2.50** LG

A location postcard of a rare street scene in Cheapside, Barnsley.

*Street scenes of Barnsley are not common. Postcards such as this are of use to local and social historians. Fashions and cars can help to date postcards.*

*c1910* *5.5in (13.5cm) wide*

**£25-30** LG

A location postcard of a flood in Derby, dated.

*Postcards of one-off events are collectable for their rarity.*

*1932* *5.5in (13.5cm) wide*

**£18-22** LG

A location postcard of Euston Station, London.

*c1920* *5.25in (13cm) wide*

**£5-6** LG

Six of twenty-three embroidered silk postcards, including a regimental badge for the Royal Berkshire Regiment, patriotic flags for the RFA and ASC, two dated cards for 1914-16 and 1918-9, the latter with a monoplane design, and various other patriotic and greeting types.

**£150-200 (SET)** DN

# FASHION & JEWELLERY

The fashion for anything 'retro' has had a big impact on this collecting market, with prices of 20th-century fashion, costume jewellery and period accessories booming in recent years. What gives the market its energy is that not only are pieces bought to form part of a collection, but are also currently worn or used in elite and high-street fashion circles as the essence of chic.

When collecting clothing, keep a keen eye out for quality in terms of the cut and material, as well as how typical a piece is of the period in which it was made – the closer the better. The same rules apply to costume jewellery – with so much of the work being affordable and fun as well as highly fashionable. The jewellery market revolves around the big names, such as Trifari or Joseff of Hollywood in the 1930s and 1940s. Although of little low material value, the quality and variety of design and association with noted names of the period, some being celebrities, makes them desirable. Men are not forgotten! Fashionable accessories such as ties, cufflinks, lighters and watches are collectable too, and once again the aim is to find anything that is the essence of its period, the finer the quality and the more typical the styling the better. In all cases, identifying a notable factory or designer adds interest, desirability and most often value.

## FASHION

The desire to gain a truly individual look, the vogue for retro fashions of bygone eras and the more scholarly approach of studying the changing styles of the past, have made fashion one of the most lively and interactive collectable markets of the 20th century.

see p.224    see p.221    see p.225

- The desirability and hence value of a vintage fashion outfit will vary according to its age, style, decoration, condition and the designer or design house responsible for it.

- Major, well-known designer names will always fetch the highest prices, partly due to the cachet of owning or wearing a piece and partly due to the inherent quality that the designer's name brings. Noted names also have an established following of collectors.

- True 'couture' pieces are of the highest quality and are made in very small quantities to special order and represent the apex of collecting. Aim to find and buy examples that typify the work of that designer. Good examples include Courreges' space-age designs, Christian Dior's 'New Look' and Vivienne Westwood's 'punk' clothes.

- Quality can be found by some lesser-known, or even unknown, names. Examine a piece closely in terms of the design, cut and material. The form, colour and any pattern should be considered.

- If you collect to wear, or are collecting on a budget, look for clothes by lesser-known names that sum up the spirit and style of a particular age. 1950s and 1960s fashions are particularly collectable for their colourful and jaunty styles, often incorporating overtly youthful or psychedelic designs.

- Changing contemporary fashions and styles have an incredibly important effect on values. While 1980s styles are said to be soon making a comeback, trusted vintage names such as Emilio Pucci never stay out of fashion lovers' eyes for long.

The design is by Andy Warhol, and features his famous 'Pop Art' Campbell's soup can motif, representing mass production.

Feeling and looking like paper, it is made from 80% cellulose and 20% cotton and was a statement on the throwaway aspects of 'Popular' culture.

The shape and cut of the dress is typically 1960s, with modern and simple lines.

The material is comparatively fragile and cannot be cleaned easily. They were marketed in quantity but were not popular so were discontinued. Today, they are rare.

An Andy Warhol design 'The Souper Dress', with original label, two tears and a few stains.

*c1960*                                             *38in (96.5cm) long*

**£700-1,000**                                             **FRE**

An Azzedine Alaïa black taffeta gored dress.

*51.5in (131cm) long*

**£300-350**      **S&T**

A Balenciaga two-piece red skirt and top.

*35in (89cm) long*

**£80-120**      **S&T**

A 1960s Balmain yellow and black silk dress.

*36.5in (93cm) long*

**£120-180**      **S&T**

A 1960s Biba plaid dress.

*54.25in (138cm) long*

**£80-100**      **S&T**

A Biba vintage floral gown.

*52.75in (134cm) long*

**£180-220**      **S&T**

A 1970s Liz Berg for Bernie Bee Pucci-style gown.

**£70-80**      **S&T**

A Byblos iridescent pink rain jacket.

*23.75in (60cm) long*

**£80-120**      **S&T**

A 1960s futuristic dress, possibly by Cardin.

*57.5in (146cm) long*

**£800-1,000**      **S&T**

An Ossie Clark elegant black dress, in crêpe tie with satin trim.

*50in (127cm) long*

**£320-380**      **S&T**

A Courrèges ivory knit dress.

*40.5in (103cm) long*

**£180-220**      **S&T**

A Courrèges size 10 skirt and blouse, with cream and beige stripes.

**£220-280**      **S&T**

A Courrèges black and white dress and belt.

*34.5in (88cm) long*

**£300-350**      **S&T**

A Courrèges museum quality couture maxi skirt, with appliqué daisies.

*40in (102cm) long*

**£1,200-1,800**      **S&T**

A Courrèges couture green dress, unlabelled.

*35in (89cm) long*

**£500-600**      **S&T**

A Courrèges couture two-piece red trouser suit.

*22.5in (57cm) long*

**£1,200-1,800**      **S&T**

A Courrèges white and blue dress.

*2.5in (108cm) long*

**£320-380**      **S&T**

A Courrèges couture green wool coat.

*37in (94cm) long*

**£1,800-2,200**      **S&T**

A Courrèges two-piece rust and cream tweed suit.

*27.5in (70cm) long*

**£250-300**      **S&T**

A rare Benny Ong blue and yellow two-piece crêpe suit.
*26.25in (67cm) long*

£250-300          **S&T**

An early Pucci size 10 dress and belt, printed with blue and green flowers.
*43.75in (111cm) long*

£350-400          **S&T**

A rare Jean Patou blue, leather trim coat and matching dress, (dress not shown).

*Jean Patou (1880-1936) saw his heyday during the 1920s and is notable for being the first European designer to present his designs on American models. Designers including Marc Bohan, Karl Lagerfeld and Christian Lacroix continued his business and name.*

*43.25in (110cm) long*

£800-1,200 (SET)          **S&T**

A 1960s Emilio Pucci blouse and skirt.
*skirt 21.5in (55cm) long*

£350-400          **S&T**

A late 1960s Emilio Pucci size 10 pink dress.
*39in (99cm) long*

£320-380          **S&T**

A 1960s Pucci Saks 5th Avenue size 12 dress and belt.
*47.25in (120cm) long*

£320-380          **S&T**

A pair of 1960s Pucci trousers, with red and purple designs on a yellow background.

*41in (105cm) long*

£220-280      S&T

A 1960s Pucci pink nylon long skirt.

*37in (94cm) long*

£200-250      S&T

A pair of Mary Quant red and white striped slacks and top.

*46.75in (119cm) long*

£150-200      S&T

A 1950s Ric Roc red and white dress.

£50-70      S&T

A Sonia Rykiel red and black knit dress.

*41.25in (105cm) long*

£120-180      S&T

An early 1970s three-piece Yves Saint Laurent outfit, including jersey, trousers and necklace.

£700-900      S&T

A Diane Von Fürstenberg black-and-white gown and jacket.

*Jacket 28in (71cm) long*

£80-120      S&T

A jacket from a Valentino two-piece print suit.

*19in (48cm) long*

£50-100 (SUIT)      S&T

A 1950s printed cotton dress, decorated with pink roses.

£25-35      CCL

A 1950s printed cotton dress, decorated with purple and pink flowers, with a bow.

£30-50      CCL

A 1950s printed cotton dress, by Montana Fashions, with orange band and decorated with poppies.

£30-50      CCL

A 1950s black and white cotton dress, with printed Aztec design highlighted with sequins.

£70-100      CCL

A 1950s printed cotton shirt dress.

£20-30      CCL

A 1950s printed cotton shirt dress.

£20-30      CCL

A 1950s black velvet full circle skirt, by McArthur Ltd, with gold thread decoration, size 10.

£40-60      CCL

A 1950s orange/red velvet full circle skirt.

£30-50      CCL

A 1950s blue felt skirt, with applied poodle motif.

£40-60      CCL

A 1950s black and white spotted prom dress, with crinoline.

**£220-260**     **S&T**

A 1950s cream and wool dress, with blue robe swirls.

**£120-160**     **S&T**

A 1950s blue and white puffball dress.

**£180-220**     **S&T**

A 1960s dress, with belt.

**£60-80**     **S&T**

A 1960s pink floral print dress.

**£60-80**     **S&T**

A 1960s flower print coat.

**£60-70**     **S&T**

A very rare and touchingly handmade tunic, with pink embroidery, buttons, metal bits, and coins, possibly Afghan.

**£850-950**     **S&T**

A vintage Chinese robe, with black appliqué embroidered grape vines.

**£380-420**     **S&T**

## HANDBAGS

The fad for all things 'retro', led by vintage clothes has meant that vintage handbags have not only become hotly collected and used as fashionable accessories, but also copied by today's handbag designers.

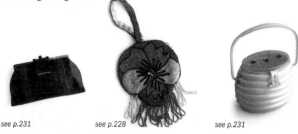

see p.231        see p.228        see p.231

- Always aim to collect bags that show typical styling from the period in which they were made in terms of form, material and decoration. Fun and quirky designs will also appeal, thanks to popular TV shows such as "Sex In The City". Most are by lesser known, or unknown, names as design quality tends to take precedence in collector's eyes.

- Beadwork bags are in demand for their intricate workmanship and bright colours. Most were made in the US, Germany, France or Belgium. Bags from the first few decades of the 20th century tend to have floral, chinoiserie or other eastern designs, often in Art Nouveau styles.

- Later beaded bags from the 1930s onwards often have complex beadwork pictures, and often fetch high values. Earlier handbags from the start of the 20th century tend to be smaller, like evening bags, as ladies still relied on men financially. Sizes grew as more items such as purses and cigarettes were carried.

- The 1930s to the 60s offer perhaps the most scope and variety to collectors, with many of the most desirable examples in novelty shapes such as telephones and poodles. Look out for Lucite bags from the 1950s, which come in a variety of colours and shapes, many with carved areas.

- As with fashion, bags by noted designer names are highly desirable. While an iconic Hermes 'Kelly' bag will be beyond the reach of most, examples by Gucci, Fendi and Judith Leiber, known for her jewelled bags, can be found at various prices.

## A CLOSER LOOK AT A HANDBAG

Judith Leiber is renowned for her glittering and individual evening bags, often known as 'minaudières'. Born in 1921 in Hungary, where also she studied handbag design, Leiber married an American GI and moved to New York in 1947. She founded her own handbag company in 1963.

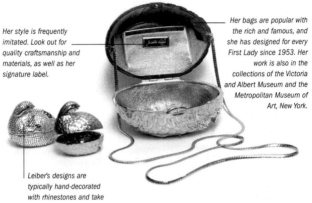

Her style is frequently imitated. Look out for quality craftsmanship and materials, as well as her signature label.

Her bags are popular with the rich and famous, and she has designed for every First Lady since 1953. Her work is also in the collections of the Victoria and Albert Museum and the Metropolitan Museum of Art, New York.

Leiber's designs are typically hand-decorated with rhinestones and take many weeks to decorate.

A Judith Leiber quail-shaped bag, with two smaller 'quails' inside.

c1980s                                           6.75(17cm) wide

**£800-900**                                                **S&T**

## TOP TIPS

- Avoid mesh and beadwork bags with holes or missing sections – they are very hard to repair.

- Many of today's handbag designs are becoming collectable, further widening the scope to collectors.

- Beware of modern reproductions of famous-name bags. Examine bags for hallmarks of quality in terms of material and stitching that a designer name should bring.

- Look out for torn linings, general daily wear and any other damage. Dried and cracked leather should be avoided.

A silver beadwork reticule or pouch, with a pink cotton ground and tassel.

*c1910*       *8in (20cm) long*

**£30-50**                    **AAC**

A 1910s grey crochet and steel beadwork reticule or pouch, with chain drawstring.

*6.75in (17cm) long*

**£50-80**                    **AAC**

A beadwork reticule or pouch, with bird design, black silk lining, with looped fringe.

*c1910*       *8.25in (21cm) long*

**£50-80**                    **AAC**

A beadwork 'pansy' bag, with cream silk lining, labelled "Hand Made in Belgium".

*c1915*       *5in (13cm) long*

**£80-120**                   **AAC**

A 1930s Austrian floral pattern beadwork 'duffle' bag, made of very fine beads.

*12in (30cm) high*

**£300-500**                 **CRIS**

A small early 20thC unlined beadwork bag.

*4in (10cm) long*

**£8-12**                     **AAC**

A 1940s French or Belgian beadwork bag, with glass bead background, embroidered with gold-plated frame.

*8.5in (22cm) wide*

**£150-200**                 **CRIS**

A 1940s French or Belgian beadwork bag, with glass bead background, embroidered with a gold-plated frame.

*8.5in (22cm) wide*

**£150-200**                 **CRIS**

A 1940s French embroidered beadwork bag, made of white, gold, pink and grey fine glass beads.

*13.25in (34cm) wide*

**£300-400**                 **CRIS**

A late 1940s French beadwork bag, with fine black glass beads and brass frame and chain handle.

*8in (20.5cm) wide*

**£100-150**                 **CRIS**

An early 1950s French or Belgian beadwork bag, with fine silvered glass beads.

*8.5in (22cm) wide*

**£150-200**                 **CRIS**

A beadwork bag, lined with white satin and with a label reading "MADE IN FRANCE".

*c1950*       *9in (23cm) wide*

**£15-20**                    **AAC**

A beaded moth purse.

*9in (23cm) long*

**£1,500-2,000** ROX

A 1940s black beaded bag, with flowers.

*10.25in (26cm) wide*

**£150-200** S&T

A 1940s black beaded purse with rose design.

*11in (28cm) wide*

**£200-250** ROX

A 1950s black beaded and jewelled bag, with poodle motif.

*14.5in (37cm) wide*

**£140-170** SM

A 1950s black jersey jewelled and beaded tapestry handbag.

*7.5in (19cm) wide*

**£80-100** SM

A 1940s white beaded figural bag.

*9in (23cm) wide*

**£300-400** ROX

A 1940s white beaded box purse.

*7in (17.5cm) wide*

**£200-300** ROX

A 1950s black Lucite compartment purse.

**£400-500** ROX

A beautiful 19thC petit point bag, with gilt frame.

*8in (21cm) wide*

**£150-200** **S&T**

A 19thC satin Turkish bag, made for the European market.

*5in (12.5cm) wide*

**£100-150** **MEN**

A 1930s tapestry bag, probably French.

*9in (23cm) wide*

**£180-230** **S&T**

A 1950s Souré black leather bag, with 3D scenic tapestry work, New York.

*15.25in (38.5cm) wide*

**£120-150** **SM**

A 1950s tapestry bag.

*10.75in (27cm) wide*

**£80-120** **S&T**

An incredibly detailed Art Nouveau bag, with celluloid clasp.

*c1900* *8.25in (21cm) wide*

**£425-475** **S&T**

A rare vintage 'Fragonard' girl on swing vanity case.

*4in (10cm) wide*

**£180-220** **S&T**

A 1950s poet bag, with 'La Maison du Poet' on the front.

*11.5in (29cm) wide*

**£80-120** **S&T**

A 1950s Rialto purse.

*Bags from the 1950s are characterised by having shorter handles.*

**£100-150** **ROX**

A 1940s American bag, with voile body and butterscotch Bakelite frame.

*8in (20.5cm) wide*

**£100-150**     **CRIS**

A 1940s black leather bag.

**£20-30**     **PC**

A 1940s python-skin bag.

**£30-40**     **PC**

A 1940s Ann Marie telephone bag, black buckskin with gilt frame.

*This example was made as a V.I.P. gift for residents of The Ritz, Paris.*

*8.25in (21cm) high*

**£1,000-1,500**     **CRIS**

A 1940s Ann Marie playing cards bag, black buckskin with gold club, spade, heart and diamond motifs and ivory dice clasp.

*11.5in (29cm) wide*

**£400-600**     **CRIS**

A 1950s American bag, with brass frame and clasp and black Lucite body, inset with abstract brass motifs.

*12in (30cm) high*

**£100-150**     **CRIS**

A 1940s Ann Marie champagne bucket bag, black buckskin with clear Lucite top and handle, and gold-plated trim.

*This bag was made as a Christmas gift for V.I.P. residents of The Ritz, Paris.*

*7.5in (19cm) wide*

**£1,500-2,000**     **CRIS**

A 1950S rigid bag, with velvet-covered exterior, brass strips and plastic lid.

*11.5in (29cm) high*

**£40-60**     **AAC**

A 1950s American 'beehive' bag.

*7in (18cm) wide*

**£150-200**     **CRIS**

A strawberry wooden box bag, with hand-painted motif.

*12.25in (31cm) wide*

| £50-60 | S&T |
|---|---|

A 1950s wooden octagonal handbag, with butterfly découpage and Lucite handle.

*7in (18cm) wide*

| £80-100 | SM |
|---|---|

A metal box bag.

*8.75in (22cm) wide*

| £60-80 | S&T |
|---|---|

A 1950s white woven basket, with felt fruit baskets.

*8.5in (22cm) wide*

| £80-100 | SM |
|---|---|

A 1930s Bakelite purse.

*5.5in (14cm) wide*

| £500-600 | ROX |
|---|---|

A 1920s brocade bag with white metal clasp.

*6.75in (17cm) wide*

| £100-150 | MEN |
|---|---|

A 1950s handmade wooden happy-house handbag.

*10.5in (26.5cm) wide*

| £130-150 | SM |
|---|---|

A 1920s tapestry petit point bag, with enamel clasp.

*9.5in (24cm) wide*

| £100-150 | MEN |
|---|---|

A 19th/20thC Native American bag.

*6in (15cm) wide*

| £200-300 | ROX |
|---|---|

A 1920s tapestry petit point bag.

*7in (18cm) wide*

| £100-150 | MEN |
|---|---|

A 1920s chocolate brown woven straw, silk-lined cloche hat, with a satin band.

*5.25in (13.5cm) high*

**£120-160**　　　　　　**LH**

A 1930s woven horse hair hat, with a velvet band, on a wire frame.

*19.25in (49cm) wide*

**£50-70**　　　　　　**LH**

A 1930s wool felt and woven horsehair hat, with silk poppies.

*14.25in (36cm) wide*

**£50-80**　　　　　　**LH**

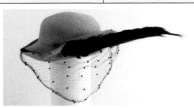

A late 1930s blush pink wool felt hat, with black feather and black dotted veil.

*15.75in (40cm) long*

**£140-180**　　　　　　**LH**

A 1930s/1940s pink felt hat, with light black veil covering and feather.

*8.25in (21cm) wide*

**£50-70**　　　　　　**MAC**

A 1940s Schiaparelli three-colour woven straw hat.

*8.75in (22.5cm) wide*

**£40-60**　　　　　　**MG**

A 1950s hat, decorated with daisies.

**£8-12**　　　　　　**CCL**

A 1950s American hat, decorated with roses.

**£18-22**　　　　　　**CCL**

A 1950s woven straw wide-brimmed hat, with velvet band and applied orange and yellow rose flower.

*15in (38cm) wide*

**£40-70**　　　　　　**LH**

A 1950s steel grey woven straw wide-brimmed hat, with organza covering.

*13.75in (35cm) wide*

**£50-80**　　　　　　**LH**

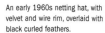

An early 1960s netting hat, with velvet and wire rim, overlaid with black curled feathers.

*11.75in (30cm) high*

**£50-80**　　　　　　**LH**

A 1950s formed woven fabric hat, with a velvet band and applied silk roses.

*14.5in (37cm) wide*

**£35-55**　　　　　　**LH**

A 1960s silk scarf, with figural pattern, produced for the "21 Club" New York, maker unknown.

*66in (167.5cm) long*

**£60-80** **REN**

A 1950s Hermes 'La Clé des Champs' pattern scarf, Jacquard silk with hand-rolled edges, designed and signed by F.R. Façonnet.

*35in (89cm) wide*

**£100-150** **REN**

A 1970s Hermes 'Les Bécanes' pattern scarf, silk twill with hand-rolled edges, designed by the Hermes Studio (unsigned).

*35in (89cm) wide*

**£100-130** **REN**

A 1970s Hermes 'Grand Apparat' pattern scarf, silk twill with hand-rolled edges, designed and signed by Jacques Eudel.

*35in (89cm) wide*

**£80-100** **REN**

A 1950s Hermes 'Chiens et Valets' pattern scarf, silk twill with hand-rolled edges, designed by C.H. Hello.

*35in (89cm) wide*

**£80-120** **REN**

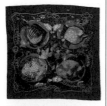

A 1980s Hermes 'Grands Fonds' pattern scarf, silk twill with hand-rolled edges, designed by the Hermes Studio (unsigned).

*35in (89cm) wide*

**£100-140** **REN**

A 1970s Hermes 'Harnais des Presidents' pattern scarf, silk twill with hand-rolled edges, designed by the Hermes Studio (unsigned).

*35in (89cm) wide*

**£80-120** **REN**

A 1940s Jacqmar 'Swan Lake' pattern parachute silk scarf.

*33in (84cm) wide*

**£60-80** **REN**

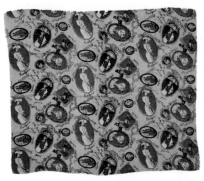

A 1940s Jacqmar 'Les Belles Dames' pattern rayon scarf.

*34in (86.5cm) wide*

**£60–90**      **REN**

A 1940s Kaystyle 'Wartime' pattern rayon scarf, signed "London by Kaystyle".

*33in (84cm) wide*

**£200–250**      **REN**

A 1970s Liberty's of London 'Paisley pattern' silk scarf.

*26.5in (67.5cm) wide*

**£15-30**      **REN**

A 1940s synthetic fabric 'Sporting' pattern scarf, designed by Thirkell.

*32in (81.5cm) wide*

**£20–40**      **REN**

A 1950s Jacqmar 'Geese' pattern silk scarf, designed by Peter Scott.

*29in (73.5cm) wide*

**£30–50**      **REN**

A Welsh Margetson & Co. Ltd 'Coronation Derby 1953 – Pinza' pattern scarf, from the series "Winners of the Derby since 1780".

*1953    34in (86.5cm) wide*

**£150–200**      **REN**

A 'Winston Churchill 80th Birthday' pattern silk scarf, designer's signature illegible.

*1954    27in (68.5cm) wide*

**£50–70**      **REN**

A 1950s 'Letters' pattern silk scarf, maker unknown.

*35.5in (90cm) wide*

**£30–50**      **REN**

A pair of American early 19thC black kid and velvet silk embroidered lace-up shoes with stacked heels.

*9in (23cm) long*

£50-70                                    AAC

A 1950s pair of Lucite and diamanté sandals, by First Editions.

£40-60                                    CCL

A 1940s pair of hollow heel shoes, made in the Phillipines, hand-embroidered and decorated with roses.

£80-120                                   CCL

A 1950s pair of Lucite and diamanté stiletto sandals, by Style Pride, with Spring-o-lators.

£50-60                                    CCL

A pair of slingback stiletto sandals, by Guildmark, with clear plastic, faux leather and faux pearl.

£25-35                                    CCL

A 1950s pair of hollow heeled peek-toe shoes, with Alpine chalets in the heels.

£80-100                                   CCL

A 1950s pair of straw mules, decorated with beadwork.

£45-65                                    CCL

A pair of American red satin slides, decorated on the open toe vamps with red feathers.

*c1955          9.75in (25cm) long*

£7-10                                     AAC

A 1950s pair of wooden platform sandals, with woven raffia toe.

£20-40                                    CCL

A 1940s painted silk tie, with purple ground and glitter details.

£120-150     **CVS**

A 1940s handpainted silk tie, by Cravate Triomphe, with starfish design.

£30-50     **CVS**

A 1940s painted silk tie, decorated with a dancing couple and a drummer, with motto "Dance Pretty Lady".

£80-120     **CVS**

A 1970s plain black silk 'peek-a-boo' tie, printed to the interior with a strawberry blonde bathing beauty.

*Peek-a-boo ties are being copied by contemporary designers such as Paul Smith.*

£100-150     **CVS**

A 1970s painted silk tie, decorated with a Neanderthal caveman dragging a woman, with the motto "Friendly Persuasion".

£50-70     **CVS**

A 1940s handpainted acetate, rayon and nylon, by Diane, decorated with a scene of a log cabin amongst palm trees.

£50-80     **CVS**

A 1950s printed silk tie, by Herb J. Hawthorns Inc, Houston, Texas, titled "Doodle Bugger, 1951".

*This was an oil rigger's club tie.*

£50-80     **CVS**

A 1940s handpainted silk tie, by Regal of California, with coloured abstract pattern.

£15-25     **CVS**

## COSTUME JEWELLERY

Popularised by glamourous stars of stage and screen during the 20th century and enjoying an enormous revival today, costume jewellery values have rocketed. The wide variety available offers both the collector and the fashionista the opportunity to experience this period sparkle and glamour at a range of values.

see p.240          see p.243          see p.241

- Collectors seek out typical designs by notable makers, most of them American. Trifari, founded in 1918, is one of the most varied and sought after with high quality designs from the 1930s and 40s by Alfred Philippe often being the most valuable. Their animal-shaped 'jelly belly' pins and those in novelty forms of leaves and fruit are also highly collectable.

- Joseff of Hollywood, whose shaped pieces can be recognised from the gold-coloured metal he used, is another popular name. His designs were worn by stars such as Per Angeli and Grace Kelly. Look out for large pins in the shape of the sun or moon.

- Miriam Haskell, working in New York from the 1920s to the 1950s, is another important name. Known for her intricate use of beads and faux pearls, her best designs have a multi-layered construction that give an impressive three-dimensional effect.

- Well-known designers produced pieces which often fetch high values today. Chanel, who began the rage for costume jewellery in fashion, Dior and Schiaparelli are among the most desirable.

- For those on a budget, look for smaller, lesser-known names such as Avon and J.J. More modern names such as Kenneth J. Lane, Dinny Hall and Butler & Wilson are popular, as are unmarked pieces.

- Bakelite jewellery, appearing during the 1920s and 30s, is now highly prized. Authentic pieces can usually be identified by signs of wear, such as light, irregular scratches. They also tend to be heavier and the clasps attached with screws or pins rather than glue. Bright colours, quirky, novelty shapes and deeply cut designs are usually the most valuable.

## A CLOSER LOOK AT A TRIFARI PIN AND EARRINGS

This pin and earrings were designed by Alfred Philippe, who had worked for Van Cleef & Arpels and Cartier. He joined Trifari in 1930 and worked for them for 40 years. His use of multi-coloured stones led to Trifari being known as the 'Rhinestone Kings'.

The stones are in an 'invisible setting'. This technique was developed by Van Cleef & Arpels in the 1930s, and is used here 10 years later.

The clear rhinestones offset the brightly coloured stones.

The stones are calibre cut, which means they were cut to fit the shape of the design. This is a sign of high quality and is rarely seen in costume jewellery.

A 1940s Trifari pin and earrings.

Earring 1.25in (3.5cm) long

**£1,000-1,500**

**ROX**

## TOP TIPS

- Look for makers' marks on clasps, earring back or brooch backs, and inside catches or closures.

- Big names aside, the immediate visual appeal and 'glitter factor' often count the most towards desirability and value.

- Remove tarnish from silver-gilt pieces with a jeweller's polishing cloth; don't buff hard as gold plating can rub off.

- Avoid soaking costume jewellery in liquids, which can loosen crystals from their settings and discolour the finish.

A mid-late 1950s Christian Dior necklace and earrings set with clear paste stones and green marble effect cabochons, by Mitchell Maer.

**£500-700** RG

A mid-late 1950s Christian Dior rhinestone and paste unicorn brooch, by Mitchell Maer.

**£100-150** RG

A mid-late 1950s Christian Dior clear paste and faux pearl flower brooch, by Mitchell Maer, signed Christian Dior.

**£120-200** RG

A Christian Dior pin, set with royal blue and aurora borealis stones, signed and dated 1958.

**£150-200** RG

A Christian Dior necklace and earrings, set with iridescent glass and aurora borealis stone, signed by Christian Dior.

*c1958*

**£400-600** RG

A 1960s Christian Dior necklace, bracelet and earrings, by Kramer.

*Earrings 1in (3cm) long*

**£200-300** ROX

A Christian Dior pearl and diamanté pin.

*1963          4in (9cm) long*

**£200-300** ROX

A Christian Dior necklace and earrings, set with faux rubies and diamonds.

*1959 Earrings 1.5in (4cm) long*

**£450-650** ROX

A 1960s Christian Dior heart-shaped brooch, set with clear stones with pink or white inclusions and pastel yellow, blue and green stones, signed Christian Dior.

**£150-200** RG

A 1940s Miriam Haskell multi-coloured bead bracelet and earrings.
*Earrings 2.25in (6cm)*

**£400-600**                                    **ROX**

A pair of 1940s Miriam Haskell yellow flower earrings.
*1.25in (3.5cm) long*

**£150-200**                                    **ROX**

A 1940s Miriam Haskell gold, blue and green pin.
*3in (7.5cm) long*

**£150-200**                                    **ROX**

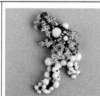

A 1940s Miriam Haskell white bead pin.
*3in (7.5cm) long*

**£150-200**                                    **ROX**

A 1940s Miriam Haskell amber and gold necklace.
*Drop centre 2in (5cm) long*

**£300-400**                                    **ROX**

A 1940s Miriam Haskell amber and pearl bead pin and earrings.
*Earrings 1in (3cm) long*

**£250-300**                                    **ROX**

A 1950s Miriam Haskell stick pin, with baroque pearls and filigree stampings.
*2.75in (7cm) long*

**£75-125**                                    **CRIS**

A 1960s Miriam Haskell pearl pin and earrings.
*3.5in (9cm) long*

**£200-250**                                    **ROX**

A 1960s Miriam Haskell pink and white necklace.
*15.75in (40cm) long*

**£150-200**                                    **ROX**

A 1960s Miriam Haskell tutti-frutti necklace.
*16in (41cm) long*

**£150-200**                                    **ROX**

A Joseff of Hollywood pin, set with faux emeralds and diamonds.

c1930      2.5in (6cm) high

£150-200      **ROX**

A pair of Russian gold and amethyst glass butterfly earrings, by Joseff of Hollywood.

c1940

£100-150      **PC**

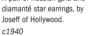

A pair of Russian gold and diamanté star earrings, by Joseff of Hollywood.

c1940

£90-120      **PC**

A 1940s star pin, by Joseff of Hollywood.

4.5in (11cm) wide

£350-400      **CRIS**

A pair of 1940s Art Deco-style red cabochon earrings, by Joseff of Hollywood.

2.5in (6cm) long

£100-150      **CRIS**

A monarch butterfly pin, by Joseff of Hollywood.

3.5in (9cm) wide

£250-300      **CRIS**

A 1940s bee chatelaine pin, by Joseff of Hollywood.

Large bee 2.25in (5.5cm)

£250-300      **CRIS**

A 1940s horse chatelaine pin, by Joseff of Hollywood.

Shortest chain 7in (18cm) long

£150-200      **CRIS**

A 1940s French bull dog pin, by Joseff of Hollywood.

1.5in (3.5cm) diam

£80-120      **CRIS**

Three 1940s fish pins, by Joseff of Hollywood.

1.5in (4cm) wide

£30-35 EACH      **CRIS**

A pair of 1940s owl earrings, by Joseff of Hollywood.

2.25in (5.5cm) high

£150-200      **CRIS**

A Trifari 'Jelly Belly' chick in egg pin.

*2in (5cm) long*

**£700-800**     **TR**

A Trifari 'Jelly Belly' fly pin.

*2in (5cm) long*

**£600-700**     **TR**

A Trifari 'Jelly Belly' crab pin.

*3in (7.5cm) long*

**£600-700**     **TR**

Three Trifari duck pins and a duck emerging from egg pin.

*Largest 1.45in (2.5cm)*

**£200-300**     **ROX**

A 1940s Trifari sterling silver and gold-plated bird of paradise pin, designed by Alfred Philippe.

**£250-350**     **RG**

A 1940s Trifari sterling silver and gold-plated bird on a branch pin.

*£150-200*     **RG**

A very rare 1940s Trifari swan pin.

*2.75in (7cm) wide*

**£600-800**     **ROX**

A 1940s Trifari bug pin.

*2.25in (6cm) long*

**£250-300**     **ROX**

A 1940s Trifari leaf and bug pin.

*2.75in (7cm) long*

**£200-250**     **ROX**

A 1940s Trifari bug pin.

*1.75in (4.5cm) long*

**£200-250**     **ROX**

A 1940s gold-plated Trifari pin, with blue and green stones.

**£150-200**     **RG**

A rare Trifari crab pin.

*3.25in (8.5cm) wide*

£1,200-1,500     **ROX**

A early 1950s Trifari blue and gold stylized fruit pin.

*2in (5cm) long*

£100-150     **CRIS**

A 1950s gold-plated Trifari pin, set with red, blue, green and clear stones.

£100-150     **RG**

A 1950s Trifari "jewels of India" necklace and earrings.

*Earring 1in (3cm) long*

£250-300     **ROX**

A Trifari crown pin, set with pearls.

*2.25in (5.5cm) long*

£150-300     **TR**

A 1950s Trifari peapod pin, with faux pearls mounted in cold enamel on gilt metal.

*2.75in (7cm) long*

£150-200     **CRIS**

A 1950s Trifari shell pin, decorated with cold enamel.

*3.25in (8cm) long*

£150-200     **CRIS**

A 1950s sea motif Trifari pin and earrings, set with cabochon imitation rose-pink and white moonstones.

*Pin 3.5in (8.5cm) long*

£150-200     **CRIS**

A Cristobal-designed Christmas tree pin, set with ruby-red and emerald-green stones.

*2.75in (7cm) high*

£25-35 **CRIS**

A Cristobal Christmas tree pin, set with emerald, ruby-red and green glass stones.

*4in (10cm) high*

£65-85 **CRIS**

A 1980s Eisenberg Ice Christmas tree pin, with multi-coloured crystal rhinestones on gold-plated casting, with copyright mark.

*2in (5cm) high*

£20-25 **CRIS**

A 1980s Eisenberg Ice Christmas tree pin, with emerald-green navette, with ruby-red and clear crystal rhinestones.

*2.25in (5.5cm)*

£25-35 **CRIS**

A 1950s Hollycraft Christmas tree pin, with multi-coloured crystal rhinestones.

*2.25in (5.5cm) long*

£50-70 **CRIS**

A 1960s English Sphinx Christmas tree pin, with green enamel leaf with ruby-red crystal rhinestones.

*2.25in (5.5cm) long*

£40-60 **CRIS**

A Mylu Christmas tree pin, set with pink and green stones.

*2.75in (7cm) long*

£250-350 **ROX**

A 1950s Trifari Christmas pin.

*This is one of three designs that Trifari made.*

*2in (5cm) high*

£75-95 **CRIS**

A carved 'apple juice' Bakelite heavy bangle, with three large and one small flowerhead-carved sections, evenly spaced with painted accents.

*0.75in (2cm) wide*

**£350-450**                    **DAW**

A reverse-carved 'apple juice' Bakelite bangle, with eight different floral and foliate-carved lobed sections.

*1.25in (3cm) wide*

**£200-300**                    **DAW**

A reverse-carved 'apple' juice Bakelite bangle, with fine cross-hatched pattern.

*1in (2.5cm) wide*

**£150-200**                    **DAW**

A 1930s 'apple juice' Lucite hinged bangle, with reverse-carved and coloured flowers and foliage.

*2.75in (7cm) wide*

**£400-500**                      **BY**

A carved butterscotch Bakelite bangle, with four ribs with alternating ribs centring three floral-carved reserves.

*1.5in (4cm) wide*

**£150-200**                    **DAW**

A heavily carved butterscotch Bakelite bangle, two clusters of three flowerheads with two single flowerheads and foliage.

*1in (2.5cm) wide*

**£400-600**                    **DAW**

A carved butterscotch Bakelite bangle, deep-carved floral and foliate carving.

**£300-400**                    **DAW**

A two-tone Bakelite and metal bangle, joined with four green bars banded by metal.

*1.5in (4cm) wide*

**£200-300**                    **DAW**

A butterscotch and black hinged bangle, with foliate carving.

*1.5in (4cm) wide*

**£700-900**                    **DAW**

A 1930s black, cast phenolic bracelet, carved with chrysanthemum designs, with inset-faceted diamanté stones.

*6.25in (16cm) long*

**£250-300** BY

A coral-coloured Bakelite expandable bracelet, with a carved floral motif, hinge loose and missing pins.

**£100-150** DAW

A carved brown Bakelite bangle, with deep-carved raspberry and trailing vine decoration.

*0.75in (2cm) wide*

**£250-300** DAW

A carved and painted apple juice bangle, domed with green painted five-groove swirls.

*0.25in (0.5cm) wide*

**£150-200** DAW

A translucent green carved Bakelite bangle, the interior lined with brass.

*1.25in (3cm) wide*

**£200-250** DAW

A 1930s multicoloured striped 'laminated' cast phenolic bangle.

*3.25in (8cm) wide*

**£250-300** BY

A 1920s brass bangle with an applied, carved cast phenolic scarab, with gold-painted and inset steel faux-jewel finish.

*Scarab 2in (5cm) high*

**£200-250** BY

A 1930s green carved cast phenolic banjo-playing frog pin, the arm moving to 'play' the banjo.

*2.75in (7cm) high*

**£1,500-2,000** BY

A pair of 9ct gold oval cuff links, in a fitted case.
*c1885*

**£180-220**                    WIM

A pair of 18ct gold and enamel oval cuff links, in a fitted case.
*c1900*

**£500-800**                    WIM

A pair of Edwardian 18ct gold and enamel bar cuff links, set with sapphires, in a fitted case.
*c1905*

**£700-1,000**                    WIM

A pair of 15ct gold 'coffee-bean' cuff links, in a fitted case.

*c1900*

**£180-220**            WIM

A pair of 9ct gold 'bowling' cuff links and pin, in a fitted case.

*c1900*

**£200-300**            WIM

A pair of Edwardian 18ct gold and enamel bar cuff links, set with sapphires, in a fitted case.
*c1905*

**£700-1,000**            WIM

A pair of 18ct gold and guilloche enamel cuff links, in a fitted case.

*c1915*

**£800-1,200**            WIM

A pair of 15ct gold and mother-of-pearl cuff links, with enamel decoration and set with seed pearls, in a fitted case.
*c1915*

**£300-500**            WIM

A pair of 18ct gold and mother-of-pearl cuff links, decorated with enamel and gold "button threads", in a fitted case.
*c1915*

**£400-600**            WIM

A pair of enamel double-sided cuff links.

*1920-30s*

**£70-100** CVS

A pair of French black and white enamel double-sided cuff links.

*1920-30s*

**£50-80** CVS

A pair of green and blue double-sided cuff links.

*1920-30s*

**£70-100** CVS

A pair of 1950s black and Bakelite oversized dice cuff links.

**£50-80** CVS

A pair of 1950s leather and metal gun-in-holster cuff links.

*1.5in (4cm) wide*

**£40-60** CVS

A pair of sterling silver Volkswagen cuff links and tie pin.

**£80-100** KOZ

A pair of silver Georg Jensen cuff links, marked "Georg Jensen", "925 S Denmark" and "114".

*1961*

**£150-200** SSP

A pair of 1960s 18ct gold Kutchinsky "D" cuff links.

**£300-500** SSP

A pair of 18ct gold, onyx and citrine cuff links.

*1970*

**£100-150** SSP

One of a pair of 1980s silver gilt, lapis lazuli and pearl bar cuff links, by Mappin & Webb.

**£80-120 PAIR** SSP

## LIGHTERS

Smoking may be falling out of fashion today, but during the 20th century it was all the rage, generating all manner of luxury products aimed at the smoker. Lighters are one of the most varied and collectable areas. Today, these are hotly sought after, causing prices to rise.

see p.253          see p.254          see p.255

- Lighters can be divided into three types; pocket lighters, table lighters and combined cigarette cases and lighters. Pocket examples are the most popular, due to size, quality and variety. Earlier 'petrol' lighters are generally more desirable than post-1950s gas-filled lighters.

- Look out for key makers' names. Dunhill, who released their first lighter c1923, has the largest following. Of very high quality, look out for examples in precious materials, or with inset or hidden accessories such as watches or powder compacts. Variety in terms of shape abounds.

- Other desirable names include Thorens, known for their mechanisms, Colibri, Parker and Ronson. Fleming's 'James Bond' owned a Ronson and stylish and finer-quality pocket and table lighters from the 1930s to the 1960s by them are popular.

- Consider the materials used, as those using precious metals or having finely decorated surfaces will be desirable. Cartier and Van Cleef & Arpels are two notable names, but examples by a lesser name can also be collectable if they are visually appealing.

- Lighters incorporating extra features or in a novelty design, such as a ring or figurine, can be desirable. If the shape has cross-market appeal, such as an aeroplane or gun, prices can rise. 'Trench art' lighters made by WWI soldiers are numerous and generally affordable.

## A CLOSER LOOK AT A DUNHILL LIGHTER

*The panels are made from Perspex carved and painted on the inside.*

*Fish designs are more commonly found and less valuable than bird designs which are extremely rare and desirable.*

*Lighters with fish are known as 'Aquarium' lighters, and those with birds are 'Aviary' lighters.*

*'Aquarium' lighters were made throughout the 1950s, and 'Aviary' lighters only c1951, making them rarer.*

A Dunhill 'Budgies' petrol table lighter, of 'fish tank' form, decorated in reverse with budgies perched on branches and trees and enclosing the brass mechanism.

*c1951*                                              *4in (10cm) long*

**£2,200-2,800**                                                **DN**

### TOP TIPS

- As many lighters were carried and used, some wear is expected. Avoid those with dents or splits, considerable wear to plating or any missing or replaced parts, particularly filling screws.

- Look closely at the markings, as the marks of well-known retailers like Asprey usually add interest and value.

- Combined cigarette cases and lighters, and some quality ceramic table lighters, may be undervalued and could rise in the future.

- Zippo lighters, produced from 1933, are tremendously popular with collectors. Look for advertising, precious-metal or WWII examples.

A 1940s Swiss silver-plated Dunhill 'Unique Standard' pocket lighter.

*2.5in (6cm) high*

**£80-120** LC

A 1950s silver-plated Dunhill 'Giant' table lighter, with engine-turned decoration.

*4.5in (11cm) high*

**£180-220** LC

An American Magic 'spinner' semi-automatic petrol pocket lighter.

*c1897* *2.5in (6cm) h*

**£150-200** RBL

A scarce 1950s American Dunhill 'tinder pistol' lighter.

*6in (15cm) long*

**£500-700** GS

An English Striker manual petrol pocket lighter, with 9ct gold outer case marked "H&A", Birmingham hallmarks.

*1918* *2.5in (6cm) high*

**£120-180** RBL

A 1930s French Flamidor manual petrol pocket lighter, with silver body.

*2.25in (5.5cm) high*

**£100-150** RBL

A 1930s German Triumph manual petrol pocket lighter, silver-cased with auto tank, and wind shield.

*2in (5cm) high*

**£100-120** RBL

A 1940s American Evans trigger manual petrol pocket lighter, with lacquer decoration.

*2in (5cm) high*

**£40-50** RBL

A late 1940s French Dunhill Salaam manual petrol pocket lighter, with lacquer-over-aluminium decoration.

*Thanks to the aluminium case, this lighter is very light in weight. The Salaam was introduced in 1946.*

A Swiss Dunhill Unique Sport manual petrol pocket lighter, brass and leather with lift-arm.

*Early Unique lighters have a single wheel to trigger the lighter; after 1932 they consistently have two – one for the user to turn which is below the wheel that strikes.*

A Swiss Dunhill Unique Sports manual petrol pocket watch lighter, silver with lift-arm.

2.25in (5.5cm) high | 1926  2.25in (5.5cm) high | 1927    2.25in (5.5cm) high

**£120-150**  RBL | **£180-200**  RBL | **£1,500-2,000**  RBL

A 1940s English Dunhill Unique manual petrol table lighter, silver-plated and shagreen decoration with lift-arm.

A Swiss Dunhill Unique manual petrol pocket lighter, silver with lift arm and engine-turned decoration.

A 1940s French silver Dunhill Handy manual petrol pocket lighter.

*Earlier versions of this model were called the 'Savory'.*

3.75in (9.5cm) high | c1926    2.25in (5.5cm) high | 2in (5cm) high

**£250-300**  RBL | **£300-400**  RBL | **£120-180**  RBL

A 1940s Dunhill Squareboy manual petrol pocket lighter, silver-plated with engine-turned decoration.

*The Squareboy was introduced by Dunhill in 1937.*

1.5in (4cm) high

**£90-100**  RBL

A no-name 1940s simple manual petrol pocket lighter, chrome-plated the lift-arm with cigar-cutter.

*2in (5cm) high*

**£150-200** RBL

A 1940s French no-name manual petrol pocket lighter, with celluloid wrap and lift-arm.

*1.75in (4.5cm) high*

**£10-30** RBL

A 1940s German no-name manual petrol pocket lighter, with mother-of-pearl wrap and lift-arm, marked "Foreign".

*1.75in (4.5cm) high*

**£50-60** RBL

A late 1940s Ronson Banker automatic petrol pocket lighter, 14ct gold with engine-turned decoration.

*2.25in (5.5cm) high*

**£250-300** RBL

A 1930s American Ronson Standard automatic petrol pocket lighter, with wind shield, leather wrap and monogram shield.

*2in (5cm) high*

**£120-180** RBL

A 1940s French Atomy manual petrol pocket lighter, aluminium with interesting fuel and flint access system.

*2in (5cm) high*

**£70-100** RBL

A 1930s ladies' semi-automatic petrol pocket lighter, chrome-plated, unknown maker, probably German.

*1.75in (4.5cm) wide*

**£50-60** RBL

A WWII hand-made Trench manual petrol pocket lighter, with the body formed from a two penny.

*2in (5cm) high*

**£50-70** RBL

An artisan's netsuke miniature tinder pistol, in the form of a walnut, decorated with silver and copper on brass with florettes on a hammered surface.

*The flint produces a spark which ignites charred silk floss in the base, creating a flame.*

*c1880    1.75in (4.5cm) high*

**£1,400-1,800** RBL

A WWII Trench miniature manual petrol pocket lighter, with engraved initials.

*1.5in (4cm) high*

**£25-35** RBL

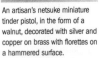

An early 1960s Zippo Coca-Cola advertising manual petrol pocket lighter, with lanyard, mint and boxed.

*2.25in (5.5cm) high*

**£250-350** RBL

A French Sarhon "spinner" manual petrol pocket lighter, with clockwork mechanism and niello-style and engraved decoration.

*c1880* *2in (5cm) high*

**£250-300** RBL

An Austrian TCW Pretty manual petrol pocket lighter, chrome-plated in fitted leather case.

*c1920* *2.25in (5.5cm) high*

**£80-100** RBL

A Carlton Ware 'Rouge Royale' table lighter.

*8.5in (22cm) long*

**£60-70** OACC

A 1930s American Ronson automatic petrol table lighter.

*The standard model, without feet, is worth about £5.*

*4.25in (7cm) high*

**£100-150** RBL

A Dorset Light Industries petrol table lighter, Bakelite with electronic ignition, special Coronation edition.

*1953* *4.5in (11.5cm) high*

**£100-120** RBL

A 1930s Thorens bar fuel dispenser, nickel-plated.

*5.75in (14.5cm) high*

**£80-120** RBL

An early 1920s Austrian Juwel silver semi-automatic petrol ring lighter.

*These ring pocket lighters were also made in brass, which is more common.*

*Face 0.75in (2cm) high*

**£600-700** RBL

*c1930*

**£150-200** RBL

An American Ronson Beauticase combination cigarette case and automatic petrol lighter, chrome-plated with lacquer decoration.

*4.5in (11.5cm) high*

A 1990s Breitling Automatic II gentleman's wristwatch, for the European market.

**£500-800** ML

A 1950s gold-plated Bulova stone-set gentleman's wristwatch.

**£70-100** ML

A 1950s 17-jewel Incabloc Buser Precision Explorer gentleman's wristwatch.

**£100-150** ML

A 1950s 10ct gold-plated Bulova 'Chevrolet' gentleman's logo wristwatch.

*These watches were made by Bulova and printed with a company logo for the company to give out as gifts.*

**£70-100** ML

A 1940s Swiss-made Certina gold-plated wristwatch.

**£20-30** TAB

A 1960s stainless steel CWC European military watch, with broad arrow marking.

**£80-120** ML

A 1930s gold-plated Elgin gentleman's wristwatch, with stepped case and two-tone dial.

**£80-120** ML

A 1930s gold-plated Art Deco-styled Elgin gentleman's wristwatch.

*This is desirable because the case is elongated, which is a popular feature.*

**£150-200** ML

A 1930s 14ct gold-plated Lord Elgin 'Driver's' watch, with swinging lugs.

*The lugs swing and allow the face to be positioned on the wrist so that it can easily be read without the driver needing to move his hand.*

**£80-120** ML

A 14ct white gold-plated Lord Elgin 'Dunbar' gentleman's wristwatch, with asymmetrical case, with original box.
c1951

**£150-200** ML

A 1950s Elgin logo watch, with Porsche logo.

**£80-120**                    **ML**

A 1930s 10ct gold-plated Gruen Curvex wristwatch, with Art Deco-styled case.

**£60-70**                    **TAB**

A 1930s Swiss nickel-cased Gruen gentleman's wristwatch, with Radium hands and dial.

**£100-150**                    **ML**

A 14ct gold-plated Hamilton Boulton gentleman's wristwatch, with clear crystal.

*c1941*

**£100-170**                    **ML**

A 14ct Hamilton Boulton gentleman's wristwatch, with original Art Deco Bakelite box.

*The striking blue crystal is highly unusual, making this watch more valuable than other similar Hamilton Boultons.*

*c1941*

**£200-250**                    **ML**

A 1960s gold-plated cased Hamilton automatic gentleman's wristwatch, with original plastic box.

*The box, particularly with its 'atomic' motif, shows the 1960s fascination with futuristic design, outer space and atomic power.*

**£100-150**                    **ML**

A 1940s Swiss-made Helvetia 18ct gold-cased two register chronograph, designed for the European market.

**£350-550**                    **ML**

A 1970s Heuer gentleman's Carrera automatic chronograph wristwatch, with black finished square case, round black dial, luminous baton markers and fluorescent orange chronograph hands.

*This watch was named after the famed Carrera Race and was made before and during the transition of Heuer to Tag Heuer. The high quality '510' movement is still used today.*

*Case 1.5in (4cm) diam*

**£350-400**                    **F**

A 1950s Rolex gentleman's 9ct gold strap watch, with circular white dial, mixed markings and manual movement, case marked.

£300-350                      F

A Tudor gentleman's automatic steel Prince Oysterdate bracelet watch, with round silvered baton dial, milled bezel and fitted to integral steel bracelet.

*Tudor is another brand name used by Rolex.*

£280-320                      F

A 1950s Tudor lady's steel-cased Oyster Princess bracelet watch, with silver baton dial, automatic movement and Oyster bracelet.

£150-200                      F

A 1930s 14ct gold case and band Tiffany & Co. triple date gentleman's wristwatch, with movement by Movado.

£550-750                     ML

A 1930s 14ct gold-case Tiffany & Co. gentleman's wristwatch, with Longines movement.

£300-370                     ML

A 1970s Tissot gentleman's 18ct gold Stylist wristwatch, with oval gold baton dial and date facility, on a woven bracelet, engraving to case back.

£400-450                      F

A Zenith lady's gold-plated manual wristwatch, with square silver baton dial.

*Case 0.75in (2cm) diam*

£45-55                        F

A 1970s Tissot gentleman's 18ct gold Stylist wristwatch, with oval gold baton dial and date facility, on a woven bracelet, engraving to case back.

An early 20thC gentleman's silver-cased waterproof watch, with black full-figure dial, later movement.

*Case 1.5in (3.5cm) diam*

£40-50                        F

An early 20thC lady's 9ct gold wristwatch, with decorative white enamel dial and hinged case back.

£30-40                        F

An American 1990s stainless steel quartz British military NATO-type wristwatch.

£60-80                       ML

A gentleman's 18ct gold wristwatch, by Omega, the dial with seconds subsidiary.

**£250-300**      **FRE**

A gentleman's 14ct gold wristwatch, by Omega, the dial with seconds subsidiary.

**£150-200**      **FRE**

A gentleman's 14ct gold wristwatch, by Omega, broken strap.

**£300-400**      **FRE**

A gentleman's gold and steel automatic Miester Constellation chronograph wristwatch, by Omega, the dial with centre second sweep and calendar aperture, the 24-jewel movement no. 24757082.

**£150-200**      **FRE**

A 1970s stainless steel Rolex Comex Sea Dweller, ref: 1665, with plastic face.

**£8,000-12,000**      **WG**

A stainless steel Rolex GMT Master, ref: 1675, with painted crown guard and dial with gold or gilt chapter ring.

c1961     1.5in (3.5cm) width

**£2,000-3,000**      **WG**

A gentleman's 14ct gold wristwatch, by Longines, the dial with seconds subsidiary, the 17-jewel movement no. 8275833.

**£120-180**      **FRE**

A gentleman's 14ct gold wristwatch, by Longines, the dial with seconds subsidiary, the 17-jewel movement no. 8100554.

**£300-400**      **FRE**

A gentleman's 14ct gold wristwatch, by Longines, the dial with seconds subsidiary, lacking winder, band broken.

**£100-150**      **FRE**

# ENTERTAINMENT & SPORTS

The appeal of entertainment and sports has much to do with the nostalgia we have for individual decades – with the faces, sights, sounds, products, shapes, colours and designs of any period a tangible reminder of times and successes now past but fondly remembered.

Quality collectables from blockbuster films such as James Bond, "Star Wars" or Harry Potter are easy winners, and in both film and television the return of any popular past series, such as a new film version of the classic Batman character or a new series of "Doctor Who", is likely to have an instant impact on each one's respective collectables.

With rock and pop it's the big names – particularly Elvis Presley and The Beatles amongst others – that are the ones with real staying power, but always aim to get certificates of authenticity because there are no shortage of fakes. Memorabilia associated with cult names where die-hard fans are dedicated to their idols also attracts great interest.

Football and boxing court a huge collector's market because of the size of the fan base and the continuing enthusiasm with which the sports are followed. Sporting collectables, though, is another area where provenance should be established carefully.

# HOT COLLECTING AREA

## FILM & TV

Owning props and memorabilia are the closest most fans can get to being part of their favourite film or TV series. While ever-increasing demand for top Hollywood pieces has led prices for these to skyrocket, affordable pieces from much-loved favourites are still up for grabs.

see p.269

see p.264

see p.269

- The market for screen-used props has grown significantly and in response studios often release props after production or give them away at premieres rather than discarding or re-using them. Provenance is of vital importance. Letters or certificates of authenticity should always accompany an item.

- Props or memorabilia from blockbusters or cult films that remain popular in the long term are the most likely to hold their value, or rise. Good examples include "Titanic" and the Harry Potter series, as well as classics like James Bond or "Star Wars".

- Props used in key scenes or in association with central characters represent the apex of collecting. Condition can affect value, although many will have been damaged from use during filming. Props used in close-up shots will usually be detailed, those only seen from far off will be more rudimentary in terms of finish.

- Cult TV series from the 1960s such as "The Avengers", "Batman" and "Thunderbirds" remain popular, in a nostalgia-driven market. Original games and memorabilia from the period can be hard to find. Items in excellent, complete condition will fetch a premium. "Star Trek" and "Doctor Who" have the largest followings.

- If a new series is released after a long break and proves to be successful, interest in original pieces peaks. This is likely to happen with "Battlestar Galactica". A similar effect is created when a past series is re-run or released on DVD.

- Look for pieces from the most popular cult TV shows and particularly those connected to popular seasons. Pieces made at the beginning of a show's run are usually a good investment as these were often made in smaller numbers.

## A CLOSER LOOK AT A DOCTOR WHO GAME

*This is in unusually fine and complete condition for a child's toy, which increases its value.*

*It was made by respected English toy manufacturer Chad Valley and was made in the show's second year of production. This makes it both early and desirable.*

*The excellent box artwork shows the first Doctor and his arch enemies, the Daleks.*

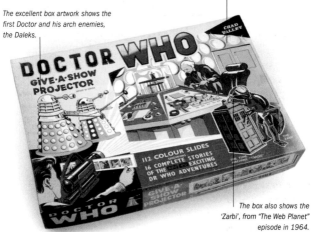

*The box also shows the 'Zarbi', from "The Web Planet" episode in 1964.*

A rare 'Doctor Who Give-A-Show Projector', by Chad Valley.
*c1965*

**£150-200**                                                      **TH**

## TOP TIPS

- Consider props or memorabilia from contemporary films or TV series if you wish to speculate. Prices often drop a year or so after the release when mass excitement has subsided a little.

- Pieces that are representative of the characters or the storyline itself will have the most powerful collecting appeal.

- Successful recent series, such as "The X-Files" and "Buffy the Vampire Slayer", may become even more collectable in the future.

- Be aware that only limited editions that are produced in smaller numbers are likely to rise significantly in value.

A pre-production scale model of 'Rocky' from "Chicken Run", mounted on aeroboard together with a tiny paper outhouse, mounted over a custom-made background with digital stills and descriptive text, in a perspex display case.
*2000      11in (28cm) high*
£60-80                          CO

A 'Taelon' bridge costume from "Gene Roddenberry's Earth Final Conflict", the all-in-one nylon suit, with painted on body markings.
*c1997*
£120-180                       CO

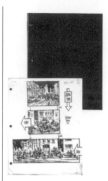

An original script from the pilot episode of the Warner Bros. TV series "The Flash", together with storyboards for scene 65, involving a bike chase.
*1990*
£70-100                        CO

A black MA2 crew jacket from "Event Horizon", with fur collar with "Event Horizon Crew '97" embroidered on the left breast with the Event Horizon logo on the back.

*1997*
£120-180                       CO

A Roman Infantry shield from "Gladiator", a rectangular brown canvas shield with wooden handle used by an extra in battle sequences in the film.
*2000      44in (112cm) high*
£250-350                       CO

A green crew T-shirt from "Harry Potter and the Philosopher's Stone".
*These T-shirts were given to cast and crew as a Christmas gift during filming.*
*2001*
£60-70                         CO

A pilot's khaki-coloured flight suit from "James Bond - Die Another Day", with badges on left arm.
*2002*
£180-220                       CO

A 19thC-style lady's day dress from "Sleepy Hollow", comprising a bodice of black sheer fabric embroidered with gold floral detail trimmed with lace over a gold full skirt, with bustle.

*1999*

**£180-220** CO

A prop Daily Planet newspaper from "Superman III", with the headline "Superman Scandal", featuring a photograph of Superman (Christopher Reeves), framed and glazed.

*25in (63cm) high*

**£200-250** CO

A current flow filter from "Star Wars: Episode I - The Phantom Menace", used in the Pit Droid scenes, mounted over a custom-made background featuring digital stills and descriptive text, in a perspex display case.

*1999 11in (28cm) h*

**£220-280** CO

A replica White Star Line Moët & Chandon champagne bottle from "Titanic", labelled "White Star Moët & Chandon Eperney".

*1997 12in (30cm) high*

**£180-220** CO

A part of the replica ship's hull and a section of bench from "Titanic", both mounted on a custom-made background featuring digital stills from the film, in a perspex display case.

*For certain scenes, a scale model of the Titanic was built at Rosarito Beach in Mexico. After filming had finished, the area was littered with left-over parts and 'props' such as this one.*

*1997 11in (28cm) h*

**£70-100** CO

A montage of digital images from "Terminator 2: Judgment Day", signed by Edward Furlong (John Connor), in silver ink, mounted with a descriptive plaque, framed and glazed.

*1991 29in (74cm) wide*

**£200-250** CO

A 'Doctor Who An Unearthly Child' BT phone card, by Jonder International Promotions.

*1994-7*      *Card 3.5in (9cm) wide*

**£10-15**      **TP**

A 'Doctor Who The Daleks' BT phone card, by Jonder International Promotions, with factsheet.

*1994-7*      *Card 3.5in (9cm) wide*

**£10-15**      **TP**

A limited edition 'Doctor Who The Trial of a Time Lord' video box set, by the BBC.

*1993*      *8.5in (21.5cm) high*

**£40-60**      **TP**

A 'Doctor Who The Five Doctors' video, by the BBC.

*1985*      *8in (20.5cm) high*

**£25-35**      **TP**

A 'Doctor Who Revenge of the Cybermen' video, by the BBC.

*1985*      *8.5in (21.5cm) high*

**£15-25**      **TP**

A rare 'Doctor Who The Five Doctors' video gift pack, issued by Dapol for Boots.

*1990*      *10in (25.5cm) wide*

**£50-70**      **TP**

A 'Doctor Who The Missing Stories - The Evil of the Daleks' audio cassette, by the BBC.

*1992*      *5.5in (14cm) wide*

**£15-25**      **TP**

A limited edition 'Dalekmania' box set, by Lumiere.

*1995*      *16.75in (42.5cm) wide*

**£40-60**      **TP**

Lydecker, John, 'Doctor Who and Warriors' Gate', published by Target.

*1982*      *7in (18cm) high*

**£15-25**      **TP**

Davis, Gerry, and Bingeman, Alison, 'Doctor Who - The Celestial Toymaker', published by Target.

*1986*      *7in (18cm) high*

**£15-25**      **TP**

A 'Dr Who 1974' annual, published by World Distributors.

*1974*      *11.5in (29cm) high*

**£8-12**      **TP**

A 'Dr Who 1977' annual, published by World Distributors.

*1977*      *11.5in (29cm) high*

**£8-12**      **TP**

A 'Doctor Who 1981' annual, published by World Distributors.

*1981*      *11.5in (29cm) high*

**£7-10**      **TP**

A 'Doctor Who 1984' annual, published by World Distributors.

*1984*      *11.5in (29cm) high*

**£6-9**      **TP**

A 'Doctor Who 1992' year book, published by Marvel.

*1992*      *11.5in (29cm) high*

**£6-9**      **TP**

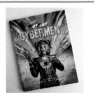

A 'Doctor Who 1995' year book, published by Marvel.

*1995*      *11.5in (29cm) high*

**£5-8**      **TP**

A 'Doctor Who Cybermen' book, published by Virgin Publishing.

*1995*      *11.5in (29cm) high*

**£7-10**      **TP**

A 'Doctor Who 1996' year book, published by Marvel.

*1996*      *11.5in (29cm) high*

**£5-8**      **TP**

An 'A-Team' M-16 rifle, by Daisy Toy.

c1983

**£15-25** TH

A rare 'Airwolf' die-cast gift set, by ERTL.

*These gift sets are rarely found complete.*

c1984

**£40-60** TH

An 'Aliens vs Corp. Hicks' limited edition set of figures, by Kenner, from an edition of 25,000 made exclusively for Kaybee Toys.

c2000

**£35-45** TD

A 1960s 'Avengers Stead's Sword Stick' display card, by Lone Star.

*With the sword stick, this would be worth approximately £350-400.*

**£65-75** TH

A box of 1966-style 'Batman' trading cards, by Topps.

c1989

**£40-50** TH

A pair of Batman and Robin figures, by Warner Bros., from the Golden Age Collection.

2000

**£45-55** TH

A "Battlestar Galactica" Ovion figure, by Mattel.

c1978

**£30-40** TH

A 'The Bionic Woman Bionic Beauty Salon', by Kenner.

*USA Cable Entertainment are developing a re-make of this classic 1970s show.*

c1976

**£30-40** TH

A sealed box of 'Terminator 2 - Judgement Day' stickers, by Toppes.
c1991

£10-15    TH

A 'Terminator 2 - Judgement Day Cyberdyne T-800 Endo Skeleton' kit, by Tsukuda.
c1991

£20-25    TH

A 'Terrahawks Action Zeroid' figure, by Bandai.
c1983

£45-50    TH

A 'Thunderbirds Lady Penelope' painting book.

c1971

£10-15    TH

A 'Tron' glow in the dark yo-yo, by Duncan.
c1982

£20-25    TH

A rare 'Wanted Dead or Alive' Josh Randall/Steve McQueen figure, by Toys McCoy.
c1997

£250-300    TH

# HOT COLLECTING AREA

## DISNEYANA

The characters and films created by Walt Disney (1901-66)
have become among the most loved of the 20th century across
many generations of children and adults. Disney's incredible
success at merchandising has led to a whole wealth of
collectables ready to be snapped up by keen fans.

*see p.275*  *see p.272*  *see p.275*

- Mickey Mouse, created in 1928, is undoubtedly Disney's most
  famous character. His appearance has changed over the decades
  and early examples from the 1930s are usually rare and valuable.
  Look for 'pie slice' eyes, a tail and a more rodent-like form.

- Early authorized merchandise from the 1930s is usually the most
  valuable. Examine any markings for the words 'Walt Disney
  Enterprises' which denote a 1930s production. Items marked 'Walt
  Disney Productions' date from the 1940s onwards, other Disney
  marks later still.

- Many unauthorised items were also produced, often in Germany or
  Japan. These are also collectable, especially if from the 1930s-40s,
  but tend to fetch lower values than for authorised items.

- Figurines, soft toys, toys and games tend to fetch the highest prices.
  Tins, greetings cards, badges, tea sets and other smaller pieces of
  memorabilia are usually more affordable.

- Pinocchio, Snow White and the Seven Dwarfs and other popular
  characters are also sought after and look likely to hold their values.
  Look out for desirable makers such as Chad Valley and Steiff.

- As pre-war Disneyana is scarce, items from the 1950s-70s,
  and even from classic films of the 1990s, are rapidly becoming
  more valuable. Animation art, centred around production 'cels'
  used in films, as well as original drawings, fetches high values.
  Always ensure that the vendor is reputable and look for certificates
  or stamps of authenticity from Disney.

## A CLOSER LOOK AT A MICKEY MOUSE DOLL

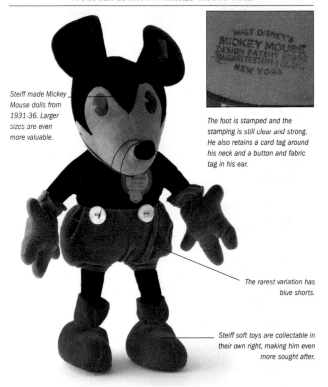

Steiff made Mickey Mouse dolls from 1931-36. Larger sizes are even more valuable.

The foot is stamped and the stamping is still clear and strong. He also retains a card tag around his neck and a button and fabric tag in his ear.

The rarest variation has blue shorts.

Steiff soft toys are collectable in their own right, making him even more sought after.

A Steiff Mickey Mouse doll, with brightly coloured open mouth and area of sewing repair on neck, shorts faded, missing tail.

*1931-36*                                                  *12in (30.5cm) high*

**£3,000-4,000**                                                **NB**

## TOP TIPS

- Handle as much early Disneyana as possible or seek expert advice about value and authenticity before buying or selling these pieces.

- If buying modern or contemporary pieces, focus on classics and aim to buy strictly limited editions, keeping them in mint condition with the packaging.

- Look for pieces with bright colours and immediate visual impact which show the characters, as these are likely to remain popular.

- Also consider materials when examining objects – tin, Catalin and celluloid, for example, are likely to date from before the 1950s.

A 1930s Mores 'Sneezy' tooth brush holder.

*3.75in (9.5cm) high*

£100-150      **BEV**

A 1930s Mores 'Bashful' tooth brush holder.

*3.75in (9.5cm) high*

£100-150      **BEV**

A 1930s Mores 'Doc' tooth brush holder.

*3.75in (9.5cm) high*

£100-150      **BEV**

A Funny Flex Mickey and Minnie, Minnie in polka dot skirt, wood-jointed with original decals.

*5in (12.5cm) high*

£200-300      **NB**

A pair of Schmidt limited-edition ceramic musical 'Mickey and Minnie Mouse' figures.

*14in (36cm) high*

£80-100      **F**

A rare Charbens Salco series die-cast model No. 3 'Mickey and Minnie's Barrel Organ', in original box.

£200-250      **F**

An American Ideal Pinocchio fully jointed painted wood and composition doll, with original oil cloth collar and felt bow tie, light paint wear and crazing on head.

*7.5in (19cm) high*

£80-100      **NB**

A rare French cast aluminium Mickey Mouse penny bank, by Depeche Company.

*6in (15cm) high*

£150-200     **ATK**

A Walt Disney's Mickey Mouse "Maestro Michel Mouse" figure.

*1993*

£120-180     **MSC**

A ceramic Mickey Mouse figure, together with two smaller figure, by Severn China.

*c1970*     *3.25in (8cm) high*

£40-50     **WHP**

A 1930s Walt Disney's Pinocchio figure, made by Knickerbocker.

£550-650     **FRA**

A Walt Disney's Pinocchio "I'll Never Lie Again ..." figure.

*2000*

£120-180     **MSC**

A Walt Disney's Sneezy from Snow White and the Seven Dwarfs felt toy.

£120-180     **FRA**

A Walt Disney's Snow White and the Seven Dwarfs "Soup's On" group.

*2000*

£1,000-1,500     **MSC**

A pair of 1950s Walt Disney's Snow White and the Seven Dwarfs ceramic toothbrush holders, by Walt Disney Designs.

*Snow White 6in (15cm) high*

£180-220     **WHP**

A painted composition Donald Duck bank, serious wear.

6.5in (16.5cm) wide

£20-40 **NB**

A Chein Donald Duck lithographed tin mechanical bank.

6.5in (16.5cm) wide

£50-70 **NB**

A Swiss Walt Disney Productions Mickey Mouse biscuit tin.

c1932        8.25in (21cm) wide

£400-600 **DH**

A 1930s 'Official Mickey Mouse Store' badge, marked "Walt Disney 1937", made by Kay Kamen Ltd of New York and London.

1.25in (3cm) wide

£15-25 **HGS**

A 1930s Continental Mickey Mouse tin.

6in (15cm) wide

£200-250 **DH**

An early 20thC baby's rattle, the brass ring suspending painted celluloid figures of Snow White and the Seven Dwarfs.

£40-60 **F**

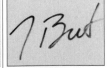

A rare autographed sketch of Jack Skellington, by Tim Burton from his film "The Nightmare Before Christmas".

£250-350 **MSC**

A Walt Disney's Toy Story Buzz Lightyear "To Infinity and Beyond" figure.
*1998*

**£80-120** MSC

A Walt Disney's Peter Pan Tinkerbell 'A Firefly! A Pixie! Amazing!' figure.
*1993*

**£250-350** MSC

Barks, Carl, 'The Fine Art of Walt Disney's Donald Duck', published by Rainbow Publishing, Inc., hardcover edition featuring glossy prints and fold-outs of the work of 'the good Duck artist', autographed by the author, limited edition 0096/1875.
*1981*

**£700-800** HC

A boxed set of Mazda Disneylights, manufactured by the British Thomson-Houston Co, consisting of 12 bell-shaped Christmas tree lights printed with Disney characters including Mickey Mouse, Dumbo, the Seven Dwarfs and Bambi, complete in original box.

**£45-55** DN

A typed letter signed by Walt Disney, a personal letterhead, boldly signed "Walt Disney", dated December 29, 1964, written to John Hurt of the Curtis Publishing Company, with a letter of authenticity.
*1964*

**£1,800-2,200** HC

A 1970s Mickey Mouse Disneyland promotional badge.

*3.5cm (9cm) diam*

**£15-20** CVS

A Wadeheath six piece nursery tea set, transfer-printed by Walt Disney Designs.

*Teapot 3.25in ( 8cm) high*

**£15-20** WHP

Left: A Walt Disney Blow-Up Thumper figure, by Royal Albert.
*1961-65*

**£150-200** PSA

Right: A Walt Disney Blow-Up Bambi, by Royal Albert.
*1961-65*

**£100-120** PSA

A Hanna Barbera original production cel from "The Flintstones", featuring Fred doing a dance.

*1961*                                                  *12in (30.5cm) wide*

**£1,000-1,400**                                        **AAG**

---

A limited edition Hanna Barbera hand-painted cel 'Fred's Windscreen Wipers' from "The Flintstones", from an edition of 300, signed by Bill Hanna and Joe Barbera.

*1989        14in (35.5cm) wide*

**£750-850**                    **AAG**

A Hanna Barbera original production cel and background artwork from "The Flintstones", featuring Barney and Betty Rubble, signed by Bill Hanna and Joe Barbera.

*13.25in (33.5cm) wide*

**£450-550**                    **AAG**

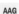

A Hanna Barbera original production cel of "Hong Kong Phooey, Number 1 Super Guy".

*12.25in (31cm) wide*

**£500-600**                    **AAG**

---

A limited edition Hanna Barbera hand-painted cel 'Classic Scooby Doo', from an edition of 500, signed by Scooby creator Iwao Takamoto.

*2000        13.5in (34.5cm) high*

**£500-600**                    **AAG**

A limited edition Hanna Barbera hand-painted cel 'Yankee Doodle Mouse', from an edition of 300, signed by Bill Hanna, Joe Barbera and Iwao Takamoto.

*12in (30.5cm) wide*

**£800-1,200**                  **AAG**

A Hanna Barbera original production cel from "Tom and Jerry: The Movie", signed by Bill Hanna and Joe Barbera.

*1992        11.75in (30cm) wide*

**£350-450**                    **AAG**

---

A limited edition Hanna Barbera hand-painted cel 'Mouse Trouble', signed by Bill Hanna, Joe Barbera and Iwao Takamoto.

*12in (30.5cm) wide*

**£800-1,200**                  **AAG**

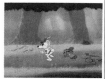

A Cosgrove Hall original production cel from the "Danger Mouse" episode "Once Upon a Time Slip", featuring Danger Mouse.

*1984*        *12.75in (32.5cm) wide*

**£150-250**        **AAG**

A Cosgrove Hall original production cel from the "Danger Mouse" episode "Cat-Astrophe", featuring Danger Mouse and Baron Greenback's mechanical cat.

*1985*     *16in (40.5cm) wide*

**£220-280**        **AAG**

A Cosgrove Hall original production cel from the "Danger Mouse" episode "Once Upon a Time Slip", featuring Danger Mouse and Penfold, signed by the voice of Danger Mouse, David Jason.

*1984*    *15.5in (39.5cm) wide*

**£650-750**      **AAG**

A Cosgrove Hall original production cel from the "Danger Mouse" episode "Once Upon a Time Slip", featuring Baron Greenback, Colonel K and Stiletto.

*1984*    *16in (40.5cm) wide*

**£300-400**      **AAG**

A Cosgrove Hall original production cel from the "Danger Mouse" episode "Remote Controlled Chaos", with original production background, featuring Baron Greenback.

*16in (40.5cm) wide*

**£350-450**        **AAG**

A Cosgrove Hall promotional artwork from "Count Duckula", featuring the Count, Igor and Nanny.

*"Count Duckula" was a spin-off from "Danger Mouse".*

*15.25in (38.5cm) wide*

**£350-400**        **AAG**

A Cosgrove Hall original production cel from "Count Duckula", featuring the Count, Nanny and Igor.

*1988-93*    *12.25in (31cm) wide*

**£150-250**        **AAG**

# HOT COLLECTING AREA

## FILM POSTERS

Film posters have evolved their own collectors' cult with prices to match. The recipe that makes a poster strongest in the collectors' market is a classic film, collectable stars and good artwork. Any single one of these elements will also give an individual poster interest and value.

see p.282            see p.284                    see p.285

- Posters of films that captured the public imagination or were considered cult hits or classics are the most desirable. "James Bond" is a dramatic example, with posters from the early films mushrooming in price over the past decade. Look out for other classics, such as "Reservoir Dogs", "Get Carter", "Straw Dogs" and any films by Alfred Hitchcock.

- The artwork will help to determine much of the value, with the work of key artists, such as Saul Bass, and the use of striking images or those typical of the film or character fetching higher prices. Designs that adhere to period style are also popular. Variations in poster artwork will also affect the value.

- More modern posters are usually produced in large quantities, but if the film retains wide popularity, some may rise in value. Look out for 'teasers' produced before the film's release as these are often scarcer and feature different artwork.

- Different countries often used different artwork. As well as the wording, the style of artwork can identify the country and national variations will usually have different values. Examples from the country of a film's original release tend to be the most popular.

- Before 1980, posters were made in several different sizes. British quad posters (30 x 40in) and US one-sheet posters (27 x 41in) are the most popular. Re-issue posters were produced when a film was re-released and are usually of lower value than the initial version.

This US one-sheet poster is both rare and in a popular size.

The robot image is considered one of the best in film poster artwork.

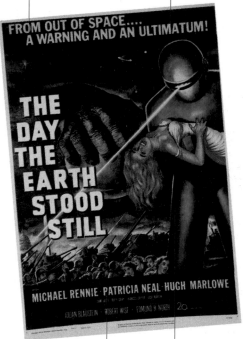

This classic title is highly sought after, as is the dramatic artwork.

The film was released during the golden age of the horror/sci-fi genre during the 1950s.

"The Day The Earth Stood Still", US one sheet poster.

*1951*                                            *41in (104cm) high*

**£10,000-13,000**                                                 **P**

## TOP TIPS

- Avoid posters with pinholes or tape marks, and don't consider those that have been trimmed into the image or dry-mounted, unless extremely rare.

- Store posters flat in between sheets of acid-free tissue paper, or have them mounted on linen by a professional.

- Reproductions and fakes are common. Consider the paper, size, colours and printing method. Recent posters are double-sided.

- Although condition is very important, many early 20th-century film posters were folded and stored badly, so some wear is expected.

"James Bond – From Russia with Love", US one sheet 'B' style poster, linen-backed.

*1964*          *40in (101cm) high*

**£2,500-3,500**          ATM

"James Bond - You Only Live Twice", US 'C' style one sheet poster, artwork by Robert McGinnis, linen-backed.

*1967*     *40in (101cm) high*

**£800-1,200**          ATM

"James Bond - Moonraker", US one sheet poster, linen-backed.

*1979*     *41in (104cm) high*

**£100-200**          ATM

"James Bond - Tomorrow Never Dies", UK quad poster.

*This version was withdrawn from circulation as 'Tommorrow' is mis-spelt in the credits.*

*1997*          *40in (101cm) wide*

**£60-80**          ATM

"Breakfast At Tiffany's", US 40x60 poster, linen-backed, framed and glazed.

*1961*     *60in (152.5cm) high*

**£10,000-15,000**          ATM

"James Bond – Die Another Day", advance US one sheet poster.

*2002*     *41in (104cm) high*

**£30-50**          ATM

"Triple-O-Seven", UK one sheet triple bill promotional poster, advertising 'Three James Bond Adventures In One Action Packed Programme': "Octopussy", "For Your Eyes Only", "Thunderball", together with a double bill poster for "The Spy Who Loved Me" and "Moonraker".

**£200-250**          CO

"Bunny Lake Is Missing", Spanish one sheet poster.

*1965*     *39in (99cm) high*

**£80-120**     **CO**

"Cat on a Hot Tin Roof", US 'B' style half sheet poster, paper-backed, framed and glazed.

*1958*     *28in (71cm) wide*

**£500-600**     **ATM**

"Charade", US one sheet poster, paper-backed, framed and glazed.

*1963*     *41in (104cm) wide*

**£520-580**     **ATM**

"Chinatown", German language A1 poster, artwork by Amsel, framed and glazed.

*1974*     *33in (84cm) high*

**£480-520**     **ATM**

"Get Carter", international one sheet poster, lined-backed.

*1971*     *41in (104cm) high*

**£320-380**     **ATM**

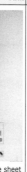

"The Godfather", UK one sheet poster.

*1972*     *41in (104cm) high*

**£500-600**     **ATM**

"The Graduate", US one sheet poster, first year release 'B' Style Academy Award poster, linen-backed.

*1967*     *41in (104cm) high*

**£200-300**     **ATM**

"Halloween", one sheet promotional poster, signed by Jamie Lee Curtis, in black ink, framed and glazed.

*1978*     *37in (94cm) high*

**£220-280**     **CO**

"La Dolce Vita", Argentine stone lithographed poster.

*1960*     *43in (109cm) high*

**£700-1,000**     P

"Last Tango in Paris", re-release US one sheet poster.

*1982*     *41in (104cm) high*

**£70-100**     P

"Le Mans", Japanese poster.

*1971*     *29in (73.5cm) high*

**£350-400**     P

"The Lord Of The Rings: The Fellowship of the Ring", style A teaser US one sheet poster.

*Teaser posters are released before the film's release. Teaser and advance posters are often very similar, but the teaser poster will not carry the film title. The rarer B style poster shows Frodo looking downwards at the ring and has a different tagline.*

*2001*     *41in (104cm) high*

**£70-100**     P

"The Man Who Wasn't There", US one sheet poster.

*The design of the artwork and the title play on Alfred Hitchcock's 1960s classic 'The Man Who Knew Too Much'.*

*2001*     *41in (104cm) high*

**£30-50**     P

"Marihuana", Argentine poster, with artwork by Raf.

*1950*     *43in (109cm) high*

**£300-500**     P

"Moulin Rouge", style C advance US one sheet poster.

*2001*     *41in (104cm) high*

**£70-100**     P

"My Fair Lady", Italian locandino poster, with artwork by Nistri.

*1964*     *28in (71cm) high*

**£280-320**     P

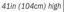

"My Fair Lady", East German A1 poster, with artwork by Westphal.

*1967*     *32in (81.5cm) high*

**£280-320**     P

"The Night Belongs To Us", Swedish poster, with artwork by Rohman.

*1929        39in (99cm) high*

**£700-1,000**                               P

"The Nightmare Before Christmas", US one sheet poster.

*1992        41in (104cm) high*

**£100-150**                               P

"Planet of the Apes", Japanese one sheet poster.

*The Japanese version of this poster is extremely rare, hence a higher value than other countries' versions.*

*1968        29in (73.5cm) high*

**£700-1,000**                               P

"The Outlaw Josey Wales", US one sheet poster.

*1976        41in (104cm) high*

**£280-320**                               P

"Planet of the Apes", Belgian poster.

*1968        22in (56cm) high*

**£200-250**                               P

"The Producers", rare style B US one sheet poster.

*1967        41in (104cm) high*

**£480-520**                               P

"Psycho", US one sheet poster.

*1960        41in (104cm) high*

**£1,700-2,000**                               P

"Ran", Japanese poster.

*1985        29in (73.5cm) high*

**£350-400**                               P

"Rear Window", Belgian poster.

*1954        22in (56cm) high*

**£400-600**                               P

"Rebel Without A Cause", US one sheet poster.

*1956        41in (104cm) high*

**£2,500-3,000**                               P

"Raiders of the Lost Ark", US one sheet poster.

*1981*          *41in (104cm) high*

**£100-150**                    **CO**

"Return to Oz", design for promotional posters, highlighted in paint and pen, by artist Michael Ploog, mounted, framed and glazed.

*1985*                    *27in (68cm) high*

**£450-500**                    **CO**

"Blanche Neige et les Sept Nains (Disney's Snow White and the Seven Dwarfs)", Belgian language one sheet poster, paper-backed, framed and glazed.

*1937*                    *34in (86.5cm) high*

**£1,500-2,000**                    **ATM**

"The Sound of Music", US roadshow-style one sheet poster, linen-backed.

*1965*          *41in (104cm) wide*

**£850-950**                    **ATM**

"Star Wars V: The Empire Strikes Back", 'Gone with the Wind'-style US one sheet poster, linen-backed.

*1980*          *41in (104cm) high*

**£350-450**                    **ATM**

"Spider-Man", advance US one sheet double-sided poster.

*This poster is extremely rare; re-called by Sony after the September 11th tragedy, it features the World Trade Center reflected in Spider-Man's eyes.*

*2002*          *40in (101cm) high*

**£200-300**                    **ATM**

"The Shining", UK quad poster.

*1980*        *40in (101.5cm) wide*

**£200-250**        P

"The Silence of the Lambs",
advance US one sheet poster.

*1990*     *41in (104cm) high*

**£120-180**        P

"Terror From The Year 5,000",
US one sheet poster.

*1958*     *41in (104cm) high*

**£480-520**        P

"Slacker", rare US one sheet
poster.

*1991*     *41in (104cm) high*

**£30-50**        P

"Trois Couleurs: Bleu", French,
country of origin poster.

*1992*     *63in (160cm) high*

**£100-150**        P

"Vertigo", Argentine one sheet poster,
with artwork by Saul Bass.

*Designer and animator Bass worked
closely with Hitchcock, possibly
influencing the "Psycho" shower scene.
He is credited with revolutionizing film
credit sequences through use of
bizarre, emotional and psychologically
disturbing animation techniques.*

*1958*     *43in (109cm) high*

**£800-900**        P

"Star Wars", re-release style D or
'circus' US one sheet poster, with
artwork by Drew Struzan and
Charles White III.

*The 'D' style was made for summer
1978 re-release and is highly
collectable. In 1992 a different
sized fan club reissue was issued
rolled – the original was folded.*

*1978*     *41in (104cm) high*

**£350-450**        P

"Through a Glass Darkly",
French language petite poster.

*1962*     *32in (81.5cm) high*

**£70-100**        P

# HOT COLLECTING AREA

## ROCK & POP

Rock and pop memorabilia has been collected since the first popsters strutted their stuff in the 1950s. Like the stars themselves, their personal items are beyond the reach of most of us, but other memorabilia produced in association with them is more accessible, but no less treasured by fans.

see p.290    see p.289    see p.293

- Items associated with well-known artists will command the highest prices as they have a wider base of fans keen to collect. The biggest names, among many, include The Beatles, Elvis Presley, Jimi Hendrix and Led Zeppelin.

- Memorabilia connected to artists who have been successful and remain in the public eye for a long time will generally hold its value better than that from bands and artists 'manufactured' recently by record companies.

- Signed instruments, particularly those associated with notable concerts, have a strong market, with guitars being the most popular. A signed instrument will not always have been used by the artist who signed it and the signature may not be authentic.

- Avoid buying without a clear guarantee of an item's provenance, which should be available from a good auction house or dealer. This could be a letter from the original vendor or star, or research showing an item's history.

- Posters and concert tickets are often an affordable way of recording an artist's career. The highest prices will be paid for those related to significant performances. Memorabilia from early on in an artist's career are often scarcer and more valuable as less were produced.

- Be aware that the autographs of superstar performers, which would have been in enormous demand, were often signed by assistants, or by other members of the band. Undedicated autographs are also preferred by collectors, unless written to another famous personality, or someone connected to the star.

First issues of any magazine are usually rare and always more desirable. This example is in excellent and complete condition, with no fading, graffiti or missing sections.

The artwork is both appealing and shows the complete band in their prime.

Magazines such as this give interesting period insights into the lives and activities of the band members.

An American 'The Beatles' official magazine, issue No.1, for Sept.-Nov. 1964, published by Dell.

10.25in (26cm) high

**£250-350**                                                                 **NOR**

## TOP TIPS

- Seek professional authentication for valuable autographs from recognised authorities like established dealers or auction houses.

- Any items that are identifiable from a video, TV appearance or album cover will attract higher prices.

- Look out for 1960s psychedelic posters with appealing and typical artwork as this is a growing market.

- Recordings made for individual markets (widespread in the 1980s), rare promotional records and first pressings are of collecting interest.

A John Lennon autograph, signed in blue ballpoint pen and additionally signed "Paul McCartney", "George Harrison" and "Ringo Starr" by Neil Aspinall, with typed heading "The Beatles Sunderland Empire - Saturday, 30th November 1963", framed with a sepia-coloured print of John Lennon with Pete Best in the background.

*16in (41cm) high*

**£2,000-2,500**          **CO**

A handbill for The Beatles at City Hall, Sheffield, Saturday, 2nd March, 1963, supporting Helen Shapiro, with postal booking form printed at the bottom.

*10in (25.5cm) high*

**£900-1,000**          **CO**

A printer's proof handbill for "Pops Alive!", featuring The Beatles billed for Sunday 31 May, Roy Orbison, Freddie and the Dreamers, Gerry and the Pacemakers and others.

*c1964          11in (28cm) high*

**£350-400**          **CO**

A 'Beatles for Sale' promotional flat, featuring the front cover of the mono album, printed in England.

*1964          12.5in (31cm) wide*

**£120-180**          **CO**

A rare Italian 'I Favolosi Beatles' (With The Beatles) mono LP, No. PMCO 31503, near mint.

*1964*

**£220-280**          **CO**

A Performance Return record for Colston Hall, Bristol, dated 10 November 1964, for The Beatles' performance with Mary Wells, together with a tour programme.

*1964          10in (25.5cm) high*

**£120-180**          **CO**

A Beatles commemorative coin, minted to commemorate their first visit to the US.

*c1964   Display 8in (20cm) high*

**£45-55**          **CO**

A double-sided promotional flyer for The Beatles' "A Hard Day's Night", by the Daily Express.

*1964          11in (28cm) high*

**£120-180**          **CO**

A Beatles Fan Club Christmas 45 rpm flexi disc, from December 1964, with original sleeve and newsletter, signed "Best Wishes Anne Collingham".

*It appears that Anne Collingham was the fictitious head of The Beatles Fan Club in Great Britain and was an invention of The Beatles' Press Officer Tony Barrow. 'Anne' also wrote a regular column in The Beatles Monthly magazine.*

*1964*

**£55-65**          **CO**

A US promotional poster for The Beatles' "White Album", near mint.

1968      37in (94cm) high

**£280-320**      CO

A rare synopsis pamphlet for The Beatles' "Yellow Submarine", produced by United Artists.

1968      10in (25.5cm) high

**£180-220**      CO

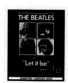

A Beatles "Let It Be" exhibitors campaign book, the five-page book listing the various promotional and advertising tools available from United Artists.

1970      12.5in (32cm) high

**£150-200**      CO

An Apple Corps. John Lennon promotional cloth doll, with a model Rickenbacker signature guitar, marked "The Beatles... Made in China."

1987      21in (53 cm) high

**£60-70**      CO

An unpublished colour photograph of Paul and Linda McCartney, photographed with an extra on the set of "Give My Regards to Broad Street" at Silvertown, London Docklands, annotated on the reverse in an unknown hand.

1984      5in (13cm) high

**£45-55**      CO

An inflatable John Lennon doll, made in Hong Kong, originally part of a set.

c1966      13in (33cm) high

**£80-120**      CO

To DOMINIC

A signed Paul McCartney promotional postcard.

8in (20cm) high

**£180-220**      CO

A Paul McCartney doll, moulded painted composition shoulder-head with painted features, black real hair wig, cloth body with painted rubber hands, wearing a black velvet suit, white shirt and black felt tie, black leather imitation boots, together with a photograph showing the four Beatles wearing similar suits.

1963-64      24.5in (62cm) high

**£2,000-2,500**      BONC

A set of four Royal Doulton Beatles toby jugs, numbered "D6725", "D6724", "D6727" and "D6726".

1984      6in (15cm) high

**£550-650**      CO

A souvenir menu from the Summer Festival at the International Hotel, Las Vegas, signed Elvis Presley in black ballpoint pen, on the front cover.

*11in (28cm) h*

£450-550    CO

A Summer Festival at the Las Vegas Hilton souvenir concert menu, signed by Elvis Presley, in black ballpoint pen on the front.

*15in (38cm) high*

£600-700    CO

A souvenir concert photo album, signed by Elvis Presley in blue ballpoint pen on the front cover.

*14in (36cm) high*

£350-450    CO

A Christmas card signed by Elvis Presley, the one-sided printed card dedicated "To Mary from Elvis Presley" in blue ballpoint pen, with an image of Elvis and "Seasons Greetings Elvis and the Colonel 1966" on the front.

*8.5in (16cm) high*

£420-480    CO

A Japanese Elvis Presley Panel Delux double album boxed set, on RCA RP-9201-2, both records unplayed.

*This exotic album package has become the most coveted Elvis boxed set ever made.*

*c1970       16in (40.5cm) h*

£800-1,200    G

A typed letter from Elvis to Colonel Parker, dated March 23, 1971 and signed by Elvis in blue ink, includes Certificate of Authenticity.

£4,000-5,000    G

A Graceland Security badge, marked "Cauley 5".

£550-650    G

Elvis Presley's black leather briefcase, covered with various tour stickers from Elvis's shows and other music groups, including International Kenpo Karate Association sticker, slightly worn, includes an Elvis Presley Museum Certificate of Authenticity.

£7,000-8,000    G

A reproduction AC/DC 1995 'Ball Breakers' World Tour poster, with facsimile autographs printed in gold.

24in (61cm) high

£55-65     CO

A rare The Doors promotional poster, for their 1967 self-titled debut album.

28in (71cm) high

£750-850     G

An early 1960s Folk Artistes Productions Ltd Champion Jack Dupree concert poster, at the Town Hall, Islington, Saturday, 17th September.

27in (69cm) high

£70-100     CO

A giant Frankie Goes to Hollywood German tour poster. *This poster was banned in Germany.*

1985     46in (117cm) high

£70-100     CO

An Elton John UK silkscreen concert poster, for gigs at Leeds University Union 10/11 March.

28in (71cm) high

£120-180     CO

A Led Zeppelin 'Tour Over Europe 1980' poster, framed and glazed.

26in (66cm) high

£100-150     CO

A Jerry Lee Lewis boxing-style playbill, for the Gaumont, Doncaster, Tues. 17th June, together with a second notice reading "Important Announcement Re. Jerry Lee Lewis" and "The Rank Organisation feel they are carrying out the wishes of the majority in withdrawing this name from the bill, but appreciate that there may be some who will not come to this show. For these, refund in cash will be made at the Booking Office in exchange for tickets already purchased".

c1958

£800-900     CO

Playbill 15in (38cm) high

A large "Monsters of Rock Festival, Donington" poster, featuring AC/DC, Van Halen, Ozzy Osbourne and Gary Moore.

c1984     59in (150cm) high

£120-180     CO

A Rolling Stones signed photograph, signed by Keith Richard, Ronnie Wood, Mick Jagger and Charlie Watts, all in blue marker pen, together with a piece of card signed Bill Wyman in black pen.

A Rolling Stones "It's Only Rock 'n' Roll" album sleeve, signed by Mick Jagger, Keith Richards, Bill Wyman, Charlie Watts and Mick Taylor, in blue marker pen, vinyl not included.

**£700-800**                                    CO

**£250-300**                                    CO

A Rolling Stones 'Beggars' Banquet' album sleeve, signed by Mick Jagger in green ink, vinyl included.

A Mick Jagger signed photograph, signed in gold marker pen, framed and glazed.

*13in (33cm) high*

A Simon & Garfunkel 'The Concert in Central Park' album sleeve, signed by Paul Simon in blue marker pen and and Art Garfunkel in silver marker, vinyl not included.

**£70-100**          CO

**£150-200**          CO

**£100-150**          CO

A Van Halen debut album sleeve, signed by David Lee Roth in silver marker, Eddie Van Halen, Alex Van Halen and Michael Anthony all in gold marker pen, vinyl not included.

A Wham signed photograph, signed in black marker pen.

A Who 'Who Are You' album sleeve, signed by John Entwhistle, Pete Townshend and Roger Daltrey in blue marker pen, vinyl not included.

**£180-220**          CO

**£55-65**          CO

**£150-200**          CO

An Artist Rights Today poster, signed by Stanley Mouse, Alton Kelley, Victor Moscoso, Wes Wilson, and Rick Griffin created for a fund raising concert in August, 1986.

**£800-1,200**    **G**

A Sonny & Cher blacklight responsive poster.

*This rare poster is one of only two known copies.*

*1967   23in (58.5cm) high*

**£1,000-1,500**    **G**

A rare Fantasy Faire and Magic Music Festival poster, listing bands including Jefferson Airplane, The Doors, and Country Joe and the Fish.

*21in (53.5cm) high*

**£800-1,200**    **G**

A Donovan "Sunshine Superman" poster, designed by Martin Sharp, metallic finish with black and blue print on a silver ground, framed and glazed.

*c1967   32in (81cm) high*

**£120-180**    **CO**

A Family Dog 'Mist Dance' poster, artwork by Victor Moscoso, photography by Paul Kagan, promoting the Youngbloods, Other Half at the Avalon Ballroom, No. 81-1.

*21in (53cm) high*

**£80-120**    **CO**

A rare concert poster for Jimi Hendrix and The Move at The Albert Hall, Tuesday 14 November, designed by Osiris Visions.

*c1967   20in (51cm) high*

**£600-800**    **CO**

A rare Middle Earth 1968 calendar poster, designed by Monk, reading "Truth Is Freedom Beauty Is Love", designed by Monk.

*1968   30in (76cm) high*

**£300-350**    **CO**

A hand-coloured Jimi Hendrix New York/Madrid Feeling Ibiza Rock Conexion poster, hand-coloured, titled "New York Rock Conexion Madrid", with further annotation "Rock & Roll Joint Show 1 Ibiza Spain Feeling Ibiza", attributed to Pietro Psaier, mounted, framed and glazed.

*34in (86cm) high*

**£600-700**    **CO**

A Millwall Football Club 1912/13 season bound volume of Southern League Programmes, including an FA Cup match vs Middlesbrough, London Senior Cup Semi Final and Final, Inter League London vs Paris, Irish League vs Southern League and Southern Charity Cup Final, bound with blue boards.

£3,500-4,000                                    MM

A unique collection of 14 Manchester United signatures, including all 11 players from the 1968 European Cup winning team, including Matt Busby and Dennis Law, in red pen signed on hexagonal sections arranged in football design with club crest to centre.

£280-320                                        MM

An enamelled silver cigarette case, painted with a footballing scene.

*3.5in (9cm) high*

£800-1,000                    TAG

A purple and cream eight-panelled England Trial cap, embroidered initials "F.A." to front and "1906-7" to peak, with maker's label A.W. Gamage Ltd. inside.

£500-600                        MM

A black and white Manchester United squad photograph, depicting 16 players in full kit, trainer and manager, titled "League Champions 1964-65" with the championship trophy and charity shield to either side, autographed below by nine players including Styles, Foulkes, Brennan, Law, Charlton, etc.

£120-180                        MM

A limited edition Manchester United FC European Cup Winners 25th Anniversary football, signed by 11 players and Matt Busby, mounted on Perspex stand with full legend engraved, wooden base with brass plaque, No. 0216/1968, in glass dome.

£400-500                        MM

An official Manchester United football shirt, bearing 21 team signatures, mounted, framed and glazed with annotation sheet on the reverse.

*Overall 37.5in (95cm) high*

**£750-850** DN

An Arsenal shirt worn by Thierry Henry, in the league game on 8 September 2001 with Premiership flashes, sponsor's logo "Dreamcast" and letter of authenticity.

**£800-1,200** MM

A "Cup Final, 1932 "Regal Souvenir" Zonaphone record, of the Cup Final, Newcastle v Arsenal, in its original paper cover featuring photographs of both teams.

**£180-220** MM

Three 8mm films of the 1962 and 1966 World Cup Finals, plus the 1970 Semi-Final, West Germany v Italy, all in original boxes.

**£50-70** MM

An early edition of Subbuteo, containing players, goalposts with nets and instructions, boxed.

**£70-100** MM

A pair of size five brown leather boots, with laces, a pair of Skues shin pads, an AGM whistle and a linesman's flag.

**£60-80** MM

A six-panelled brown and white sportsman's cap, with an interesting gold embossed shield to the front with a motto "Persto et Praesto" below and dated 1930/1 to peak, slight repair to number otherwise very good condition, complete with a wooden supporter's rattle with turned wooden handle in good working order.

**£80-120** MM

A fine set of six Royal Worcester 'Viceroy' cups and saucers, with the 'three lions' logo to each, plus a matching sugar basin and milk jug, all very good condition.

**£60-80** MM

A Henry Armstrong autographed photo, full body pose of this boxing Hall of Fame member who held three World Championships at the same time, personalized in black ink, signature is strong.

*10in (25.5cm) long*

£100-150                    HA

A Benny Leonard autographed photograph, classic bust shot of this boxing great, autographed in bold black ink, personalized.

*1947      10in (25.5cm) long*

£450-550                    HA

An autographed colour press photograph of Cassius Clay, standing over Sony Liston, signed in felt-tip pen "Muhammed Ali aka Cassius Clay", mounted with engraved plaque, framed and glazed.

*21.5in (54.5cm) high*

£150-200                    MM

An autographed colour press photograph of Muhammed Ali, standing over a floored Ken Norton signed by both fighters in blue felt-tip ink, engraved plaque "The Rumble in the Jungle", matching frame.

*21.5in (54.5cm) high*

£180-220                    MM

An autographed colour press photograph, signed in gold felt-tip pen by Ali, Joe Frazier, Ken Norton, George Foreman and Larry Holmes, plaque "Champions Forever", in matching frame.

£250-350                    MM

A signed boxing glove, mounted on mahogany based display case with engraved brass name plate "Ali, Foreman, Frazier, Norton, Lennox Lewis, Holmes, Tyson, Holyfield and Riddick Bowe".

*16.5in (42cm) wide*

£600-700                    MM

A Joe Louis funeral service programme, dated April 12, 1981.

£40-60                      SL

A Joe Louis World's Heavyweight Champion pinback button, featuring Joe in classic white training tanktop.

*1.25in (3cm) diam*

£40-50                      HA

A full-size replica Grand Prix racing helmet, signed on visor in silver marker pen by Michael Schumacher, World Champion, with Ferrari, Marlboro and Asprey sponsors' logos.

**£1,800-2,200** MM

A large signed colour photograph of Ayrton Senna, on the winners' podium, signed in black felt-tip, mounted, framed and glazed.

*16in (40.5cm) long*

**£550-650** MM

A signed limited edition print of Ayrton Senna, fighting off Nigel Mansel's challenge in the closing laps of the Monaco Grand Prix on 31st May 1992 where he clinched victory driving Marlboro McLaren, the border signed in pencil by Ayrton Senna and artist Alan Fearnley, No. 14/850.

**£2,500-3,500** MM

Three Winter Olympic Programmes in Oslo 1952, covering ice hockey, skiing and Nordic events on 5th, 6th and 11th day of the Games held during the month of February.

**£50-70** MM

Four pieces of Olympic ephemera, including two tickets for 1936 Games in Berlin; 1974 Munich Games Athletic Ticket; and programme for the Closing Ceremony in Helsinki 1952.

**£100-150** MM

Mannock, J.P., 'Billiards Expounded – to all Degrees of Amateur Players', two early first editions, red cloth and gilt boards, some wear and dust staining.

*c1920*

**£50-70** MM

An interesting silver-plated and enamel Albion Auto Racers winged motif, mounted on silver hallmarked plate, with three matching silver hallmarked name plates, each decorated with rose motifs including enamel red rose.

**£45-55** MM

A scarce signed sepia photograph of national champion H.W. Payne, on his racing cycle, signed in ink "Yours sincerely H.W. Payne 1899".

**£45-55** MM

A good R. Wylie Hill & Co, Glasgow boxed table tennis set, including accessory price guide and Thos. de la Rue Illustrated Retail Price List Guide.

**£150-200** MM

# TOYS, DOLLS & TEDDIES

Collections of children's toys are often driven by nostalgia, with individuals often focusing their collection on familiar objects from their childhood – or items they always wanted as children!

The affordable, mass-produced plastic dolls from the 1950s introduced names such as Barbie and Tiny Tears, both now prominent players for collectors. The ever-popular area of teddy bears and soft toys has its spotlight firmly focused on Steiff, notable for achieving sometimes jaw-dropping prices at auction. But English companies such as Merrythought, Chad Valley and especially J. K. Farnell should not be ignored, the latter considered the English equivalent of Steiff. Beware, though, as there are plenty of low-quality and fake examples around.

Dinky and Corgi are the two big players in the toy car and truck market, with Corgi recently eclipsing Dinky in relation to popularity and pricing. Star Wars is one of the most merchandised brands of all time, and their 1980s toys have had a massive upturn in the wake of the latest Star Wars films. For new growth areas, look to handheld computer games by companies such as Nintendo and Bambino with collectors who owned them as children in the 1980s and 90s driving the market.

# HOT COLLECTING AREA

## PLASTIC DOLLS

Plastic overtook bisque and other materials from the 1950s to become the leading material for dolls. Whilst everyone knows that your mother's or grandmother's delicate ceramic doll can be valuable today, your or your mother's favourite plastic doll may also have grown up into a hot collectable.

see p.306          see p.303          see p.304

- As plastic dolls were mass-produced and sold in large numbers, they should be in perfect condition, with the body and face fresh and clean and the hair set in its original style, in order to fetch the highest prices.

- Clothes should be original, clean and unfaded. Dolls in unusual, bright or complex original clothing will be prized. Original tags and boxes add value. Desirability is also increased by a rare or appealing design, or by a well-known maker with a large fan base, then and now.

- Dolls by named mid-20th-century makers are currently the most sought after, so look for names such as Pedigree, Sasha, Roddy, Terri Lee and Vogue. Examine size and features such as hair colour or movements, as this can affect value considerably.

- Mary Hoyer's dolls were shipped all over the world by the 1950s, with production ending in 1960 and only recommencing in the 1990s. Her hard plastic dolls made from 1946 are desirable today.

- Sasha dolls were realistic-looking dolls available with different hair colour, eyes and skin. Designed to break down cultural stereotypes, they were a statement of the 1960s. Clean faces add value.

- Introduced in 1959 in the USA, Barbie became the most successful doll ever made. Collectors look for vintage models produced before 1972, with the most valuable being the first Barbie. Some of Barbie's friends and relations can also be sought after and collectable, especially if early in date.

## A CLOSER LOOK AT A PLASTIC DOLL

*This doll has its original box, which is also in excellent condition.*

*Not only is the hair set in its original style, it also retains the delicate hairnet and curlers.*

*She still retains her original accessories including hatbox and fashion award.*

*It is important Madame Alexander dolls retain their tag, as in this example.*

A Madame Alexander 'Margot Ballerina' doll, with original clothing, hairnet, fashion award, medallion, hatbox and curlers and box.

*1953*                                        *14in (35.5cm) high*

**£650-750**                                        **DE**

### TOP TIPS

- Clothing on its own can also fetch high values as collectors match a mint-condition costume to a similar doll.

- Avoid buying dolls with their hair cut by previous owners as this is impossible to replace or repair.

- Tiny Tears is also attracting growing interest and may rise in value further in the future.

- Barbie can be dated to a period by the design of her face and her hair colour and style. Dates on her body indicate a patent date, not the year she was made.

An extremely rare dressed Mattel Barbie No1.

*1959*

**£4,000-6,000** ATA

A black-haired 'Bubble Cut' Barbie, with swimsuit and 'greened' ears.

*Barbie used to have copper earrings. When the copper degraded, it stained the ears green. This reduces the value, although it can be cleaned off.*

*12in (30cm) high*

**£30-50** DE

An unclothed 'Bubble Cut' Barbie.

*1963* *12in (30cm) high*

**£40-60** DE

A 1960s brunette 'Bubble Cut' Barbie, with original box and brochure.

*Box 12.25in (31cm) high*

**£100-150** DE

A mint and boxed Platinum Bubble Barbie, with red swimsuit, red shoes and booklet.

*c1963 Box 12.25in (31cm) high*

**£200-250** ATA

A 'Titian Bubble Cut' Barbie with swimsuit.

*'Titian' was the name given to this colour of Barbie's hair.*

*12in (30cm) high*

**£80-120** DE

An early Mattel Inc. 'Barbie' doll, dressed as Guinevere, in original box.

*11.5in (29cm) high*

**£220-280**  F

A TNT Barbie.

*11.5in (29cm) high*

**£40-60**  DE

A 'Miss America' Barbie, with clicking legs.

*12in (30cm) high*

**£40-60**  DE

A boxed Supersize Barbie, with 'Super Hair'.

*c1978*  *18.5in (47cm) high*

**£80-120**  DE

A Malibu Barbie.

*12in (30cm) high*

**£15-20**  DE

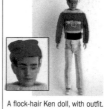

A flock-hair Ken doll, with outfit.

*Ken, Barbie's boyfriend, was first introduced in 1961 with blond flock hair and beach clothing and towel.*

*12.25in (31cm) high*

**£20-30**  DE

A TNT brunette 'Flip Francie'.

*Francie was Barbie's 'modern cousin' and was produced from 1966-76.*

*11in (28cm) high*

**£120-180**  DE

A Mattel Francie with bent legs.

*11.25in (28.5cm) high*

**£80-120**  DE

A Mattel 'Skipper'.

*1964-1970*  *9in (23cm) h*

**£15-25**  DE

A very rare 1930s early Mary Hoyer doll, with twist waist, unmarked.

*This was one of her first dolls.*

**£150-200** DE

A vintage Mary Hoyer doll, with tagged outfit, original shoes and replaced wig.

**£280-330** DE

A vintage Mary Hoyer 'Southern Belle' doll.

**£350-400** DE

A 1950s Mary Hoyer doll, with rare platinum blonde hair, doll marked and outfit tagged.

**£600-700** DE

A vintage Mary Hoyer doll, in hard plastic with tagged dress, marked on back, all original.

**£250-300** DE

A 1950s vintage Mary Hoyer doll, with factory-made clothes and hat, original shoes and socks.

*14in (35.5cm) high*

**£250-300** DE

A vintage Mary Hoyer 'Rollerskating' doll.

**£300-350** DE

A vintage Mary Hoyer 'School Time' doll.

**£420-480** DE

A vintage Mary Hoyer 'At The Beach' doll, all original.

**£420-480** DE

A 1950s Mary Hoyer boy doll, with tagged shirt and pants, marked and boxed.

**£550-600** DE

A blonde-haired blue-eyed Sasha doll.

*17in (43cm) high*

**£60-70** WHP

A dark-haired brown-eyed Sasha doll, with some original clothing and original Sasha wrist tag.

*17in (43cm) high*

**£150-180** WHP

A brunette gingham 103 Sasha doll, in original clothing and box.

*15.75in (40cm) high*

**£160-200** WHP

A Sasha boy, with brown hair and eyes, some original clothing and Sasha wrist tag.

*17in (43cm) high*

**£100-150** WHP

An early 1950s Vogue Doll Company strung 'Ginny' doll, with tagged dress and later plastic Ginny shoes.

**£250-300** DE

A Cheryl Vogue Doll Company 'Ginny' doll.

*c1953*

**£350-400** DE

An April Vogue Doll Company composition strung 'Ginny' doll, all original.

*c1953*

**£420-480** DE

An early rare Vogue 'Toddler Cowboy' doll, with lasso and signed shoe, all original, mint condition.

**£300-350** DE

A 1960s W. Goebel plastic boy doll.

*10.75in (27cm) high*

**£80-120**      **DE**

A 'LuAnn Simms' hard plastic doll, by Roberta, Horsmann & Valentine.

*1953*      *18in (46cm) high*

**£100-170**      **DE**

A Revlon plastic doll, by Ideal, with original clothing, necklace and label.

*This doll has rare red hair, which adds to her desirability and value. The colour is usually brown. She is also in mint condition.*

*18in (46cm) high*

**£300-350**      **DE**

A 1980s 'Tiny Tears' plastic doll.

*The Tiny Tears doll by American Character Doll was 'fed' water in a bottle through the mouth allowing her to wet herself and shed tears. The first version hit the shelves c1950 and her subsequent popularity ensured she went through a number of updates over the following decades. Early examples have solid heads, often with moulded hair, and jointed rubber bodies. Later examples are deemed less attractive by collectors.*

*12in (30cm) high*

**£70-100**      **DE**

A 1950s German celluloid boy doll, with original box.

*8in (20cm) high*

**£40-60**      **DE**

A Lenci 'Mascotte' doll, with rare costume, labelled.

**£180-200** DE

An Italian Lenci 'Schoolboy' felt doll, all original.

*c1930* *17in (43cm) high*

**£400-500** BEJ

A 1930s Lenci mechanical store display mannequin, from Lord & Taylor with Lord & Taylor tag, all original.

**£750-800** DE

A 1930s Nora Wellings black doll, with painted plush velvet face, flirty glass eyes and smiling mouth.

**£55-65** WHP

A Nora Wellings 'Mountie' doll.

*9.75in (25cm) high*

**£15-25** WHP

A 1930s Empire-marked 'Sailor', often mis-sold as a Nora Wellings doll.

*8in (20cm) high*

**£20-25** BEJ

Left: An early Setti 'Farmer' doll, handmade and painted by John R. Wright.

*19in (48.5cm) high*

**£900-1,100** DE

Right: An early Setti 'Farmer's Wife' doll, handmade and painted by John R. Wright.

*18in (45.5cm) high*

**£800-1,000** DE

A large size Steiff 'Pucki', with tag and money bag.

**£160-180** DE

A boxed Pelham puppet type SL 'Cinderella', with original control bar and coloured strings, and complete with instruction sheet, very good condition in very good original second type yellow box with lid.

*11.5in (29cm) high*

**£35-45** DN

A boxed Pelham puppet type SS 'Clown', dressed in red jump suit with white spots and red felt hat, with original control bar and coloured strings, complete with instruction sheet, good condition in good original card box with red and blue label to the lid.

**£70-100** DN

A boxed Pelham puppet 'Baby Dragon', with 1963 tag beneath left wing, original control bar and coloured strings, complete with instruction sheet, good condition second type yellow box, minor graffiti to lid.

**£250-300** DN

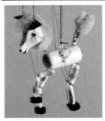

A boxed Pelham puppet A5 'Foal', with original crossbar and coloured strings, yellow box with lid also good except for one part-split corner and graffiti to underside of base.

*7.75in (20cm) high*

**£30-40** DN

A boxed Pelham puppet Jumpette 'Girl', with original control bar and strings, very good condition in good small-size yellow box with lid.

*9in (23cm) high*

**£30-40** DN

A boxed Pelham puppet type SS 'Golliwog', dressed in red trousers and green and white striped shirt, with original control bar and coloured strings, complete with instruction sheet and untangling chart; good condition in good original card box with red and blue label to the lid.

**£250-350** DN

A boxed Pelham puppet type SS 'Gypsy', with original control bar, coloured strings and additional clothing, very good condition in very good original second type yellow box with lid.

*11.75in (30cm) high*

**£30-40** DN

A boxed Pelham puppet type SS 'Gypsy', with original control bar and coloured strings, good condition in good original second type yellow box with lid.

*12.25in (31cm) high*

**£25-35** DN

A boxed Pelham puppet type LL 'Lulabelle', with coloured strings, early version with bamboo limbs and rubber-ring lips, some paint loss but generally very good condition in fair to good original card box with blue label to the lid.

*23.5in (60cm) high*

**£150-200** DN

A boxed Pelham puppet type SL 'Merlin', dressed in blue robes and hat with original coloured strings, complete with instruction sheet; moth damage to robes but in good condition in good original second type yellow box.

**£200-250** DN

A boxed Pelham puppet type SL 'Mickey Mouse', with original control bar and coloured strings and complete with instruction sheet, excellent condition in good original second type yellow box with lid.

*10.25in (26cm) high*

**£80-100** DN

A boxed Pelham puppet 'Muffin the Mule', early example with original control bar, good condition in fair to good original yellow-striped box.

*6.75in (17cm) long*

**£220-280** DN

A boxed Pelham puppet type SL 'Pinocchio', version with plastic legs, with original control bar and coloured strings and complete with instruction sheet, excellent condition in good but incorrect second type yellow box with lid, marked for "Tyrolean Boy".

*11.75in (30cm) high*

**£40-60** DN

# HOT COLLECTING AREA

## TEDDY BEARS

As important to collectors today as they were to the children who loved them, teddies are well known as sought-after collectables. Although the market is dominated by big names and high prices, nothing grabs a collector's heart more than a cute, characterful expression.

see p.312                  see p.314                  see p.315

- Bears in excellent condition fetch the highest prices. Original pads, eyes, stitching and intact fur will all add value. Also vital are size, maker and condition.

- Pre-WWI bears are rare and expensive; even interwar bears fetch high prices, especially those by German makers such as Steiff, Gebruder Bing and Schuco. Those in large sizes, unusual colours, early shapes or with mechanical features will fetch premium prices.

- Bears changed in form after WWII and those by makers such as Chad Valley, Merrythought and Pedigree of Britain are commonly found. Prices for 1940s and 50s teddies are rising as supplies of earlier bears dry up. Later bears are currently less collectable.

- Steiff teddies remain the most sought after, being solidly built, well stitched and full of character. J.K. Farnell, known as the 'English Steiff' and Chiltern also produced desirable bears.

- Miniature and novelty bears by makers such as Schuco and Steiff of Germany are popular collectables, and often more affordable than their larger relations. Look out for examples that conceal a hidden function such as perfume bottles.

- An interesting or heart-warming story or history will add extra interest and thus value to a bear. Look out particularly for early photographs of bears with their original owners.

- During the late 1970s bears started to be made exclusively as collectors' pieces. They may have potential future investment, but prices are not yet rising. Always keep the paperwork and box.

## A CLOSER LOOK AT A TEDDY BEAR

*Although unmarked, this bear shows many characteristics of early bears.*

*His snout is long, whereas bears made after World War II generally have shorter snouts.*

*He is covered with mohair, whereas later bears used a 'shinier' synthetic plush material.*

*His eyes are early 'boot buttons'. Glass was used after the late 1920s, with plastic being used from the 1950s onwards.*

*His jointed arms are long and curved. Bears from the 1950s onwards usually have shorter arms.*

An early 20thC teddy bear, the fully-jointed golden body stuffed with wood wool, with felt pads and black button eyes.

*13in (33cm) high*

**£900-1,100**

**DN**

### TOP TIPS

- Always sniff an old bear – it's impossible to fake the smell of years of love, attention and accidents.

- Get to know the defining features of well-known makers and of different countries as this will help you identify a teddy.

- Avoid suspiciously clean 'old' bears, or any bear with an old label on new paw pads – pre-World War II bears are often faked.

- The date of a Steiff bear can be told from its shape and the style of the characteristic metal Steiff button in the ear. Beware of reproduction buttons placed on non-Steiff bears.

A Steiff brown plush 'Teddy Bear'.

8.5in (24cm) high

£500-800     **HGS**

A Steiff brown mohair teddy bear, straw-filled with black boot button eyes, pointed snout, stitched nose, mouth and claws, swivel head, jointed at shoulders and hips, felt paw pads, button to left ear, nose covered with black felt.

*This bear has many of the characteristics of early bears including 'boot button eyes', jointed limbs, long curved arms, a humped back and a shaved muzzle.*

c1910     12in (31cm) high

£500-700     **BONC**

A Steiff brown teddy bear, dressed in military clothing, some losses.

*The addition of a contemporary costume makes this bear attractive to collectors. Steiff bears, made in Germany, are highly desirable and usually have a button in their ear, the style of which can help to date the bear. This button was used from 1920 to 1950, and the shape of the bear suggests it was made in the 1920s or 1930s.*

17in (43cm) long

£1,500-2,000     **DAW**

A Chiltern blond mohair teddy bear, with orange glass eyes, brown stitched nose, mouth and claws, shaved muzzle, swivel head and jointed at shoulders and hips, velvet paw pads.

c1930     16in (41cm) high

£220-280     **BONC**

A Chiltern light brown mohair 'Hugmee' teddy bear, with glass eyes, stitched features, swivel head and jointed at shoulders and hips, velvet paw pads, some wear and damage.

c1930     15in (38cm) high

£70-100     **BONC**

A Chad Valley brown mohair teddy bear, with orange glass eyes, black stitched nose and mouth, swivel head and jointed at shoulders and hips, cloth paw pads, label to foot.

c1930     11in (28cm) high

£180-220     **BONC**

A 1970s Merrythought 'Cheeky' dark gold mohair teddy bear, fully jointed, felt pads, wool-stitched mouth on velvet snout, label reading "Merrythought/ Ironbridge, Shropshire" to foot.

15.25in (39cm) high

£280-320     **DN**

A 1930s British Pedigree teddy, with label.

*19in (48cm) high*

**£200-250** BEJ

A 1930s British Chad Valley teddy bear.

*20in (50cm) high*

**£500-600** BEJ

A German bear, with round muzzle and growler.

*c1950 18in (46cm) high*

**£400-450** BEJ

A British Chiltern 'Hugmee' bear.

*One of English company Chiltern's (1908-1967) most popular ranges was the Hugmee bear. It was introduced in 1923 and there were many different designs, including this one with its unusual unshaved muzzle. After the war Hugmees had shorter arms and legs to conserve materials. Chiltern bears typically have upturned paws.*

*c1930* *16in (40.5cm) high*

**£400-600** BEJ

A British cubbie bear, with short limbs, maker unknown.

*c1930* *14in (35.5cm) high*

**£300-350** BEJ

A British glum bear cub, unmarked.

*c1950* *11in (28cm) high*

**£350-400** BEJ

A 1920s Schuco 'Yes/No' golden mohair teddy bear, straw-filled with black boot button eyes and tail, mohair worn, paw pads damaged.

*A concealed mechanism allows the head to nod or shake by moving the tail. Had he not been so well-loved and worn, the value would have been over £500.*

15in (38cm) high

£180-220          BONC

A 1920s English golden mohair teddy bear, known as 'Lionel', fully jointed wood wool-stuffed body with a small hump, glass eyes and black wool-stitched snout, inoperative growler.

26.5in (60cm) high

£100-150          DN

A 1930s English golden plush teddy bear, possibly by Lines Bros., fully jointed with a small hump, glass eyes and black wool-stitched snout, the rear centre seam with an embroidered label reading "Made in England", replacement felt pads.

£120-180          DN

A small 1930s English light blond teddy bear, possibly by J.K. Farnell, fully jointed wood wool-stuffed body, with glass eyes and wool-stitched snout.

11.5in (29cm) high

£50-80          DN

A 1940s English golden plush teddy bear, with remains of a label, minor damage to snout.

17.75in (45cm) high

£80-120          DN

A 1930s German cinnamon-coloured mohair teddy bear, possibly by Schuco, fully jointed, with glass eyes and wool-stitched snout.

*Provenance: Known as 'Larry', this bear spent some time as a window display in the teddy bear shop in Swanage.*

15in (38cm) high

£180-220          DN

A German dual-colour mohair teddy bear, fully jointed, kapok and wood wool-stuffed body, with glass eyes and wool-stitched snout, replacement felt pads.

14.5in (37cm) high

£50-80          DN

An English blue mohair teddy bear, straw-filled, with orange glass eyes, black stitched nose, mouth and claws, swivel head and jointed at shoulders and hips, felt paw pads.

c1950          16in (41cm) high

£120-180          BONC

A 1950s Schuco golden plush bear.

*Schuco miniature bears from the 1950s are rounder in form than earlier versions from the 1920s which have thinner limbs and larger, stitched noses.*

2.75in (7cm) high

**£80-120** HGS

A Schuco plush panda bear.

3.25in (8.5cm) high

**£120-180** HGS

A miniature Steiff white mohair teddy bear, with black bead eyes, black stitched nose and mouth, swivel head and jointed at shoulders and hips.

c1920        3.5in (9cm) high

**£180-220** BONC

A miniature Steiff golden mohair teddy bear, with black bead eyes, black stitched nose and mouth, swivel head and jointed at shoulders and hips.

c1920        3.5in (9cm) high

**£180-220** BONC

An English WWI 'Mascot' golden mohair teddy bear, with clear glass eyes, black felt nose, swivel head and jointed at shoulders and hips.

c1915        3.5in (9cm) high

**£200-250** BONC

A 1950s Steiff golden plush bear, with original tag.

6in (15cm) high

**£400-500** HGS

A miniature Schuco brown mohair monkey, with painted metal face, felt ears, hands and feet, swivel head and jointed at shoulders and hips.

c1920        3.5in (9cm) high

**£80-120** BONC

A Steiff grey felt elephant on wheels, with black button eyes and white felt tusks, with red felt saddle with gold embroidery, on a metal frame and with wooden wheels, button to left ear.

c1918          10in (25cm) high

£200-300          BONC

A Steiff elephant, with original ear and neck tags, blanket with bells.

7.5in (19cm) long

£50-100          NB

A 1950s Steiff 'Mecki' Hedgehog.

10.52in (27cm) high

£80-100          BONC

A Steiff rhinoceros, with wood wool stuffed body, felt horn, glass eyes and grey felt pads, with metal tag and yellow label in left ear.

11.5in (29cm) long

£50-70          DN

A Steiff white plush lamb, with black boot button eyes, pink stitched nose and mouth, button in left ear.

c1920          10in (25cm) high

£35-55          BONC

A Schuco Yes/No monkey, with painted metal eyes, plush head and mask face, felt ears, wearing sewn-on bellboy felt clothes of red cap, jacket and boots, black trousers, mechanism to tail for Yes/No movement to head.

*Moving his rigid tail allows you to make his head nod, or for him to shake his head, hence the 'Yes/No' name. A Yes/No teddy bear was also made, which can be more valuable, depending on condition and size.*

c1920          8in (20cm) high

£120-180          BONC

A Steiff Santa, clown and gnomes, all with rubber heads, Santa wearing red felt outfit and hat, three gnomes wearing felt clothes and hats with large pointed leather shoes.

c1960

£150-200          BONC

A miniature ladybird, possibly Steiff, with red bristle coat and black bristle wire legs and antennae.

2.75in (7cm) long

£20-30          F

A Schuco plush and pipe cleaner ladybird.

3.25in (8cm) long

£150-200          HGS

A 1950s Agnes Brush Winnie The Pooh.

*Agnes Brush of Long Island, New York made characters from Winnie The Pooh during the 1940s and 1950s.*

13.5in (34cm) high

£200-300          HGS

A Steiff 'Snobby' black poodle hand puppet, with original paper label and button in ear.

**£150-200**　　　**SL**

A Steiff 'Gaty' hand puppet, with original paper label and button in ear, model number 317.

**£100-150**　　　**SL**

A 1950s British Merrythought piglet, with label.

*9in (23cm) high*

**£80-120**　　　**BEJ**

A 1930s German mohair clockwork kitten.

*6in (14cm) high*

**£200-250**　　　**BEJ**

A pale blue plush lamb, boxed, unmarked.

*c1930*

**£100-150**　　　**BEJ**

A 1960s Chad Valley Golly, with felt eyes and plastic suede-effect mouth and teeth, typically dressed in yellow waistcoat, striped trousers and blue jacket, with printed label.

*2.5in (62cm) high*

**£25-35**　　　**DN**

A 1970s Wendy Boston Basil Brush.

*15.75in (40cm) high*

**£25-35**　　　**WHP**

# HOT COLLECTING AREA

## DIE-CAST TOYS

No young boy's toybox was complete without metal cars to race around and planes to propel around the living room. Many of us still have some of our childhood collections, or else today vie against others to own the models we always wanted. Just as well, as interest does not diminish with age and prices can be high.

see p.321          see p.322                    see p.325

- Dinky, produced by Meccano, is one of the most famous and traditional names. Their first vehicles were released in 1931 as accessories for train sets. The 1930s was Dinky's golden age, with over 200 models to choose from. As so few survived, pre-war toys in excellent condition are rare and desirable.

- As well as the form of the car, features such as white rubber wheels identify early models. Also look at the model number on the base to identify the production period. Due to the variety, many focus on one type, with civilian cars, planes and lorries being popular.

- 1947 saw the introduction of Dinky's 'Supertoys', with their characteristic blue-and-white striped boxes. Today, many models from the 1950s and 60s with their yellow boxes, are sought after by adults who played with them as children. 'Speedwheels' arrived in the 1970s, in response to competition from other companies.

- Corgi was Dinky's main competitor in Britain. Released in 1956 by Mettoy, they appealed to young boys of the 1960s and 70s attracted by their windows and moving parts. Although Dinky has traditionally overshadowed Corgi, the balance is now reversing.

- Corgi also had great success producing vehicles from popular film and TV series of the period. James Bond is perhaps the most memorable and valued, but look for versions from "Batman" and other TV series such as "The Avengers".

- Examine toys closely as different colours or details such as 'flashes' on cabs can indicate rare models, made for short periods of time or for export. Wheels, interiors, accessories and transfers are other areas to consider. Rare variations often command premium prices.

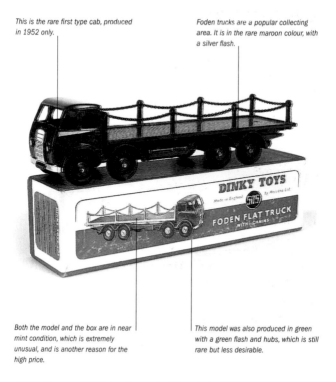

*This is the rare first type cab, produced in 1952 only.*

*Foden trucks are a popular collecting area. It is in the rare maroon colour, with a silver flash.*

*Both the model and the box are in near mint condition, which is extremely unusual, and is another reason for the high price.*

*This model was also produced in green with a green flash and hubs, which is still rare but less desirable.*

A Dinky Toys no. 505 Foden flat truck with chains, with first-type cab, maroon cab, chassis, back and ridged hubs, silver side flash, near mint including blue lift-off lid box.

**£11,000-13,000**                                                    **VEC**

## TOP TIPS

■ Never repaint or touch-up a worn die-cast toy as this can reduce the value even more.

■ Look out for boxes – matching a correct box in excellent condition to the right toy in similar condition can add up to 40% of the value.

■ Look out for complete and original Dinky gift sets with their boxes as these are rare and rising rapidly in value.

■ Corgi's 'Whizz Wheels' range look set to rise in value. Look for appealing cars in excellent condition with their original boxes to take proper advantage of this.

A Dinky No. 30c Daimler, fawn body, black chassis, black ridged hubs, excellent condition, slight mark to roof.
*1946-50*

**£70-80** VEC

A Dinky No. 30d Vauxhall, olive green, black open chassis, black ridged wheels, good condition.
*c1946*

**£70-80** VEC

A Dinky No. 30f Ambulance, cream, black chassis, black ridged hubs, good condition.

*1947-48*

**£55-65** VEC

A Dinky No. 38c Lagonda, green, dark green interior, black ridged hubs, silvered windscreen, excellent condition.
*1947-50*

**£90-120** VEC

A Dinky Streamlined Fire Engine, red, black ridged hubs, ladder and bell, together with a Streamlined Coach, grey, dark blue mudguards, black ridged wheels, and a Motor Breakdown Truck, red, black ridged wheels, all in good condition.

**£90-120** VEC

Two Dinky cars, a No. 238 Jaguar D type racing car in turquoise, no racing number and a No. 181 Volkswagen Beetle in grey with blue wheels, boxed, minor age wear, minor paint chips.
*1951-60*

**£60-70** W&W

A Dinky No. 157 Jaguar XK 120 coupe, two-tone in cerise and duck egg blue, in associated box, some wear to box, minor wear to vehicle.
*1957-59*

**£130-180** W&W

A Dinky No. 448 Chevrolet Pick-Up and Trailers, good condition.
*1963-68*

**£90-120** CHEF

A No. 501 Foden Dinky Diesel eight-wheeled wagon, with first-type brown cab and back, black chassis, silver side flash, brown ridged wheels, herringbone tyres, no hook, back with some corrosion, in buff box, split at one end.

**£150-200**  **VEC**

A rare US export No. 501 Dinky Foden eight-wheeled wagon, in early Supertoy box with red spot on end label.

*The US export only issue had a red cab and back, silver cab flash and black chassis. In mint condition it can be worth up to £4,000.*

**£800-1,000**  **VEC**

A Dinky Toys 504 Foden 14-ton tanker, first type cab and chassis, in red with silver flash to cab, fawn tank, red wheel hubs, boxed, some wear, vehicle in good condition, minor chipping, rusting to tank.

**£250-300**  **W&W**

A Dinky Toys 942 Foden 14-ton tanker "Regent", with red hubs, fair condition with paint chipping and wear, blue-stripped box.

**£55-65**  **DN**

A Dinky Toys 905 Foden flat bed truck with chains, boxed.

*7.25in (18.5cm) long*

**£150-200**  **CB**

A Dinky Toys 959 Foden dump truck, red with silver chassis and yellow wheel hubs, complete with plough blade to front, boxed, minor wear, minor chips.

**£300-350**  **W&W**

A Dinky Toys 903 Foden flatbed truck with tailboard, dark blue cab and chassis, orange flatbed and light blue hubs, unboxed.

**£80-120**  **DN**

Two Dinky Toys commercial vehicles, a 533 Leyland Comet Cement Wagon "Ferrocrete", unboxed and a 922 Big Bedford Lorry with maroon cab and chassis and fawn truck body.

**£55-65**  **DN**

A scarce French Dinky Kart No. 512, midget racer with driver, in original box, minor wear.

£140-180      **W&W**

A Dinky No. 901 Foden Diesel 8-wheel Wagon, second type cab, excellent condition in poor box.

*1954-57*

£100-150      **VEC**

A Dinky Supertoys No. 943 Leyland Octopus Tanker - Esso, fair condition, boxed.

*1958-64*

£80-120      **CHEF**

A Dinky Supertoys No. 563 Crawler Tractor, good condition, boxed.

*1948-54*

£50-80      **CHEF**

A Dinky Supertoys No. 923 Big Bedford Van 'Heinz', fair to good condition, box worn.

*Look out for the variation advertising Heinz Tomato Ketchup, which is much scarcer, having been produced between 1958 and 1959 only, and which can be worth eight times the value of this version in mint condition with mint packaging.*

*1955-58*

£130-180      **CHEF**

A scarce prewar Dinky No. 30b Rolls Royce car, with open chassis finished in dark blue with black chassis, white tyres, signs of chassis expansion leading to some bowing, minor chips to paint.

*1935-40*

£120-180      **W&W**

A scarce pre-war Dinky No. 12 Postal Set, comprising Air and GPO Pillar Boxes, Telephone Call Box in red, additional Call Box in white, Postman, and No. 34b Royal Mail Van, GR to sides, open windows, all in original blue card box with yellow insert, with original blue string, minor fading to box.

*1937-41*

£450-500      **W&W**

A Dinky Supertoys No. 965 Euclid Rear Dump Truck, very good condition, boxed.

*1955-61*

£90-110      **CHEF**

A scarce pre-war Dinky 33 series No. 33a Mechanical Horse, No. 33d Box Van Trailer with "Hornby Trains", "British Guaranteed" to sides, and No. 33e Dust Wagon Trailer, open wagon, tinplate cover with shutter, and flat truck.

*c1935*

£220-280      **W&W**

A Corgi No. 259 Le Dandy Coupé, blue, white, wire wheels, near mint condition, in excellent condition box.

*1966-69*

**£150-200** VEC

A Corgi No. 328 Hillman Imp 'Rally Monte Carlo', blue, racing No. 107, spun hubs, mint condition apart from weak rear suspension weak, in good condition blue and yellow box.

*If the advertising leaflet is present with this car and the box, add roughly 20% to the value.*

*1966-67*

**£70-100** VEC

A Corgi No. 351 Land Rover 'RAF', blue, tin rear canopy, flat spun hubs, excellent condition, slight roof mark, in good condition box.

*1958-62*

**£70-100** VEC

A Corgi No. 438 Land Rover, metallic green, grey plastic canopy, spun hubs, excellent condition apart from very slight roof marks, in good but grubby blue and yellow carded box.

*1963-77*

**£70-100** VEC

A Corgi No. 230 Mercedes Benz 220SE Coupé, red, lemon interior, spun hubs, excellent condition, showing slight surface corrosion to base and interior slightly sun faded, in good condition.

*1962-64*

**£55-65** VEC

A Corgi No. 253 Mercedes Benz 220SE Coupé, mint condition, blue and yellow box.

*1964-68*

**£70-100** VEC

A Corgi No. 226 Morris Mini Minor, dark red, lemon interior, cast hubs, excellent condition, couple of very minor marks to roof, in excellent condition box.

*Sky blue or yellow bodies are the rarest colourway and can be worth more than twice the value of the more common red and maroon versions.*

*1960-68*

A Corgi No. 333 Mini Cooper 'International Rally', red, white roof, spun hubs, racing No. 21.

*c1966*

**£180-220** VEC

**£90-120** VEC

A Corgi No. 202 Morris Cowley, grey, flat spun hubs, near mint condition, has been restored, in good condition box.

*This example is worth less than the other example as it has been damaged and then restored, so is not original.*

1956-61

**£45-55** VEC

A Corgi No. 202 Morris Cowley Saloon, grey, flat spun hubs, near mint condition, in good condition although grubby all-carded blue box.

1956-61

**£90-120** VEC

A Corgi No. 205 Riley Pathfinder Saloon, red, flat spun hubs, good condition, in fair but complete all-carded blue box.

1956-62

**£55-65** VEC

A Corgi No. 209 Riley Pathfinder Police Car, black, flat spun hubs, aerial, roof box, good condition in good condition all-carded blue box.

1958-61

**£80-120** VEC

A Corgi No. 281 Rover 2000TC, purple, yellow interior, WhizzWheels, near mint condition in excellent condition orange and yellow window box, one end flap slightly marked.

1971-72

**£70-100** VEC

A Corgi No. 207 Standard Vanguard Saloon, red over pale green, flat spun hubs, good condition in good condition box.

1957-62

**£80-120** VEC

A Corgi No. 203 Vauxhall Velox Saloon, flat spun hubs, near mint condition, slightly re-touched, in excellent condition.

*Also available in red or yellow at the same value range. Early versions came with a leaflet.*

1956-61

**£90-120** VEC

A Corgi 256 Volkswagen 1200, with East African Safari Trim and rhino, very good condition, boxed.

1965-68

**£170-200** CHEF

A Corgi No. 404 Bedford Dormobile Personnel Carrier, cream, flat spun hubs, near mint condition in good condition box.

*Look for the yellow and blue two-tone version. This earlier version is identified by its 'split' windscreen.*

1956-62

**£80-120** VEC

A Corgi No. 266 Chitty Chitty Bang Bang, complete with all four figures, near mint condition, with a few minor marks, in good condition blue and yellow window box, which has been professionally re-cellophaned.
*1968-72*

**£120-180**     VEC

A Corgi No. 268 'The Green Hornet's' Black Beauty, near mint condition, boxed.
*1967-72*

**£200-250**     CHEF

A Corgi No. 805 'The Hardy Boys' Rolls Royce Silver Ghost, yellow, blue, red, figures still in dome, excellent condition, with slight chips to bonnet, in good but crushed blue and yellow picture box.
*1970-71*

**£80-120**     VEC

A Corgi No. 277 'The Monkees' Monkeemobile, red, white roof, cast wheels, near mint condition in good condition blue and yellow window box.
*1968-72*

**£200-250**     VEC

A Corgi No. 802 'Popeye' Paddle wagon, complete with all original parts and in working order, in a reproduction box, some age wear and chipping.
*1969-72*

**£80-120**     W&W

A Corgi No. 258 'The Saint's Car' Volvo P1800, very good condition, boxed.
*1965-70*

**£150-200**     CHEF

A Corgi No. 9004 'The World of Wooster' Bentley, near mint condition, with slightly discoloured wheels, in excellent pack.
*1967-69*

**£100-150**     VEC

A Star Wars 'Luke Skywalker' Early Bird action figure.

*Overwhelming demand meant that Kenner Toys were unable to produce enough figures leading up to Christmas 1977. Instead, they supplied retailers with 'Early Bird Certificates' which could be later redeemed for toys. This 'Early Bird' Luke figure can be identified as he has a double-extending light sabre.*

4in (10cm) high

£150-250          KF

A Star Wars 'Princess Leia' action figure.

c1978          3.75in (9.5cm) h

£25-30          KF

A Star Wars 'Darth Vader' action figure.

c1978          4in (10cm) high

£7-10          KF

A Star Wars 'Sand Person' carded action figure, by Palitoy.

*These figures were originally called 'Tusken Raiders'.*

c1978          9in (22.5cm) high

£300-400          KF

A Star Wars 'Greedo' carded action figure, by Kenner.

c1979          9in (22.5cm) high

£180-220          KF

A Star Wars - The Empire Strikes Back 'Han Solo (Bespin Outfit)' carded action figure, by Palitoy.

c1981          9in (22.5cm) high

£120-180          KF

A Star Wars - The Empire Strikes Back 'AT-AT Commander' carded action figure, by Palitoy.

c1982          9in (22.5cm) high

£70-100          KF

A Star Wars - The Empire Strikes Back 'Imperial TIE Fighter Pilot' carded action figure, by Palitoy.

c1982          9in (22.5cm) high

£70-100          KF

A Star Wars - The Empire Strikes Back 'AT-AT All Terrain Armoured Transport', by Palitoy, mint and boxed.

*c1980*                    *18in (45.5cm) high*

**£200-250**                                    **KF**

A Star Wars - Return of the Jedi 'Slave 1' vehicle, by Palitoy.

*c1981  15.5in (39.5cm) width*

**£50-70**                    **KF**

A Star Wars - Return of the Jedi 'B-Wing Fighter' vehicle, by Kenner.

*c1984*

**£150-200**            **KF**

A Star Wars - The Power of the Force 'Tatooine Skiff' vehicle, by Kenner, sealed in the box.

*This toy was a late addition to the Kenner range and few were made, they are also quite fragile which makes them hard to find complete or sealed in the box.*

*c1985*                    *Box 15.5in (39.5cm) high*

**£400-600**                                    **KF**

A Star Wars 'Imperial Troop Transporter', by Palitoy.

*c1979 Toy 10in (25.5cm) wide*

**£60-90**                    **KF**

A Star Wars - The Empire Strikes Back 'Rebel Armoured Snowspeeder', by Palitoy.

*c1980  Toy12in (30.5cm) high*

**£40-60**                    **KF**

A Star Wars - The Empire Strikes Back 'MTV-7 Multi-Terrain' vehicle mini-rig, by Kenner.

*c1982        9in (22.5cm) wide*

**£20-25**                    **KF**

A Star Wars - Return of the Jedi 'AST-5 Armoured Sentinel Transport' vehicle mini-rig.

*'Mini-rigs' were a range of small vehicles or appliances, designed by Kenner toys and which never appeared on screen.*

*c1983    3.75in (9.5cm) high*

**£15-20**                    **KF**

A Bing 0-gauge 4-4-0 electric motored green RN 3422 locomotive, with litho-finish, some age wear to finish.

**£100-120** W&W

A Bing 0-gauge clockwork George the Fifth RN 2663, 4-4-0 and tender, well refinished with two-colour lining, three control levers to cab, central handle missing, minor wear to finish, distortion to cab roof.

**£65-75** W&W

A Carette for Bassett Lowke clockwork 4-4-0 George the Fifth locomotive RN 2663, and six wheel tender finished overall in black with two-colour fine lining, with two-control rods to cab, minor wear to finish, some damage to cab.

*Many of the trains sold by British company Bassett-Lowke (1899-1969) between 1900 and 1933 were supplied by the German companies Gebruder Bing and Carette. They also had their own factory, called George Winteringham, which they relied on after their relationships ended with Carette c1917 and Bing in 1933.*

**£150-180** W&W

A Bassett Lowke 'Duke of York' green clockwork 0-gauge train. c1927

**£225-265** WOS

A Hornby 0-gauge clockwork 4-4-0 no. two special tender locomotive, Yorkshire, RN 234, in LNER green livery with black running plate, LNER to tender sides, some repainting, tender reworked and refinished.

**£130-150** W&W

A Hornby 0-gauge clockwork no. two tender locomotive, 4-4-0 with six wheel tender, refinished in green, with brass plate no. 2711 to cab sides, bolt together construction, minor wear, rust through to corner of tender, one driving wheel loose.

**£200-240** W&W

A Hornby 0-gauge clockwork 2-6-0 Mogul and six wheel tender, based on Bassett Lowke mechanism with adapted body, valve gear, finished black with RN2867 to cab side, and associated six wheel tender finished LMS maroon, loco cab's coupling missing.

**£180-220** W&W

A Hornby 0-gauge 0-4-0 clockwork tank locomotive No. 1 special, finished in Southern 516 green and black livery.

**£100-150**                                  **W&W**

A Hornby 0-gauge 4-4-4 special tank locomotive, a well restored three rail 20v electric, finished in Southern E492 black livery.

**£150-200**                                  **W&W**

A Hornby 0-gauge 4-4-4 tank locomotive, a well restored clockwork No. 2, finished in Southern E492 black livery.

**£180-220**            **W&W**

A Hornby 0-gauge 4-4-0 locomotive and tender, a well restored clockwork No. 2 finished in Southern A760 green and black livery.

**£180-220**            **W&W**

A Hornby R372 Class A4 'Seagull' locomotive, in LNER blue livery, number 4902, near mint condition, boxed.

**£40-50**            **DN**

A Hornby Series E3200 Electric Passenger set, 20-volt electric 4-4-2 Royal Scot engine No. 6100, together with three LMS coaches and track, front bogie wheels to engine detached with one wheel missing and one fatigued.

**£600-700**            **BONC**

A Hornby 0-gauge No. 101 tank passenger set, in the scarce LNER teak livery, comprising 101-type LNER RN 460, 0-4-0 locomotive, clockwork, two 1st/3rd composite four wheel coaches and guards/baggage van, in original blue card set box with inner packing card, circle of rail, two straights, clip box clips and key and packet of four lights, box, minor outer marks, worn.

**£120-180**                                  **W&W**

A Hornby R49 limited edition 'Lord of the Isles' set, comprising GWR 4-2-2 locomotive number 3048 and three chocolate and cream coaches, near mint boxed.

**£80-120**            **DN**

A Tomy Desert Race hand-held clockwork game.
*c1979* 5.75in (14.5cm) wide

**£10-15** HLJ

A Bambino Basketball tabletop game.
*c1979* 7.5in (19.5cm) wide

**£30-40** HLJ

A Toytronic Racetrack hand-held game.
*c1980* 3.5in (9cm) wide

**£25-35** HLJ

A Bambino Safari tabletop game.
*c1980* 9.5in (24cm) wide

**£30-50** HLJ

A CGL Grand Prix hand-held game.
*c1981* 5in (13cm) wide

**£30-50** HLJ

A CGL Galaxy Twinvader tabletop game.
*c1981* 6.5in (17cm) wide

**£25-35** HLJ

A Grandstand Astro Wars tabletop game.
*c1981* 5.7in (14.5cm) wide

**£30-50** HLJ

A Tomy Lupin tabletop game.
*c1981* 6in (15cm) wide

**£30-50** HLJ

A Grandstand Mini-Munchman hand-held game.
*c1981* 4in (10.5cm) wide

**£30-40** HLJ

A Nintendo Fire FR-27 wide screen game and watch.
*c1981* 4.25in (11.5cm) wide

**£40-70** HLJ

A Nintendo Popeye PP-23 wide screen game and watch.

*c1981*     *4.25in (11cm) wide*

**£50-80**     **HLJ**

A Grandstand BMX Flyer hand-held game.

*c1982*     *6in (15cm) wide*

**£30-50**     **HLJ**

A Tomy Caveman tabletop game.

*c1982*

**£25-35**     **HLJ**

A Tomy Thundering Turbo 3-D hand-held game.

*c1983*     *5.5in (14cm) wide*

**£25-35**     **HLJ**

A Tomy Tron tabletop game, based on the 1982 Walt Disney movie.

*c1982*     *6in (15cm) wide*

**£50-70**     **HLJ**

A Nintendo Donkey Kong DK-52 multiscreen game and watch.

*c1982*     *4.25in (11.5cm) wide*

**£35-45**     **HLJ**

A silver Nintendo Fireman RC-04 game and watch.

*c1980*     *3.75in (9.5cm) wide*

**£150-200**     **HLJ**

A Nintendo Greenhouse GH-54 multiscreen game and watch.

*c1982*     *4.25in (11.5cm) wide*

**£40-60**     **HLJ**

A Nintendo Mickey & Donald DM-53 multiscreen game and watch.

*c1982*     *4.25in (11.5cm) wide*

**£40-60**     **HLJ**

A Nintendo Donkey Kong Jr. DJ-101 new wide screen game and watch.

*c1982*     *4.25in (11cm) wide*

**£30-50**     **HLJ**

A Nintendo Oil Panic OP-51 multiscreen game and watch.

*c1982*     *4.25in (11.5cm) wide*

**£30-50**     **HLJ**

A 1970s Acapulco souvenir snowdome, with an octopus.

3in (7.5cm) high

£12-20      NWC

A 1970s souvenir snowdome from Florida, with a dolphin and a see-saw inside.

4in (10cm) high

£12-20      NWC

An early 1980s Hawaii souvenir snowdome, in the form of a treasure chest.

2.75in (7cm) high

£8-12      NWC

An early 1990s Las Vegas souvenir snowdome, with dice inside.

2in (5cm) high

£8-15      NWC

An early 1980s New York City souvenir snowdome, with the Twin Towers.

2.75in (7cm) high

£8-15      NWC

A 1970s souvenir snowdome from San Francisco, with a mermaid.

4.5in (11.5cm) high

£12-20      NWC

A late 1950s souvenir Washington 'Water Globe' salt and pepper container, with sliding lid.

2.75in (7cm) high

£15-25      NWC

A 1940s glass and bakelite Niagra Falls souvenir snowdome.

4in (10cm) high

£20-45      NWC

A 1930s glass and bakelite snowdome 'Uncle Alfred - The Hermitage, Tenn.', by Pine.

*The Hermitage in Nashville was the home of seventh American President Andrew Jackson and Uncle Alfred was his favoured house servant.*

2.5in (6.5cm) high

£30-60      NWC

An early 1970s Walt Disney Productions 'Mickey and Donald' snowdome, with Mickey Mouse and Donald Duck on a see-saw.

*3in (7.5cm) high*

**£20-30**    **NWC**

An early 1970s Walt Disney Productions 'The Wonderful World of Disney' snowdome, with Mickey and Minnie Mouse.

*3in (7.5cm) high*

**£20-30**    **NWC**

An early 1960s Walt Disney Productions Raggedy Anne snowdome.

*5in (12.5cm) high*

**£65-90**    **NWC**

A set of three 1980s McDonalds snowdomes.

*This set was given away with Happy Meals in Germany only.*

*2.25in (5.5cm) each*

**£15-22 (EACH)**    **NWC**

An early 1960s Walt Disney Productions Pinocchio snowdome.

*This is one from a set of five snowdomes which include Raggedy Anne and Bugs Bunny.*

*5in (12.5cm) high*

**£65-90**    **NWC**

A set of four McDonalds "101 Dalmatians" snowdomes.

*c1996*    *4.5in (11.5cm) high*

**£8-12 (EACH)**    **NWC**

A 1970s Christmas tree snowdome, with Santa Claus.

*6in (15cm) high*

**£20-30**    **NWC**

A late 1960s Snowman snowdome, with see-saw action.

*5in (12.5cm) high*

**£15-25**    **NWC**

A 1970s Christmas snowdome, with Santa climbing into a chimney.

*5.25in (13.5cm) high*

**£15-25**    **NWC**

Meet
the
Spring-
fly **BEA**

BRITISH EUROPEAN

**CELLULAR TELEPHONE**

GSM CM-DX1000

The speed of technological change in the 20th century and its vast range is reflected in the now collectable objects of each decade. From the popularity of the cruise liner during the first few decades, to the development of television and air travel and the recent arrival of the mobile phone, each period offers a platform for collecting.

A general rule is to find objects in excellent condition associated with prominent brands and showing superb design evocative of the period in which they were made. Memorabilia from the "Titanic" remains highly sought after and is set to continue to achieve high prices in the light of the disaster's centenary in 2012. Cameras, available in every decade of the 20th century and now eclipsed by digital models, vary in their appeal from the low-value Box Brownie to eminently collectable and valuable Leica cameras.

Radios are still an active collecting area and although 1930s models are the apex, stylishly shaped 1950s and 60s examples are climbing in value on the back of the 'retro' trend. Then there is the still fast-developing world of the mobile phone, possibly an important collecting area of the future, with the speed of new models being introduced driven as much by a need to update to the latest style as by technological convenience.

# TRAVEL

Mundane and taken for granted today, much 20th-century travel was incredible in its scope and rapid development. From the elegance of cruise liners to the roar of a mighty steam train or an aeroplane's jet engines, the changing nature of getting from A to B has left collectors with a vast array of desirable memorabilia.

see p.244                see p.241                see p.343

- The first few decades of the century saw rigid-frame balloons taking us across the Atlantic as well as being used in wartime air raids. Items bearing the instantly recognisable shape of the Zeppelin are hotly sought after.

- While advertising posters, games and general memorabilia are more affordable, items from famous airships such as the fated "Hindenburg" fetch the highest prices. Aviation collectors also seek out items related to famous aviators and prices soar if they are directly related to their daring trips.

- Cruise liners had become a popular, and often luxurious, way to travel by the 1900s. Names from the golden age, such as "Olympic", "Mauretania" and "Normandie" dominate the market. Look for related items in the Art Deco style. More recent liners such as the "Queen Mary" and the "Queen Elizabeth II" generated more memorabilia which is usually more affordable.

- Partly due to the 1997 film, the market for items related to the "Titanic" tragedy of 1912 has boomed. Evocative images of the ship or, more rarely, items related to the survivors or from the ship itself regularly fetch newsworthy prices. Prices may continue to rise in the lead up to the centenary in 2012, but watch out for fakes.

- The romance of travel, in all its forms, is often best illustrated in period advertising posters. Railway posters in particular, with their bright British scenes of weekends away, have seen enormous rises in value in the past two decades. The visual appeal and period style of the artwork and popularity of the artist and railway count the most towards value.

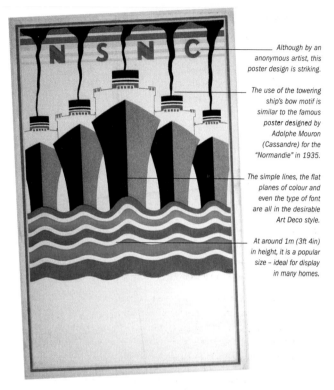

*Although by an anonymous artist, this poster design is striking.*

*The use of the towering ship's bow motif is similar to the famous poster designed by Adolphe Mouron (Cassandre) for the "Normandie" in 1935.*

*The simple lines, the flat planes of colour and even the type of font are all in the desirable Art Deco style.*

*At around 1m (3ft 4in) in height, it is a popular size – ideal for display in many homes.*

'NSNC' (Nelson Steam Navigation Company), stock poster showing a line-up of ships, signed "AW", mounted on linen.

*40.25in (102cm) high*

**£600-800**                                                     **SWA**

## TOP TIPS

- Look for striking artwork on advertising or posters, preferably with an image of the mode of transport dramatically or stylishly depicted.

- Pieces from the vessels themselves will often fetch higher prices than mass-produced memorabilia, but always check the provenance.

- Look for items depicting famous craft or vehicles, and particularly those that relate to famous events for which they were known.

- Motor-racing posters are still an emerging market. Notable marques, drivers or races at well-known tracks, as well as a good visual sense of speed, add value.

A Continental silver box commemorating the Hindenburg's first flight to North America on 14th June 1936, with applied enamelled plaque and Swastika and inscription reading "Zur Erinnerung an die erste Fahrt des Luftschiffes nach Nordamerika am 14.06.36", also stamped "EHW 850".

*4.75in (12cm) wide*

**£800-1,200** COB

A piece of outer fabric from the Graf Zeppelin, mounted on a descriptive card reading "Certified genuine piece of aluminized outer fabric of the Graf Zeppelin from a sheet presented to Clara Adams, the only woman passenger on the 1st flight to America, given to her by Dr. Hugo Eckener in October 1928".

*Fabric 0.5in wide (1.5cm) wide*

**£100-150** AGI

An aluminium girder recovered from the L-33 Zeppelin.

*This airship was damaged by anti-aircraft shelling and forced to land in Little Wigborough, Essex on 24th September 1916.*

*11in (28cm) long*

**£70-90** AGI

A Eugen Riemer airship sweet tin.

*c1905* *2.75in (7cm) wide*

**£250-300** DH

A Graf Zeppelin metal match book cover.

*c1905* *2.25in (5.5cm) wide*

**£100-150** DH

A German sweet bag, with an image of an airship.

*c1905* *9.25in (23.5cm) high*

**£8-12** DH

A 'Graf Zeppelin's Weltreise' board game, by Klee.

*c1928* *12in (30.5cm) wide*

**£200-250** DH

An American Zeppelin game.

*William Randolph Hearst promoted the first global flight of the Graf Zeppelin to raise public awareness and Lakehurst, New Jersey was the official starting point.*

*1929* *3.5in (9cm) wide*

**£30-40** DH

An airship air rifle pellet tin.

*c1920s* *3in (7.5cm) diam*

**£20-25** DH

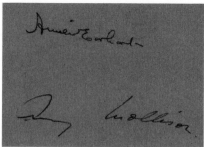

Amelia Earhart and Amy Johnson, an album page signed in blue ink, with Johnson signing her married name of "Amy Mollison", mounted, framed and glazed.

**£2,000-2,500** FA

Amy Johnson, an album page signed in black ink by Johnson, signing her married name "Amy Mollison".

*Amy Johnson was a British aviator who flew solo from England to Australia in 1930, to Japan in 1931 and Cape Town in 1932, setting new records in each case.*

**£200-300** FA

Chuck Yeager, signed lithograph.

*In 1947 Yeager flew faster than the speed of sound. In 1956 he took command of the Air Force Aerospace Research Pilots School, training pilots for the US space programme.*

10in (25.5cm) wide

**£300-350** AGI

A cast metal bust of Charles Lindbergh, marked with illegible artist's name.

6in (15cm) high

**£15-20** AGI

A cast bronze bust of Charles Lindbergh, with plaque reading "La Ville de Paris à Charles Lindbergh en commemoration de la Première Taversee de L'Atlantique en Avion".

1927

**£15-20** AGI

A copy of "Aviation Stories and Mechanics" July 1927, Vol. 1, No. 1, featuring Lindbergh's Trans-Atlantic flight, excellent overall condition.

**£15-20** AGI

An aluminium hood ornament in the form of 'The Spirit of St Louis', with attached radiator bracket.

*'The Spirit of St Louis' was the name of the plane that took Lindbergh on the first trans-Atlantic flight in 1927.*

c1927 11in (28cm) long

**£25-30** AGI

A brass petrol table lighter, in the form of a Spitfire.

1940-2 5.5in (14cm) high

**£50-60** COB

A German WWII V-2 rocket head igniter, consisting of a metal rod set into a threaded wooden base with a nail-like needle projecting from the base.

20in (51cm) long

**£250-350** AGI

Two postcards of the RMS Titanic, one pre-disaster by Reginald Silk of Portsmouth captioned "RMS Titanic on her maiden voyage, 10th April 1912", Silk 2 stern view, showing the vessels "Among the Icebergs" with caption detailing the event and further information on the back.

An RMS Titanic postcard, published by W. & T. Gaines, Leeds, posted 30th April 1912, part message reads "How distressing to read the account....", good condition, slight wear to corners.

*Along with original artefacts, any contemporary memorabilia related to the Titanic disaster is much sought after and usually fetches high prices. Whilst postcards and images of the luxury liner are not usually very valuable, if they specifically mention the Titanic, as this example sent 15 days after the ship sunk does, the value is much higher. Letters or postcards sent from the Titanic when it left Southampton or docked at Cherbourg and Queenstown, Ireland, are of even higher value.*

£350-400     DN | £700-800     W&W

A pair of postcards of the RMS Titanic, both captioned "White Star triple-screw steamer Titanic, 45,000 tons", one with subtitle "This & the sister ship Olympic 45,000 are the two largest vessels in the world", the other an identical view but issued after the disaster in the Spithead Series with subtitle "which sank on April 15th 1912, with 1635 people".

£120-180     DN

A large sepia photograph of the RMS Titanic, presumably leaving Southampton on her maiden (and only) voyage, April 1912, from an original negative.

*21.5in (54.5cm) wide*

£40-60     W&W

Harrison, Leslie, "A Titanic Myth - A Californian Incident", published by W Kimber & Co.

*Tells the story of the captain of the Californian, which was 19 miles away when the Titanic sunk and was blamed by many for the loss of 1,500 lives.*

*1992*     *9.5in (24cm) high*

£10-15     COB

An RMS Mauretania brochure.
*1955/6*

£20-30     COB

A pull-out deck plan of the RMS Mauretania.
*1939*     *10.25in (26cm) high*

£60-80     COB

An RMS Queen Mary souvenir cup and saucer, made by Aynsley, commemorating her maiden voyage on May 27th 1936.

*The RMS Queen Mary was launched in 1934 and passengers included celebrities and stars such as Greta Garbo and Clark Gable. During the war she carried over 80,000 troops and played a notable role in the Allied campaign. Now, she is moored in Long Beach, California as a hotel and tourist attraction.*

*Saucer 5.5in (14cm) diam*

**£100-150** COB

A hand-painted RMS Queen Mary commemorative water jug, by Suzanne Handcrafts.

*1936     4.5in (11.5cm) high*

**£30-40** COB

An RMS Queen Mary souvenir jigsaw puzzle.

*1936     Box 9.5in (24cm) wide*

**£30-40** COB

A Morning Post supplement from the RMS Queen Mary, dated May, 1936.

*16in (40.5cm) high*

**£20-30** COB

An RMS Queen Elizabeth dinner menu, for Sunday, October 20, 1968.

*This was used during the liner's last voyage.*

*10.5in (26.5cm) high*

**£12-18** COB

A BI Education Cruises 1983 brochure.

*11.5in (29cm) high*

**£6-7** COB

Two Canadian Pacific Steamships Limited luggage labels.

*6.5in (16.5cm) wide*

**£4-6 (EACH)** COB

A 1960s RMS Queen Elizabeth souvenir pencil.

*7in (18cm) long*

**£8-10** COB

A course book for the RMS Queen Elizabeth.

*1964     11.75in (30cm) wide*

**£30-50** COB

A Canberra souvenir key ring.

*2in (5cm) wide*

**£4-6** COB

A Canadian Pacific Triangle Route menu.

*1932*     *8.75in (22cm) high*

**£10-15**     COB

A blank radiogram form from the Cunard Steamship Co. Ltd.

*10.25in (26cm) high*

**£5-6**     COB

A Cunard West Indies Cruise in Mauretania pamphlet.

*1965*     *9in (23cm) high*

**£6-7**     COB

A 1960s French Line brochure for the mailsteamer 'Antilles'.

*11.75in (30cm) high*

**£40-60**     COB

A KMP Line sailing schedule for 1938.

*9.75in (25cm) high*

**£12-18**     COB

A 1930s fold-out deck plan for the Normandie.

*12.75in (32.5cm) high*

**£80-120**     COB

A double pack of 'Orient Line to Australia' patience cards, by John Waddington, London, in padded turquoise box.

*4in (10cm) wide*

**£12-18**     LG

A late 1950s/early 1960s Orient Line pennant for the SS Orsova.

*14.5in (37cm) wide*

**£10-15**     COB

A Deutsche Luftfahrt-Werbewoche 1932 five-colour lithograph poster, framed.

*1932     29in (48.5cm) long*

**£600-700**                        ATK

A Hamburg-Amerika Linie five-colour lithograph poster of the airship 127 Graf Zeppelin, showing the air route from Hamburg, Germany to Rio de Janeiro, South America in three days, framed.

*Due to their brief life as a reliable mode of mass transport, posters showing airships in this way are scarce. This example shows a very long distance route which seems incredible to us now.*

*1931*

**£1,500-2,000**                        ATK

A Soc. An. Aero Espresso Italiana lithograph poster, dated and signed "Keverta".

*1932     39.25in (99.5cm) long*

**£800-900**                        ATK

An Air France three-colour lithograph poster, depicting an airplane flying over the jungle in Africa, signed "Guena", printed in France, framed and dated.

*1946     39.25in (99.5cm) long*

**£800-1,200**                        ATK

A Lufthansa, Air France lithograph poster, showing the flight route Europe-South America, with an illustration of a Junker aircraft which goes around the world, with the German national emblem, showing all stopovers, framed.

*1935     26.25in (66.5cm) long*

**£1,000-1,500**                        ATK

A British European Airways 'Meet the Spring - fly BEA' lithograph poster, with expressionistic depiction of an elegant lady on the runway signed, framed.

*1948     41.25in (105cm) long*

**£500-600**                        ATK

A Frederiksberg poster.

*Frederiksberg is a popular beach in Denmark.*

1938

**£300-400**                    DO

A North Eastern Railways 'The Yorkshire Coast' quad royal poster, from the 'Alice in Holidayland' advertising campaign, designed by Frank Mason.

c1910                    50in (127cm) wide

**£8,000-10,000**                    REN

A London & North Eastern Railways double royal woodcut-style 'Batchworth Heath' poster, unnamed artist.

c1924                    40in (101.5cm) high

**£1,000-1,500**                    REN

A London & North Eastern Railways double royal woodcut-style 'Batchworth Heath' poster, unnamed artist.

c1924        40in (101.5cm) high

**£1,000-1,500**                    REN

A Great Western Railways 'Stratford Upon Avon' quad royal poster, from the series "This England of Ours", designed by Michael Reilly.

c1930        50in (127cm) wide

**£3,500-4,500**                    REN

A Shell 'Mousehole, Penzance' poster from the "To Visit Britain's Landmarks" series, originally displayed on Shell lorries, designed by A. Stuart-Hill.

c1932                    45in (114.5cm) wide

**£4,000-6,000**                    REN

A 1950s Goodward International Programme poster, for Saturday., 25th September 2p.m.

*30in (76cm) high*

£350-400     SAS

A 1950s 26th R.A.C. Tourist Trophy Race at Goodwood poster, Saturday, 19th August 12 Noon, illustration by MT, three very minor tears.

*30in (76.5cm) high*

£350-400     SAS

An International Nine-Hour Car Race at Goodwood poster, 20th August, 3 p.m. until Midnight, night-time illustration by Roy Nockolds.

*30in (76cm) high*

£450-500     SAS

An R.A.C. European Grand Prix at Brands Hatch poster, July 11th 11a.m., illustration by B.K. Bull, two small tears.

*30in (76.5cm) high*

£150-200     SAS

A Daily Mail Race of Champions at Brands Hatch poster, Saturday, 13th March 1965 1.30pm.

1965     *30in (76cm) high*

£35-45     SAS

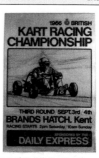

A 1966 British Kart Racing Championship at Brands Hatch poster.

1966     *30in (76cm) high*

£35-45     SAS

A mid-1950s Crystal Palace Motor Racing poster, Bank Holiday Monday 6th August 2pm, illustration by Raymond Groves, one very minor paper tear.

*29.75in (75.5cm) high*

£330-380     SAS

A 1950s Crystal Palace Motor Racing poster, Whit Monday 2 p.m., illustration by Raymond Groves, small tear to lower right corner.

*30in (76cm) high*

£300-350     SAS

# TECHNOLOGY

At no other time has technology evolved so swiftly and become as important to us as it did during the 20th century. This means that what was yesterday's latest technological achievement is, or could be, tomorrow's collectable.

see p.349    see p.353    see p.355

- 20th-century cameras are collectable and often valuable. The focus of this market is on quality and rarity, with notable names such as Franke & Heidecke, Minox, Voigtlander and Zeiss playing a large part.

- Leica cameras, commercially available from 1925, are hotly collected across the world. Condition and an early date are key, and models with unusual engravings or made for specialist functions can be yet more valuable. Even lenses and accessories can have individual values if scarce.

- The radio's golden age was from the 1920s until the 1950s, when valves were used. The brighter the colour and the more typical the styling is of the period, the more value it is likely to have. Look for hot names such as Britain's EKCO, and its Art Deco style radios, Philco, and FADA and Emerson from the US.

- Domestic television sets date from 1936 onwards. Sets from the late 1930s and 40s are rare, so consider those from the 1950s to the 70s. Significant examples will be formed in styles and materials typical of the period, the best having become design classics.

- The same applies to standard telephones, so look for landmark models, often made in Bakelite and especially in bright colours. Novelty or unusual forms are also collectable.

- Look for large early mobile phones from the 1980s and early 90s, those that were the first to use certain technologies, such as digital networks, or those that captured the public imagination. Larger brand names, such as Nokia, may become the focus for collectors.

## A CLOSER LOOK AT A CATALIN RADIO

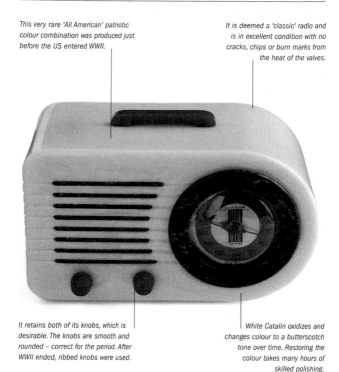

*This very rare 'All American' patriotic colour combination was produced just before the US entered WWII.*

*It is deemed a 'classic' radio and is in excellent condition with no cracks, chips or burn marks from the heat of the valves.*

*It retains both of its knobs, which is desirable. The knobs are smooth and rounded – correct for the period. After WWII ended, ribbed knobs were used.*

*White Catalin oxidizes and changes colour to a butterscotch tone over time. Restoring the colour takes many hours of skilled polishing.*

An American Fada Streamliner Model 189 'Bullet' radio in white, blue and red Catalin, with smooth knobs.

*1941*                                              10.25in (26cm) wide

**£2,000-2,500**                                              CAT

### TOP TIPS

- Never plug an electrical collectable into the mains without seeking the advice of a qualified electrician first.

- Transistor radios are becoming a hot collectable – as with older radios, look for distinctive styling. Damage to the case will reduce value.

- Sinclair products have grown in popularity over the past few years, and may continue to rise.

- The vintage mobile phone market is still developing, with fluctuating prices. Always buy in excellent condition to take advantage of any future price rises.

A Sinclair Cambridge calculator.

*This was Sinclair's second calculator.*

*c1973*

**£50-70** HLJ

A Sinclair Cambridge Memory calculator.

*c1974*

**£40-60** HLJ

A gold-plated Sinclair Sovereign calculator.

*c1977*    5.5in (14cm) long

**£120-180** HLJ

A stainless steel Sinclair Sovereign calculator, matt finish.

*c1977*    5.5in (14cm) long

**£100-150** HLJ

A Sinclair Enterprise Programmable calculator.

*c1979*

**£40-60** HLJ

A Curta calculator type 1.

*c1948*

**£450-500** ATK

A Mark 8 miniature computer, by Jonathan A. Titus, an un-assembled kit-built computer comprising six Mark 8 circuit boards, an Intel 8008 chip, two Signetics 8267 chips, two Signetics 8263 chips, and eight National semiconductor 1101 memory chips.

*The Mark 8 preceded the Altair 8800 personal computer by six months as the 'world's first' personal home computer. Only the PC boards and plans were supplied by Titus, the rest had to be bought and assembled by the owner. The '8008' was Intel's first 8-bit processor, with a staggering 5mhz speed!*

*c1974*

**£450-550** ATK

A Leica IIIa, with Summar 2/50mm lens, rewind knob damaged, with case.
*1939*

**£250-350** **ATK**

A Leica IIIb, with collapsible Summitar 2/5 cm lens, with "Leica" engraved in red, shutter needs help, with case.
*1948*

**£300-400** **ATK**

A Leica IIIa, with Elmar lens, flange "0" standardized.
*1939*

**£220-280** **ATK**

A Leica IIIf, factory converted from a 3C.
*c1948*

**£300-350** **COLC**

A Leica IIIc, with Summaron 3.5/3.5 cm lens.
*1949*

**£350-450** **ATK**

A Leica CL, with Summicron-C 2/40, lens hood, cap and maker's case.
*1973-74*

**£320-380** **ATK**

A Leica M2, with Summilux 1.4/50 lens, with self timer, protection film and lens cap.
*1960*

**£600-700** **ATK**

A Leica M3 body, single wind, with body cap.
*1957*

**£320-380** **ATK**

A black Leica M3 body, speed dial, accessory shoe and base plate probably restored, with body cap.
*1961*

**£1,200-1,500** **ATK**

A Leica M4, with Summaron 3.5/3.5 lens, filter and lens cap.
*1970-71*

**£650-750** **ATK**

A black Leica M6 body, as new, boxed.
*1996*

**£800-1,000** **ATK**

A Kodak Flash Brownie, with Bakelite body.

c1946

£12-15       COLC

A silver and cream 'Jersey' Kodak Brownie, with Bakelite body.

*This model was launched as a prototype in Jersey in black and in this rare cream version. It was not a popular camera and was not available for general release.*

c1955

£100-200       COLC

A Kodak Brownie Bullseye, with Bakelite body, made in the USA.

1958

£10-15       COLC

A Kodak Pony II.

c1959

£5-10       COLC

A Kodak Retinette 1B.

c1963

£12-15       COLC

A Kodak Disc 4000, near mint and boxed.

*The fashion for disc format cameras first hit manufacturers during the mid 1980s, spurred on by this model, Kodak's first. It was not successful and the format did not last. This was also the first mass produced camera with an aspheric lens.*

c1985

£15-25       COLC

A Russian Leitz Leningrad 35mm camera, with spring-motor drive, with Leica mount.

c1960

£70-110       OACC

A Mec 16 SB camera.

*This was the first camera with through the lens light metering (TTL), despite Pentax advertising that they were first.*

c1960

£60-80       COLC

A 1930s Zeiss Ikarette 120 camera, with adjustable 10.5cm f4.5 Tessar lens.

**£55-65** COLC

A Baby Ikonta 'Ikomat', with rare 3.5 Tessar lens.

*This camera usually comes with a Novar lens.*

*c1935*

**£160-200** COLC

A 1930s Zeiss Adoro teak, nickel-plate and leather tropical camera.

**£400-500** COLC

A Zeiss Ikon Contax II a, with Zeiss-Opton Sonnar 1.5/50 lens, lens a bit stained.

*1952*

**£150-200** ATK

An early Zeiss Ikon Contax III, with Sonnar 2/5cm lens, light meter does not work.

*1936*

**£150-200** ATK

A Zeiss Contaflex 35mm camera, with twin lens relex.

*This was the first camera with a built-in light meter. If the shutter does not function or the meter is inoperative, the value will be lower.*

*c1936*

**£700-1,000** COLC

A 1950s Ikonta 521, with Novar lens.

**£25-35** COLC

A Zeiss Ikon Contarex I, with Planar 2/50 lens, lens hood and case.

*1960-1967*

**£250-300** ATK

A Zorki 35mm camera, made in the USSR.

*c1974*

**£35-40** COLC

A black Bakelite EKCO RS2 radio.

*Visually, this is the same radio as the M23 released in 1932 and also designed by J.K. White, but a fire destroyed the tooling for the RS2 in late 1931, so a new model was rapidly designed and built with a slightly different speaker configuration. The RS2 is much rarer than the M23.*

1931    15.25in (39cm) high

**£300-400**                                    LC

An EKCO model AC85 black Bakelite wireless.

*This Art Deco styled set was designed by Wells Coates, who also designed the round EKCO radio sets.*

c1934                23in (58.5cm) wide

**£100-150**                                    LC

A black Philco Type 333 'People's Set' radio, battery powered, lacks back.

c1936

**£60-80**                                       LC

A Ferranti-type 145 wireless, AC mains.

c1945        19.5in (50cm) high

**£40-60**                                       LC

A brown Bakelite EKCO Type A22 radio.

c1945                14.5in (37cm) high

**£400-600**                                     ATK

A Kolster Brandes FB10 AC mains receiver.

*This radio is affectionately called the 'Toaster' by collectors and was available in a range of solid and sprayed colours.*

c1955

**£20-30**                                       LC

Three National Panasonic 'Toot-a-Loop' wrist radios, in red, yellow and green plastic hinged cases.

1970        6in (15cm) long

**£50-70 (EACH)**                L&T

An early 1970s radio, by Isis, Hong Kong.

9.75in (25cm) wide

**£35-45**                                       MA

A Weltron eight-track radio and stereo player, contained within swivelling white ovoid plastic case with carrying handle on pedestal base and two attendant Weltron 2004 white spherical speakers.

1968

**£200-300**                                     L&T

A 1930s black Bakelite 200 series telephone.

*These telephones are currently being reproduced in the Far East. One way to tell whether an example is genuine is to run your finger over the numbers on the handset bar. If they are not crisp, it is usually a re-moulded reproduction.*

8in (20cm) wide

£180-220     L

A 1950s black Bakelite 300 series telephone, with original lead.

6in (15cm) wide

£120-180     L

A 1960s red plastic telephone, by the Reliance Telephone Co.

5in (12.5cm) wide

£40-60     L

A 1960s red plastic telephone, by the Reliance Telephone Co.

5in (12.5cm) wide

£45-55     L

A rare 1970s orange plastic Trimphone.

8in (20cm) long

£80-100     L

A wooden Trub telephone, by Gfeller, designed in the 1970s.

c1994    8.25in (21cm) wide

£70-90     L

A 1970s cream plastic Ericofon telephone, by Ericsson.

*The Ericofon was designed in the late 1940s and went into production in 1954. The stylish one-piece design, with the dial in its base, was launched for domestic use in 1956. It came in a multitude of colours. It was discontinued in 1972. Collectors should be aware that modern copies are now on sale.*

8.25in (21cm) high

£70-100     L

A 1980s red plastic 'Hot Lips' telephone.

8.5in (21.5cm) wide

£35-45     L

A Sony CM-DX1000 GSM mobile phone, with sliding earpiece and extending aerial.

*This was also known colloquially as the 'Mars Bar' phone, due to its similarity in shape to the Mars Bar.*

c1995    7in (17.5cm) high

**£60-90**                    GC

A Swedish Ericsson EH97 Hotline ETACS mobile phone, with flip up aerial.

*This phone was a direct copy of the popular English Orbitel and was Ericsson's first handheld portable phone.*

1992-93    7in (17.5cm) long

**£15-25**                    GC

A black Motorola 8500X ETACS phone.

*This phone cost between £250 and £350 when released in the late 1980s.*

c1987    7.75in (19.5cm) high

**£60-90**                    GC

A grey Motorola 'Personal Phone' ETACS mobile phone.

*This phone cost £249 when released and is unusual in that it has no LCD or digital display.*

c1992    6.25in (16cm) long

**£25-35**                    GC

A black Motorola MR1 PCM mobile phone, with flip cover and extending aerial.

c1994    6in (15.5cm) high

**£25-35**                    GC

A grey Motorola MicroTac Duo ETACS mobile phone, with flip and extending aerial.

c1992    6.5in (16.5cm) long

**£20-30**                    GC

A Motorola 8800X ETACS mobile phone, with Motorola fitted leather case with sleeve for spare battery.

1990-91                    8in (20cm) high

**£70-100**                    GC

An American Philco Projection set 48-2500.

*1948*

**£600-1,000** TVH

A British Baird 'Everyman' tabletop television.

*The front of this television has an applied medallion showing a portrait of John Logie Baird, who died in 1946.*

*c1949* 12in (30.5cm) high

**£200-300** TVH

A British Pye LV306 television.

*c1950*

**£150-250** TVH

A British Pye VT2 television.

*c1951*

**£120-150** TVH

A Bush TV62 table television set.

*c1956*

**£80-120** LC

An American Philco Preduta television.

*c1959*

**£300-500** TVH

An American RCA 'Personal' 8-PT-7030 television, with telescopic aerials.

*c1956*

**£80-120** TVH

A 1970s National Commando 505 portable television.

12in (30.5cm) high

**£45-55** L

A Keracolour, model B722 television.

*This model with a 'teak' appearance finish is extremely scarce.*

*c1970* 33.75in (86cm) high

**£500-600** L&T

A 1970s JVC 'Videosphere' television set.

*This set was also known as the 'Sputnik' set after the Russian satellites launched in 1957.*

12.5in (32cm) high

**£250-300** L&T

# KEY TO ILLUSTRATIONS

Every collectable illustrated in the BBC *20th Century Roadshow Collectables Price Guide* by Judith Miller has a letter code that identifies the dealer or auction house that sold it. The list below is a key to these codes. In the list, auction houses are shown by the letter A and dealers by the letter D. Some items came from a private collection, in which case the code in the list is accompanied by the letter P. Inclusion in this book no way constitutes or implies a contract or binding offer on the part of any of our contributors to supply or sell the goods illustrated, or similar items, at the prices stated.

**AAC (A)**
**Sanford Alderfer Auction Company**
501 Fairgrounds Road,
Hatfield PA 19440
USA
Tel: 001 215 393 3000
Fax: 001 215 368 9055
www.alderferauction.com

**AAG (D)**
**Animation Art Gallery**
13-14 Great Castle Street,
London W1W 8LS
Tel: 020 7255 1456
Fax: 020 7436 1256
www.animaart.com

**AGI (A)**
**Aurora Galleries International**
30 Hackamore Lane, Suite 2,
Bell Canyon, CA 91307
USA
Tel: 001 818 884 6468
Fax: 001 818 227 2941
www.auroragalleriesonline.com

**AOY (D)**
**All Our Yesterdays**
6 Park Road, Kelvinbridge,
Glasgow G4 9JG
Tel: 0141 334 7788
Fax: 0141 339 8994
antiques@allouryesterdays.
fsnet.co.uk

**AS&SA (A)**
**Andrew Smith & Son**
The Auction Rooms,
Manor Farm, Itchen Stoke,
Winchester, Hampshire
Tel: 01962 735988
Fax: 01962 738879
auctions@andrewsmith
andson.fsbusiness.co.uk

**ATA (D)**
**Atomic Age**
318 E Virginia Road,
Fullerton, CA 92831 USA
Tel: 001 714 446 0736
Fax: 001 714 446 0436
atomage100@aol.com

**ATK (A)**
**Auction Team Koln**
Postfach 50 11 19, Bonner
Str. 528-530 50971 Koln,
Germany
Tel: +49 (0) 221 38 70 49
Fax: +49 (0) 221 37 48 78
www.breker.com

**ATM (D)**
**At the Movies**
17 Fouberts Place, London
W1F 7QD
Tel: 07770 777 411
Fax: 020 7439 6355
www.atthemovies.co.uk

**B&H (A)**
**Burstow & Hewett**
Lower lake, Battle,
East Sussex TN33 0AT
Tel: 01424 772 374
Fax: 01424 772 302
www.burstowandhewett.co.uk

**BA (D)**
**Branksome Antiques**
370 Poole Road, Branksome,
Poole, Dorset BH1 1AW
Tel: 01202 763 324
Fax: 01202 763 643

**BAD (D)**
**Beth Adams**
Unit G043/044, Alfie's
Antiques Market, 13-25
Church Street, London
NW8 8DT
Tel: 0207 723 5613
Fax: 0207 262 1576
www.alfiesantiques.com

**BAR (A)**
**Dreweatt Neate (Bristol)**
St John's Place, Apsley Road,
Clifton, Bristol BS8 2ST
Tel: 0117 973 7201
Fax: 0117 953 5671
www.dnfa.com

**BEJ (D)**
**Bébés & Jouets**
c/o Post Office,
165 Restalris Road,
Edinburgh EH7 6HW
Tel: 0131 332 5650
bebesetjouets@u.genie.co.uk

**BEV (D)**
**Beverley**
30 Church Street,
London NW8 8EP
Tel: 020 7262 1576

**BIB (D)**
**Biblion**
1/7 Davies Mews,
London W1K 5AB
Tel: 020 7629 1374
Fax: 020 7493 7158
www.biblion.com

**BLO (A)**
**Bloomsbury Auctions**
24 Maddox Street,
London W1S 1PP
Tel: 020 7495 9494
Fax: 020 7495 9499
www.bloomsburyauctions.com

**BONC (A)**
**Bonhams**
101 New Bond Street,
London W1S 1SR
Tel: 020 7393 3900
Fax: 020 7393 3905
www.bonhams.com

**BONS (A)**
**Bonhams**
101 New Bond Street,
London W1S 1SR
Tel: 020 7393 3900
Fax: 020 7393 3905
www.bonhams.com

**BRB (D)**
**Bauman Rare Books**
4535 Madison Ave, between
54th & 55th Streets, New
York, NY 100022 USA
Tel: 001 212 751 0011
www.baumanrarebooks.com

**BY (D)**
**Bonny Yankauer**
bonnyy@aol.com

**CA (A)**
**Chiswick Auctions**
1-5 Colville Road,
London W3 8BL
Tel: 020 8992 4442
Fax: 020 8892 0541

**CAT (D)**
**Catalin Radio**
5443 Schultz Drive, Sylvania,
OH 43560 USA
Tel: 001 419 824 2469
Mob: 001 419 283 8203
www.catalinradio.com

**CCL (D)**
**Cloud Cuckoo Land**
6 Charlton Place, Camden
Passage, London, N1
Tel: 020 7354 3141

**Chef (A)**
**Cheffins**
The Cambridge Saleroom,
2 Clifton Road, Cambridge
CB1 4BW
Tel: 01223 213 343
Fax: 01223 413 396
www.cheffins.co.uk

**CLV (A)**
**Clevedon Salerooms**
The Auction Centre, Kenn
Road, Clevedon, Bristol
BS21 6TT
Tel: 01934 830 111
Fax: 01934 832 538
www.clevedon-salerooms.com

**CO (A)**
**Cooper Owen**
2nd Floor, 21 Denmark
Street, London WC2H 8NP
Tel: 020 7240 4132
Fax: 020 7240 4339
www.cooperowen.com

**COB (D)**
**Cobwebs**
78 Old Northam Road,
Southampton SO14 OPB
Tel: 02380 227 458
www.cobwebs.uk.com

**ColC (D)**
**Collectors Cameras**
PO Box 16, Pinner, Middlesex
HA5 4HN
Tel: 020 8421 3537

**CR (A)**
**Craftsman Auctions**
333 North Main Street,
Lambertville, NJ 08530 USA
Tel: 001 609 397 9374
Fax: 001 609 397 9377
www.ragoarts.com

**CRIS (D)**
**Cristobal**
26 Church Street, London NW8
Tel/Fax: 020 7724 7230
www.cristobal.co.uk

**CVS (D)**
**Cad Van Swankster at
The Girl Can't Help It**
Alfies Antique Market, Shop
G115, 13-25 Church Street,
London NW8 8DT
Tel: 020 7723 0564
Fax: 020 8809 3923
www.alfiesantiques.com

**CW (P)**
**Christine Wildman
Collection**
wild123@allstream.net

**D (A)**
**Dickens Auctioneers**
The Claydon Saleroom,
Claydon House Park,
Calvert Road, Middle
Claydon, Bucks MK18 2EZ
Tel: 01296 714434
Fax: 01296 714492
www.dickens-auctioneers.com

**DAC (D)**
**Dynamite Antiques &
Collectibles**
Maryland, USA
eb625@verizon.net

**DAW (A)**
**Dawson's Appraisers &
Auctioneers**
(Now trading as Dawson & Nye)
128 American Road, Morris
Plains, NJ 07950 USA
Tel: 001 973 984 6900
Fax: 001 973 984 6956
www.dawsonandnye.com

**DCC (P)**
**Dee Carlton Collection**
qnoscots@aol.com

**DE (D)**
**The Doll Express**
No longer trading

**DETC (D)**
**Deco Etc**
122 West 25th Street,
(between 6th & 7th Aves.),
New York,
NY 10010 USA
Tel: 001 212 675 3326
www.decoetc.net

**DH (D)**
**Huxtins**
11 & 12 The Lipka Arcade,
288 Westbourne Grove,
London W11
Mob: 07710 132 200
www.huxtins.com

**DN (A)**
**Dreweatt Neate**
Donnington Priory
Salerooms, Donnington,
Newbury, Berkshire
RG14 2JE
Tel: 01635 553 553
Fax: 01635 553 599
www.dnfa.com

**DO (D)**
**DODO**
Alfies Antique Market,
1st floor (F073, 83 & 84),
13-25 Church Street,
Marylebone, London NW8 8DT
Tel: 020 7706 1545
dodoposters@yahoo.com

**DRA (A)**
**Rago Modern Auctions**
333 North Main Street,
Lambertville, NJ 08530 USA
Tel: 001 609 397 9374
Fax: 001 609 397 9377
www.ragoarts.com

**F (A)**
**Fellow's & Sons**
Augusta House,
19 Augusta Street, Hockley,
Birmingham B18 6JA
Tel: 0121 212 2131
Fax: 0121 212 1249
www.fellows.co.uk

**FA (A)**
**Fraser's Autographs**
399 The Strand, London
WC2R OLX
Tel: 020 7836 9325
www.frasersautographs.com

**FFM (D)**
**Festival**
136 South Ealing Road,
London W5 4QJ
Tel: 020 8840 9333
info@festival1951.co.uk

**FJA (D)**
**Feljoy Antiques**
Shop 3, Angel Arcade,
Camden Passage,
London N1 8EA
Tel: 020 7354 5336
Fax: 020 7831 3485
www.chintznet.com/feljoy

**FM (D)**
**Francesca Martire**
Stand F131-137,
First Floor, Alfie's Antiques
Market, 13-25 Church Street,
London NW8 0RH
Tel: 020 7724 4802
www.alfiesantiques.com

**FRA (D)**
**France Antique Toys**
Tel: 001 631 754 1399

**FRE (A)**
**Freeman's**
1808 Chestnut Street,
Philadelphia, PA 19103 USA
Tel: 001 215 563 9275
Fax: 001 215 563 8236
www.freemansauction.com

**G (A)**
**Guernsey's Auctions**
108 East 73rd Street,
New York, NY 10021 USA
Tel: 001 212 794 2280
Fax: 001 212 744 3638
www.guernseys.com

**GA (D)**
**Gentry Antiques**
c/o Rod & Line Shop,
Little Green, Polperro,
Cornwall PL132RF
Tel: 07974 221 343
www.cornishwarecollector.co.uk

**GC (P)**
**Graham Cooley Collection**
graham.cooley@metalysis.com

**GCA (D)**
**Griffin & Cooper Antiques**
South Street Antiques
Center, 615 South 6th
Street, Philadelphia,
PA 19147, USA
Tel: 001 215 582 0418/3594

**GGRT (D)**
**Gary Grant**
18 Arlington Way, London,
EC1R 1UY
Tel: 020 7713 1122

**GORB (A)**
**Gorringes**
Terminus Road,
Bexhill-on-Sea, East Sussex
TN39 3LR
Tel: 01424 212 994
Fax: 01424 224 035
www.gorringes.co.uk

**GORL (A)**
**Gorringes**
15 North Street, Lewes,
East Sussex BN72PD
Tel: 01273 472 503
Fax: 01273 479 559
www.gorringes.co.uk

**GS (D)**
**Goodwins Antiques Ltd**
15 & 16 Queensferry Street,
Edinburgh EH2 4QW
Tel: 0131 225 4717
Fax: 0131 220 1412

**H&G (D)**
**Hope and Glory**
131A Kensington Church
Street, London W8 7LP
Tel: 020 7727 8424

**HA (A)**
**Hunt Auctions**
75 E. Uwchlan Ave, Suite
130, Exton, PA 19341 USA
Tel: 001 610 524 0822
Fax: 001 610 524 0826
www.huntsauctions.com

**HC (A)**
**Heritage Comics**
Heritage Plaza, 100 Highland
Park Village, 2nd Floor,
Dallas, TX 75205-2788 USA
Tel: 001 800 872 6467
Fax: 001 214 520 6968
www.heritagecomics.com

**HERR (A)**
**W.G. Herr Art & Auction
House**
Friesenwall 35, D-50672
Cologne, Germany
Tel: +49 (0) 221 25 45 48
Fax: +49 (0) 221 270 67 42
www.herr-auktionen.de

**HGS (D)**
**Harper General Store**
10482 Jonestown Rd,
Annville, PA 17003 USA
Tel: 001 717 865 3456
Fax: 001 717 865 3813
www.harpergeneralstore.com

**HLJ (D)**
**Hugo Lee-Jones**
Mob: 07941 187207
electroniccollectables@
hotmail.com

**J&H (A)**
**Jacobs and Hunt Fine Art
Auctioneers**
26 Lavant Street, Petersfield,
Hampshire GU323EF
Tel: 01730 233 933
Fax: 01730 262 323
www.jacobsandhunt.co.uk

**JBC (P)**
**James Bridges Collection**
james@jdbridges.fsnet.co.uk

**JDJ (A)**
**James D. Julia Inc**
P.O. Box 830, Fairfield, Maine
04937 USA
Tel: 001 207 453 7125
Fax: 001 207 453 2502
www.juliaauctions.com

**JH (D)**
**Jeanette Hayhurst Fine Glass**
32a Kensington Church Street,
London W8 4HA
Tel: 020 7938 1539

**KF (D)**
**Karl Flaherty Collectables**
Tel: 02476 445 627
kfckarl@aol.com

**L (D)**
**Luna**
323 George Street,
Nottingham NG1 3BH
Tel: 0115 924 3267
www.luna-online.co.uk

**L&T (A)**
**Lyon and Turnbull Ltd.**
33 Broughton Place,
Edinburgh EH1 3RR
Tel: 0131 557 8844
Fax: 0131 557 8668
www.lyonandturnbull.com

**LC (A)**
**Lawrence's Fine Art
Auctioneers**
The Linen Yard, South Street,
Crewkerne,
Somerset TA18 8AB
Tel: 01460 73041
Fax: 01460 74627
www.lawrences.co.uk

**LFA (A)**
**Law Fine Art Ltd.**
Firs Cottage, Church Lane,
Brimpton, Berkshire RG74TJ
Tel: 0118 971 0353
Fax: 0118 971 3741
www.lawfineart.co.uk

**LG (D)**
**Legacy** (no longer trading)

**LH (D)**
**Lucy's Hats**
South Street Antiques Center,
615 South 6th Street,
Philadelphia, PA 19147, USA
Tel: 001 215 592 0256
shak06@aol.com

**MA (D)**
**Manic Attic**
Stand S011, Alfies Antiques
Market, 13 Church Street,
London NW8 8DT
Tel: 020 7723 6105
Fax: 020 7724 0999
www.alfiesantiques.com

**MAC (D)**
**Mary Ann's Collectibles**
South Street Antiques
Center, 615 South 6th
Street, Philadelphia,
PA 19147, USA
Tel: 001 215 592 0256
Tel: 001 215 923 3247

**MB (D)**
**Mostly Boxes**
93 High Street, Eton,
Windsor, Berkshire SL4 6AF
Tel: 01753 858 470
Fax: 01753 857 212

**MCOL (P)**
**Mick Collins Collection**
admin@sylvacclub.com

**MEN (D)**
**Mendes Antique Lace
and Textiles**
Tel: 01273 203 317
Mob: 07813 014 065
www.mendes.co.uk

**MHC (P)**
**Mark Hill Collection**
Mob: 07798 915 474
stylophile@hotmail.com

**MHT (D)**
**Mum Had That**
www.mumhadthat.com

**ML (D)**
**Mark Laino**
South Street Antiques
Center, 615 South 6th
Street,
Philadelphia, PA 19147, USA
Tel: 001 215 592 0256

**MM (A)**
**Mullock Madeley**
The Old Shippon, Wall-under-
Heywood, Church Stretton,
Shropshire SY6 7DS
Tel: 01694 771 771
Fax: 01694 771 772
www.mullock-madeley.co.uk

**MSC (P)**
**Mark Slavinsky Collection**

**NB (A)**
**Noel Barrett Antiques &
Auctions Ltd**
P.O. Box 300, Carversville, PA
18913 USA
Tel: 001 215 297 5109
www.noelbarrett.com

**NOR (D)**
**Neet-O-Rama**
93 West Main Street,
Somerville, NJ 08876 USA
Tel: 001 908 722 4600
www.neetstuff.com

**NWC (P)**
**Nigel Wright Collection**
xab@dircon.co.uk

**OACC (D)**
**Otford Antiques and
Collectors Centre**
26-28 High Street, Otford,
Kent TN14 5PQ
Tel: 01959 522 025
Fax: 01959 525 858
www.otfordantiques.co.uk

**P (D)**
**Posteritati**
239 Center Street, New York,
NY 10013 USA
Tel: 001 212 226 2207
Fax: 001 212 226 2102
www.posteritati.com

**PB (D)**
**Petersham Books**
Unit 67, 56 Gloucester Rd,
Kensington, London SW74UB
Tel/Fax: 020 7221 4035
www.modernfirsts.co.uk

**PC (P)**
**Private Collection**

**PSA (A)**
**Potteries Specialist
Auctions**
271 Waterloo Road,
Cobridge, Stoke-on-Trent,
Staffordshire ST6 3HR
Tel: 01782 286 622
Fax: 01782 213 777
www.potteriesauctions.com

**QU (A)**
**Quittenbaum**
Hohenstaufenstraße 1,
D-80801, München, Germany
Tel: +49 (0) 89 33 00 75 6
Fax: +49 (0) 89 33 00 75 77
www.quittenbaum.de

**RBL (D)**
**Richard Ball Lighters**
richard@lighter.co.uk

**REN (D)**
**Rennies**
13 Rugby Street,
London WC1 3QT
Tel: 020 7405 0220
www.rennart.com

**RG (D)**
**Richard Gibbon**
34/34a Islington Green,
London N1 8DU
Tel: 020 7354 2852
neljeweluk@aol.com

**RH (D)**
**Rick Hubbard Art Deco**
3 Tee Court, Bell Street,
Romsey, Hampshire
SO51 8GY
Tel/Fax: 01794 513 133
www.rickhubbard-artdeco.co.uk

**ROX (D)**
**Roxanne Stuart**
Tel: 001 888 750 8869
gemfairy@aol.com

**S&T (D)**
**Steinberg and Tolkien**
193 King's Road, Chelsea,
London SW3 5ED
Tel: 020 7376 3660
Fax: 020 7376 3630

**SAS (A)**
**Special Auction Services**
Kennetholme, Midgham,
Nr Reading,
Berkshire RG7 5UX
Tel: 01189 712 949
Fax: 01189 712 420
commemorative@aol.com
www.invaluable.com/sas

**SCG (D)**
**Gallery 1930 – Susie**
**Cooper Gallery**
18 Church Street, London
NW8 8EP
Tel: 020 7723 1555
Fax: 020 7735 8309
gallery1930@aol.com
www.susiecooperceramics.com

**SM (D)**
**Sparkle Moore at The Girl**
**Can't Help It**
Alfies Antique Market, Shop
G100 & G116, Ground Floor,
13-25 Church Street,
London NW8 8DT
Tel: 020 7724 8984
Mob: 07958 515 614
www.sparklemoore.com

**SOTT (D)**
**Sign of the Tymes**
2 Morris Farm Rd, Lafayette,
NJ 07848 USA
Tel: 001 973 383 6028
jhap@nac.net
www.millantiques.com

**SSP (D)**
**Sylvie Spectrum**
Stand 372, Gray's Antiques
Market, 58 Davies Street,
London W1Y 2LB
Tel: 020 7629 3501
Fax: 020 8883 5030
www.graysantiques.com

**SWA (A)**
**Swann Galleries Image**
**Library**
104 East 25th Street,
New York, NY10010 USA
Tel: 001 212 254 4710
Fax: 001 212 979 1017
www.swanngalleries.com

**TAB (D)**
**Take-A-Boo Emporium**
1927 Avenue Road, Toronto,
Ontario M5M 4A2 Canada
Tel/Fax: 001 416 785 4555
www.takeaboo.com

**TAG (D)**
**Tagore Ltd**
c/o The Silver Fund, 1 Duke of
York Street, London SW1Y 6JP
Tel: 07989 953 452

**TGM (D)**
**The Glass Merchant**
Tel: 07775 683 961
as@titan98.freeserve.co.uk

**TH (D)**
**Toy Heroes**
42 Westway, Caterham-on-
the Hill, Surrey CR3 5TP
Tel: 01883 348 001
www.toyheroes.co.uk

**TP (D)**
**Tenth Planet Ltd**
Unit 36, Vicarage Field,
Shopping Centre, Ripple
Road, Barking,
Essex IG11 8DQ
Tel: 020 8591 5357
Fax: 020 8591 3035
www.tenthplanet.co.uk

**TR (D)**
**Terry Rodgers & Melody LLC**
30 & 31 Manhattan Art and
Antiques Center, 1050 2nd
Avenue, New York, NY 10022
Tel: 001 212 758 3164
Fax: 001 212 935 6365
melodyjewelry@aol.com

**TRA (D)**
**Toy Road Antiques**
2200 Highland Street, Canal
Winchester, OH 43110 USA
Tel: 001 614 834 1786
toyroad@aol.com

**TVH (D)**
**tvhistory.tv**
www.tvhistory.tv

**V (D)**
**Ventisemo**
4 Unit S001, Alfies Antique
Market, 13-25 Church Street,
London NW8 8DT
Mob: 07767 498 766
www.alfiesantiques.com

**VEC (D)**
**Vectis Auctions Limited**
Fleck Way, Thornaby, Stockton
on Tees TS179JZ
Tel: 01642 750 616
Fax: 01642 769 478
www.vectis.co.uk

**W&W (A)**
**Wallis and Wallis**
West Street Auction Galleries,
Lewes, East Sussex BN7 2NJ
Tel: 01273 480 208
Fax: 01273 476 562
www.wallisandwallis.co.uk

**WG (D)**
**The Watch Gallery**
129 Fulham Road,
London SW3 6RT
Tel: 020 7581 3239
Fax: 020 7584 6497

**WHP (A)**
**WH Peacock**
26 Newnham Street, Bedford
MK40 3JR
Tel: 01234 266 366
Fax: 01234 269 082
www.peacockauction.co.uk

**WIM (D)**
**Wimpole Antiques**
Stand 349, Grays Antiques
Market, 58 Davies Street,
London W1K 2LP
Tel: 020 7499 2889
Fax: 020 7493 9344
www.graysantiques.com

**WOS (D)**
**Wheels of Steel**
Unit B10-11, Gray's Mews
Antiques Market, 1/7 Davies
Mews, London W1Y 2LP
Tel: 020 7629 2813
Fax: 020 7493 9344
www.graysantiques.com

**WW (A)**
**Woolley and Wallis**
51-61 Castle Street,
Salisbury, Wiltshire SP1 3SU
Tel: 01722 424 500
Fax: 01722 424 508
www.woolleyandwallis.co.uk

# USING THE INTERNET

- The internet has revolutionised the trading of collectables. Compared to a piece of furniture, most collectables are easily defined, described and photographed. Shipping is also comparatively easy, due to average size and weight. Prices are also generally more affordable and accessible than for antiques and the internet has provided a cost-effective way of buying and selling, away from the significant overheads of shops and auction rooms. Many millions of collectables are offered for sale and traded daily online, with sites varying from global online marketplaces, such as eBay, to specialist dealers' websites.

- When searching online, remember that some people may not know how to describe their item accurately. General category searches, even though more time consuming, and even purposefully misspelling a name, can yield results. Also, if something looks too good to be true, it probably is. Using this book to get to know your market visually, so that you can tell the difference between a real bargain and something that sounds like one, is a good start.

- As you will understand from looking through this book, colour photography is vital – look for online listings that include as many images as possible and check them carefully. Beware that colours can appear differently, even between computer screens.

- Always ask the vendor questions about the object, particularly regarding its condition. If there is no image, or you want to see another aspect of the object – ask. Most sellers (private or trade) will want to realise the best price for their items so will be more than happy to help – if approached politely and sensibly.

- As well as the 'e-hammer' price, you will probably have to pay additional transactional fees such as packing, shipping and possibly regional or national taxes. It is always best to ask for an estimate for these additional costs before leaving a bid. This will also help you tailor your bid as you will have an idea of the maximum price the item will cost if you are successful.

- In addition to well-known online auction sites, such as eBay, there is a host of other online resources for buying and selling, such as fair and auction date listings.

# USEFUL WEBSITES

## BBC Antiques website
**www.bbc.co.uk/antiques/**
Contains information and dates for the BBC's various antiques and collectables shows, as well as articles on collecting and dates of local auctions and fairs.

## Live Auctioneers
**www.liveauctioneers.com**
**info@liveauctioneers.com**
A free service that allows users to search catalogues from selected auction houses in Europe, the USA and the United Kingdom. Through its connection with eBay, users can bid live via the internet into salerooms as auctions happen. Registered users can also search through an archive of past catalogues and receive a free newsletter by email.

## invaluable.com
**www.invaluable.com**
**sales@invaluable.com**
A subscription service that allows users to search selected auction-house catalogues from the United Kingdom and Europe. Also offers an extensive archive for appraisal uses.

## The Antiques Trade Gazette
**www.atg-online.com**
The online version of the UK trade newspaper, comprising British auction and fair listings, news and events.

## Maine Antiques Digest
**www.maineantiquesdigest.com**
The online version of America's trade newspaper including news, articles, fair and auction listings and more.

## La Gazette du Drouot
**www.drouot.com**
The online home of the magazine listing all auctions to be held in France at the Hotel de Drouot in Paris and beyond. An online subscription enables you to download the magazine online

## Auctionnet.com
**www.auctionnet.com**
Simple online resource listing over 500 websites related to auctions online.

## AuctionBytes
**www.auctionbytes.com**
Auction resource with community forum, news, events, tips and a weekly newsletter.

## Auctiontalk
**www.auctiontalk.com**
Auction news, online and offline auction search engines and live chat forums.

## Go Antiques/Antiqnet
**www.goantiques.com**
**www.antiqnet.com**
An online global aggregator for art, antiques and collectables dealers who showcase their stock online, allowing users to browse and buy.

## eBay
**www.ebay.com**
Undoubtedly the largest and most diverse of the online auction sites, allowing users to buy and sell in an online marketplace with over 52 million registered users. Collectors should also view eBay Live Auctions (www.ebayliveauctions.com) where traditional auctions are combined with real-time, online bidding, allowing users to interact with the saleroom as the auction takes place.

# UK FAIRS

There are many fairs selling 20th-century collectables around the UK. Here is a selection of some of the better-known ones.

**Alexandra Palace**
The Great Hall
Alexandra Palace,
Wood Green, London N22
Tel: 020 8883 7061
Fax: 020 8245 8361
info@pigandwhistlepromotions.com
www.pigandwhistlepromotions.com

**The Antiquarian Book Fair**
The Antiquarian Booksellers Association
Sackville House, 40 Piccadilly,
London W1J 0DR
Tel: 020 7439 3118

**Antiques Fair**
The Prestwood Complex
County Showground, Stafford,
Staffordshire
Tel: 01743 271 444

**The Antiques Fair**
The Royal Horticultural Hall
Elverton Street (off Vincent Square)
Victoria, London SW1
Contact Adams Antiques Fairs Ltd
Tel: 020 7254 4054
www.adams-antiques-fairs.co.uk

**Antiques for Everyone**
Earls Court, London
Contact Centre Exhibitions
NEC House, National Exhibition Centre,
Birmingham B40 1NT
Tel: 0121 767 2454
Fax: 0121 767 3535
antiques@necgroup.co.uk

**Antiques for Everyone**
National Exhibition Centre,
Birmingham B40 1NT
Contact Centre Exhibitions
NEC House, National Exhibition Centre,
Birmingham B40 1NT
Tel: 0121 767 2454
Fax: 0121 767 3535
antiques@necgroup.co.uk

**Antiques for Everyone**
The Scottish Exhibition and Conference
Centre, Glasgow
Contact Centre Exhibitions
NEC House, National Exhibition Centre,
Birmingham B40 1NT
Tel: 0121 767 2454
Fax: 0121 767 3535
antiques@necgroup.co.uk.

**Ardingly International Antiques
and Collectors Fair**
South of England Showground, Ardingly,
West Sussex
Contact DMG Antiques Fairs
PO Box 100, Newark,
Nottinghamshire NG24 1DJ
Tel: 01636 702 326
Fax: 01636 707 923
www.dmgantiquefairs.com

**Arthur Swallow Fairs**
International Antiques and Collectors Fair
Held at RAF Swinderby
PO Box 43, Buxton Delivery Office,
Derbyshire SK17
Tel: 01298 27493
enquiries@arthurswallowfairs.co.uk
www.arthurswallowfairs.co.uk

**Bowman Antiques Fairs**
Held at The Bingley Hall County Showground,
Weston Rd, Stafford, Staffs ST18 0BD
Tel: Tel: 07071 284 333
info@antiquesfairs.com
www.antiquesfairs.com

**The Cambridge Glass Fair**
Oxbridge Fairs
Tel: 07887 762 872
info@cambridgeglassfair.com
www.cambridgeglassfair.com

**Detling International Antiques
and Collectors Fair**
Kent Country Showground, Detling,
Maidstone, Kent
Contact DMG Antiques Fairs
PO Box 100, Newark,
Nottinghamshire NG24 1DJ
Tel: 01636 702 326
Fax: 01636 707 923
www.dmgantiquefairs.com

**The Ephemera Society Fair**
Tel: 01923 829 079

**Giant Antiques and Collectors Fair**
The Matford Centre Exeter
Contact Devon County Antiques Fairs
Tel: 01363 82571
www.antiques-fairs.com

**The Giant Wetherby Antique and
Collectors Fair**
Wetherby Racecourse
Contact Jaguar Fairs Ltd
Tel: 01332 831 404
www.jaguarfairs.com

**Jaguar Fairs**
PO Box 158, Derby DE21 5ZA
Tel: 01322 831 404
www.antiques-atlas.com

**Leeds Royal Armouries Art Deco Fair**
Leeds Royal Armouries, Leeds, West Yorkshire
Ann Zierold Fairs
Tel: 0151 653 8606

**Magnum Antiques and Collectors Fairs**
River Park Leisure Centre
Gorden Park, Winchester
and Grange Centre
Bepton Road, Midhurst
Tel: 01491 681 009

**Malvern Antiques and Collectors Fair**
Three Counties Showground,
Malvern, Worcestershire
Contact DMG Antiques Fairs
PO Box 100, Newark,
Nottinghamshire NG24 1DJ
Tel: 01636 702 326
Fax: 01636 707 923
www.dmgantiquefairs.com

**Newark International Antiques and Collectors Fair**
Newark and Nottinghamshire Showground, Newark
Contact DMG Antiques Fairs
PO Box 100, Newark,
Nottinghamshire NG24 1DJ
Tel: 01636 702 326
Fax: 01636 707 923
www.dmgantiquefairs.com

**Newmarket Antiques and Collectors Fair**
Rowley Mile Racecourse,
Newmarket, Suffolk
Contact DMG Antiques Fairs
PO Box 100, Newark,
Nottinghamshire NG24 1DJ
Tel: 01636 702 326
Fax: 01636 707 923
www.dmgantiquefairs.com

**The Northern Antiques Fair**
Harewood House, West Yorkshire
Contact Bailey Fairs
Tel: 01277 214 699
www.baileyfairs.co.uk

**Shepton Mallet Antiques and Collectors Fair**
Royal Bath & West Showground
Shepton Mallet, Somerset
Contact DMG Antiques Fairs
PO Box 100, Newark,
Nottinghamshire NG24 1DJ
Tel: 01636 702 326
Fax: 01636 707 923
www.dmgantiquefairs.com

**Stafford Bingley Hall Antiques Fair**
3 Park Square,
Leeds LS1 2NE
Contact Bowman Antique Fairs
PO BOX 64, Shipley BD17 7YA
Tel: 07071 284 333
Fax: 07071 284 334
info@antiquesfairs.com
www.antiquesfairs.com

**Towy Antiques Fairs**
PO Box 24, Carmarthen SA31 1YS
Tel: 01267 236 569
towyfairs@btopenworld.com

# ANTIQUES CENTRES

This is just a small selection of the antiques centres around the UK. Use the annual *Guide to the Antique Shops of Britain* published by The Antique Collectors Club to locate centres selling 20th-century collectables near you.

**Alfies Antiques Market**
13-25 Church Street, London NW8 8DT
Tel: 020 7723 6066
www.alfiesantiques.com

**Antiquarius**
131-141 King's Rd, London SW3 4PW
Tel: 020 7351 5353

**Northcote Road Antiques Market**
155 Northcote Rd, Battersea, London SW11
Tel: 020 7228 6850

**Bartlett Street Antiques Centre**
5-10 Bartlett Street, Bath BA1 2QZ
Tel: 01225 466 689

**Bermondsey Market**
Crossing of Long Lane and Bermondsey
Street, London SE1
Tel: 020 7351 5353

**Brackley Antique Cellar**
Drayman's Walk, Brackley,
Northamptonshire NN13
Tel: 01280 841 841

**Brighton Lanes Antiques Centre**
12 Meeting House Lane, Brighton,
East Sussex BN1 1HB
Tel: 01273 823 121
contact@brightonlanes-antiques.co.uk

**Brocante Antique Centre**
6 London Road
Marlborough
Wiltshire SN8 1PH
Tel: 01672 516 512

**Brown House Antiques**
High Street, Newport, Nr. Saffron Walden
Essex CB11 3QY
Tel: 01799 540 238

**Camden Passage Market**
Camden Passage, Islington, London N1

**Cookstown Antiques**
16 Oldtown Street, Cookstown,
Co. Tyrone BT80 8EF
Northern Ireland
Tel: 028 8676 5279

**Courtyard Collectables**
Cyril Noall Square, Fore Street, St Ives,
Cornwall TR26
Tel: 01736 798 809

**De Danann Antique Centre**
25/27 London Road, Dorchester,
Dorset DT1 1NF
Tel: 01305 250 066

**Empire Exchange**
1 Newton Street, Piccadilly,
Manchester M1 1HW
Tel: 0161 236 4445

**The Folly Antiques Centre**
Folly Market, College Street, Petersfield,
Hampshire GU31 4AD
Tel: 01730 266 650

**The Ginnel Antiques Centre**
The Ginnel, off Parliament Street,
Harrogate HG1 2RB
Tel: 01423 567 182
www.theginnel.co.uk

**Gloucester Antiques Centre**
1 Severn Road, Gloucester GL1 2LE
Tel: 01452 529 716
www.antiques-center.com

**Grays Antiques Market**
58 Davies Street,
London W1Y 2LP
Tel: 020 7629 7034
www.egrays.com

**Heanor Antiques Centre**
1-3 Ilkeston Road, Heanor, Derbyshire
Tel: 01773 531 181
www.heanorantiquescentre.co.uk

**Heskin Hall Antiques**
Heskin Hall, Wood Lane, Heskin, Chorley,
Lancashire PR7 5PA
Tel: 01257 452 044

**Hungerford Antiques**
Hungerford Arcade, 26 High Street,
Hungerford, Berkshire RG17 0NF
Tel: 01488 683 701

**Kaimes Smithy Antiques**
79 Howdenhall Road, Edinburgh EH16 6PW
Tel: 0131 441 2076

**Lawrence House Antiques**
87-9 Brighton Road, Redhill, Surrey RH1 6PS
Tel: 01737 779 169

**Littles Collectables**
8/10 Little Street, Congleton, Cheshire CW12 1AR
Tel: 01260 299 098

**Newcastle Antique Centre**
2nd Floor, 142 Northumberland Street,
Newcastle NE1 7DQ
Tel: 0191 232 9832

**Otford Antiques and Collectors' Centre**
26-28 High Street, Otford, Kent TN15 9DF
Tel: 01959 522 025
Fax: 01959 525 858
www.otfordantiques.co.uk

**Oxford Street Antique Centre**
16-26 Oxford Street, Leicester LE1 5XU
Tel: 0116 255 5863

**Portobello Road Market**
Portobello Road, London W11

**Potteries Antique Centre**
271 Waterloo Road, Cobridge,
Stoke-on-Trent, ST6 3HR
Tel: 01782 201 518
www.potteriesantiquescentre.com

**Quay Centre**
Topsham Quay, Nr Exeter EX3 0JA
Tel: 01392 874 006
www.antiquesontopshamquay.co.uk

**St Clement's Antiques**
93 St Clement's Street, Oxford OX4 1AR
Tel: 01865 727 010

**Selected Antiques and Collectables**
19 Newport Road, Barnstaple EX32 9BG
Tel: 01271 321 338

**Snooper's Paradise**
7-8 Kensington Gardens, Brighton,
East Sussex, BN1 4AL
Tel: 01273 602 558

**The Swan Antiques Centre**
Tetsworth, Nr Thame, Oxfordshire OX9 7AB
Tel: 01844 281 777
www.theswan.co.uk

**Tom Bland Antiques Centre**
Opposite Norwich Cathedral
Tel: 01603 619 129
www.tomblandantiques.co.uk

**Windsor House Antiques Centre**
High Street, Gloucestershire GL56 0AD
Tel: 01858 565 221

**Woburn Abbey Antiques Centre**
Woburn Abbey, Woburn,
Bedfordshire MK17 9WA
Tel: 01525 290 350

**Wolverhampton Antiques and
Collectors Market**
Basement of Retail Market, Salop Street,
Wolverhampton WV3 0SF
Tel: 01902 555 212

**Yorkhill Quay**
Antiques Warehouse
Unit 3b Yorkhill Quay Estate
Glasgow G3 8QE
Tel: 0141 334 4924

# SPECIALIST DEALERS

Together with the list of contributors at the front of this section, this forms a selection of dealers who specialise in a particular collecting field. Many of the dealers listed here have featured in the *Collectables Price Guide* by Judith Miller.

## AUTOGRAPHS

**Lights, Camera, Action**
6 Western Gardens, Western Boulevard,
Apsley, Nottingham HG8 5GP
Tel: 0115 913 1116
www.lca-autographs.co.uk

## AUTOMOBILIA

**Classic Automobilia & Regalia Specialists**
4-4a Chapel Terrace Mews,
Kemp Town, Brighton BN2 1HU
Tel: 01273 622 722
www.carsofbrighton.co.uk

## CERAMICS

**Collectors' Choice**
P.O. Box 99, Guildford, Surry GU1 1GA
Tel: 014383 576 655
louise@collectors-choice.net
www.collectors-choice.net

**China Search**
P.O. Box 1202, Kenilworth,
Warwickshire CV8 2WW
Tel: 01926 512 402
helen@chinasearch.uk.com
www.chinasearch.uk.com

**Eastgate Antiques**
S007/S009, Alfies Antiques Market.
13 Church Street, London NW8 8DT

**Mad Hatter**
Admiral Vernon Antiques Market
Unit 38, 141-149 Portobello Road,
London W11
Tel: 020 7262 0487
madhatter.portobello@virgin.net

**Louis O'Brien**
Tel: 01276 32907

**Geoffrey Robinson**
G077-78 & G091-91, Alfies Antiques Market,
13 Church Street, London NW8 8DT
Tel: 020 7723 0449

## COSTUME & ACCESSORIES

**Beyond Retro**
110-112 Cheshire Street, London E2 6EJ
Tel: 020 7613 3636
sales@beyondretro.com
www.beyondretro.com

**Linda Bee**
Gray's Antiques Market
1-7 Davies Mews, London W1Y 2LP
Tel: 020 7629 5921

**Vintage Modes**
Gray's Antiques Market
1-7 Davies Mews, London W1Y 2LP
Tel: 020 7409 0400
www.vintagemodes.co.uk

## COSTUME JEWELLERY

**William Wain**
Antiquarius, 131-141 King's Road, London
SW3 4PW
Tel: 020 7351 5353

**Eclectica**
2 Charlton Place, London N1
Tel: 020 7226 5625
eclecticaliz@yahoo.co.uk

## DOLLS

**Victoriana Dolls**
101 Portobello Road, London W11 2BQ
Tel: 0 1737 249 525
heather.bond@totalserve.co.uk

**Yesterday's Child**
1 Angel Arcade, 118 Islington High Street,
London N1 8EG
Tel: 020 7354 1601

## FIFTIES, SIXTIES & SEVENTIES

**Design 20c**
Tel: 01276 512329/0794 609 2138
sales@design20c.com
www.design20c.com

**The Multicoloured Timeslip**
S002, Alfies Antiques Market, 13 Church
Street, London NW8 8DT
d_a_cameron@hotmail.com

## FILM & TV

**The Prop Store of London**
Great Farm House, Chenies, Rickmansworth,
Herts WD3 6EP
Tel: 01494 766 485
steve.lane@propstore.co.uk
www.propstore.co.uk

## GLASS

**Antique Glass at Frank Dux Antiques**
33 Belvedere, Bath BA1 5HR
Tel: 01225 312 367
www.antique-glass.co.uk

**Nigel Benson 20th Century Glass**
58-60 Kensington Church Street, London W8 4DB
Tel: 020 7938 1137

## PLASTICS

**Paola & Iaia**
S050-S051, Alfies Antiques Market,
13 Church Street, London NW8 8DT
Tel: 07751 084 135

## POSTERS

**Barclay Samson**
65 Finlay Street,
London SW6 6HF
Tel: 020 7731 8013
richard@barclaysamson.com

**The Reel Poster Gallery**
72 Westbourne Grove, London W2 5SH
Tel: 020 7727 4488
info@reelposter.com
www.reelposter.com

## POSTCARDS

**Carlton Antiques**
43 Worcester Road, Malvern, Worcs WR14 4RB
Tel: 01684 573 092
dave@carlton-antiques.com
www.carlton-antiques.com

## ROCK & POP

**Beatcity**
PO Box 229, Chatham, Kent ME5 8WA
Tel: 01634 200 444
www.beatcity.co.uk

**Tracks**
PO Box 117, Chorley,
Lancashire PR6 0UU
Tel: 01257 269 726
sales@tracks.co.uk
www.tracks.co.uk

## SMOKING

**Tom Clarke**
Admiral Vernon Antiques Centre, Unit 36,
Portobello Road, London W11
Tel: 020 8802 8936

## SPORTING MEMORABILIA

**Fiona Taylor**
Jubilee Hall Antiques Centre, Oak Street,
Lechlade GL7 3AE
Tel: 01367 253 777

**Manfred Schotten**
109 High Street, Burford, Oxon OX18 4HR
Tel: 01993 822 302
www.schotten.com

## TOYS & GAMES

**Colin Baddiel**
Gray's Antiques Market, Stand B25, South
Molton Lane, London W1Y 2LP
Tel: 020 7629 7352

**Donay Games**
34 Gower Road, Haywards Heath,
West Sussex RH16 4PN
Tel: 01444 416 412
donaygames@btconnect.com
www.donaygames.com

## WATCHES

**70s Watches**
graham@gettya.freeserve.co.uk
www.70s-watches.com

# AUCTION HOUSES

There are numerous auction houses around the UK, often specialising in particular types of sale. Use the annually published "Collectables Price Guide" by Judith Miller for a more comprehensive listing, or look in your local directory for those in your area.

## LONDON

**Bloomsbury Auctions**
3 & 4 Hardwick Street, London EC1R 4RY
Tel: 020 7833 2636
www.bloomsbury-book-auct.com

**Bonhams**
101 New Bond Street, London W1S 1SR
Tel: 020 7629 6602
And branches nationwide
www.bonhams.com

**Christies (South Kensington)**
85 Old Brompton Road, London SW7 3LD
Tel: 020 7581 7611
www.christies.com

**Sotheby's (Olympia)**
Hammersmith Road, London W14 8UX
Tel: 020 7293 5555
www.sothebys.com

**Rosebery's**
74-76 Knights Hill, West Norwood,
London SE27 0JD
Tel: 020 8761 2522

## BEDFORDSHIRE

**W. & H. Peacock**
The Auction Centre, 26 Newnham Street,
Bedford MK40 3JR
Tel: 01234 266 366
www.peacockauction.co.uk

## BERKSHIRE

**Cameo**
Kennet Holem Farm, Bath Road,
Midgham, Reading,
Berkshire RG7 5UX
Tel: 0118 971 3772
cameo-auctioneers@lineone.net

**Dreweatt Neate**
Donnington Priory, Donnington, Nr Newbury,
Berkshire RG14 2JE
Tel: 01635 553 553
donnington@dnfa.com
www.dnfa.com

**Special Auction Services**
The Coach House, Midgham Park, Reading,
Berkshire RG7 5UG
Tel 0118 971 2949
commemorative@aol.com

## BUCKINGHAMSHIRE

**Amersham Auction Rooms**
125 Station Road, Amersham, Bucks HP7 0AH
Tel: 01494 729 292
www.amershamauctionrooms.co.uk

**Dickens Auctioneers**
Claydon Saleroom, Calvert Court, Middle
Claydon, Buckinghamshire MK18 2EZ
Tel: 01296 714 434
www.dickins-auctioneers.com

## CAMBRIDGESHIRE

**Cheffins**
2 Clifton Road, Cambridge CB1 4BW
Tel: 01223 213 343
www.cheffins.co.uk

**Hyperion Auctions Ltd**
Station Road, St Ives, Cambridgeshire PE27 5BH
Tel: 01480 464 140
www.hyperionauctions.co.uk

## CHANNEL ISLANDS

**Martel Maides**
40 Cornet Street, St Peters Port, Guernsey,
Channel Islands GY1 1LF
Tel: 01481 722 700
www.martelmaides.co.uk

## CHESHIRE

**Frank R. Marshall & Co.**
Marshall House, Church Hill, Knutsford,
Cheshire WA16 6DH
Tel: 01565 653 284
www.frankmarshall.co.uk

**Halls Fine Art (Chester)**
Booth Mansion, 30 Watergate Street, Chester,
Cheshire CH1 2LA
Tel: 01244 312 300
www.halls-auctioneers.ltd.uk

## CLEVELAND

**Vectis Auctioneers**
Fleck Way, Thornaby, Stockton-on-Tees,
Cleveland TS17 9JZ
Tel: 01642 750 616
www.vectis.co.uk

## CORNWALL

**W.H. Lane & Son**
Jubilee House, Queen Street, Penzance,
Cornwall TR18 4DF
Tel: 01736-361 447
graham.bazley@excite.com

**David Lay**
The Penzance Auction House,
Alverton, Penzance,
Cornwall TR18 4RE
Tel: 01736 361 414
dlay@pzsw.fsnet.co.uk

## CUMBRIA

**James Thompson**
64 Main Street, Kirkby, Lonsdale,
Cumbria LA6 2AJ
Tel: 01524 271 555
www.jthompsonauctioneers.co.uk

**Penrith Farmers' & Kidd**
Skirsgill Saleroom, Skirsgill, Penrith,
Cumbria CA11 0DN
Tel: 01768 890 781
penrith.farmers@virgin.net

## DERBYSHIRE

**Noel Wheatcroft & Son**
Matlock Auction Gallery,
The Old Picture Palace, Dale Road,
Matlock, Derbyshire DE4 3LU
Tel: 01629 57460
www.wheatcroft-noel.co.uk

## DEVON

**Bearne's**
St Edmund's Court, Okehampton Street,
Exeter, Devon EX4 1LX
Tel: 01392 207 000
www.bearnes.co.uk

**Onslows**
The Coach House, Manor Road,
Stourpaine, Dorset DT11 8TQ
Tel: 01258 488 838
www.onslows.co.uk

## ESSEX

**Ambrose**
Ambrose House, Old Station Road,
Loughton, Essex IG10 4PE
Tel: 020 8502 3951
www.ambroseauction.co.uk

**G.E. Sworder & Sons**
14 Cambridge Road, Stansted Mountfitchet,
Essex CM24 8DE
Tel: 01279 817 778
www.sworder.co.uk

## GLOUCESTERSHIRE

**Dreweatt Neate**
Collectors' Saleroom, Baynton Road,
Ashton, Bristol BS3 2EB
Tel: 0117 953 0803
www.dnfa.com

**Cotswold Auction Co.**
Chapel Walk Saleroom, Chapel Walk,
Cheltenham, Gloucestershire GL50 3DS
Tel: 01242 256 363
www.cotswoldauction.co.uk

**Mallams (Cheltenham)**
26 Grosvenor Street, Cheltenham,
Gloucestershire GL52 2SG
Tel: 01242 235 712
www.mallams.co.uk

## HAMPSHIRE

**Andrew Smith & Sons**
The Auction Rooms, Manor Farm, Itchen
Stoke, Nr Winchester SO24 0QT
Tel: 01962 735 988
auctions@andrewsmithandson.com
www.andrewsmithandson.com

**Jacobs and Hunt**
Fine Art Auctioneers, 26 Lavant Street,
Petersfield, Hampshire GU32 3EF
Tel: 01730 233 933

## HEREFORDSHIRE

**Brightwells**
The Fine Art Saleroom, Ryelands Road,
Leominster, Herefordshire HR6 8NZ
Tel: 01568 611 122
www.brightwells.com

## HERTFORDSHIRE

**Brown & Merry**
Tring Market Auctions
Brook Street, Tring, Hertfordshire HP23 5EF
Tel: 01442 826 446

## ISLE OF WIGHT

**Ways The Auction House**
Garfield Road, Ryde, Isle of Wight PO33 2PT
Tel: 01983 562 255
www.waysauctionrooms.fsbusiness.co.uk

## KENT

**Dreweatt Neate**
The Auction Halls, Linden Park Road, Pantiles,
Tunbridge Wells, Kent TN2 5QL
Tel: 01892 544 500
www.dnfa.com

**Hogben Auctioneers**
Unit C, Highfield Estate, off Warren Road,
Folkestone, Kent CT19 6DD
Tel: 01303 246 810
hogbenauctions@btconnect.com

## LANCASHIRE

**Capes Dunn & Co.**
The Auction Galleries, 38 Charles Street,
Manchester M1 7DB
Tel: 0161 273 1911

## LEICESTERSHIRE

**Gilding's**
Roman Way Market, Harborough,
Leicestershire LE16 7PQ
Tel: 01858 410 414
www.gildings.co.uk

**Heathcote Ball & Co.**
Castle Auction Rooms, 78 St Nicholas Circle,
Leicester LE1 5NW
Tel: 0116 2536 789
heathcoteball@clara.net

## LINCOLNSHIRE

**Golding Young & Co.**
Old Wharf Road, Grantham, Lincolnshire
NG31 7AA
Tel: 01476 565 118
www.goldingyoung.com

**Marilyn Swain**
The Old Barracks, Sandon Road, Grantham,
Lincolnshire NG31 9AS
Tel: 01476 568 861
swain.auctions@virgin.net

## MERSEYSIDE

**Cato, Crane & Co**
6 Stanhope Street, Liverpool L8 5RE
Tel: 0151 709 5559
www.cato-crane.co.uk

## NORFOLK

**T.W. Gaze & Son**
49 Roydon Road, Diss, Norfolk IP22 4LN
Tel: 01379 650 306
www.twgaze.com

**Keys**
8 Market Place, Aylsham, Norfolk NR11 6EH
Tel: 01263 733 195
www.aylshamsalerooms.co.uk

## NORTHAMPTONSHIRE

**Heathcote Ball & Co.**
Albion Auction Rooms, Commercial Street,
Northampton NN1 1PJ
Tel: 01604 622 735

## NOTTINGHAMSHIRE

**Mellors & Kirk Fine Art Auctioneers**
Gregory Street, Nottingham NG7 2NL
Tel: 0115 979 0000
www.mellors-kirk.co.uk

**Neales**
192-194 Mansfield Road, Nottingham NG1 3HU
Tel: 0115 962 4141
www.neales.co.uk

## OXFORDSHIRE

**Mallams (Oxford)**
Bocardo House, St Michaels Street, Oxford,
Oxfordshire OX1 2EB
Tel: 01865 241 358
www.mallams.co.uk

**Soames Country Auctions**
Pinnocks Farm Estate, Witney, Oxfordshire OX8 1AY
Tel: 01865 300 626
www.soamesauctioneers.co.uk

## SHROPSHIRE

**Halls Fine Art (Shrewsbury)**
Welsh Bridge Salerooms, Shrewsbury,
Shropshire SY3 8LA
Tel: 01743 231 212
www.halls-auctioneers.ltd.uk

**Mullock Madeley**
The Old Shippon, Wall-under-Heywood,
Nr Church Stretton, Shropshire SY6 7DS
Tel: 01694 771 771
www.mullock-madeley.co.uk

## SOMERSET

**Clevedon Salerooms**
Herbert Road, Clevedon, Bristol BS21 7ND
Tel: 01275 876 699
clevedon.salerooms@cableinet.co.uk

**Gardiner Houlgate**
The Bath Auction Rooms, 9 Leafield Way,
Corsham, Bath, Somerset SN13 9SW
Tel: 01225 812 912
www.invaluable.com/gardiner-houlgate

**Lawrence's Fine Art Auctioneers Ltd**
South Street, Crewkerne, Somerset TA18 8AB
Tel: 01460 73041
www.lawrences.co.uk

## STAFFORDSHIRE

**Potteries Specialist Auctions**
271 Waterloo Road, Cobridge, Stoke-on-Trent,
Staffordshire ST6 3HR
Tel: 01782 286 622
www.potteriesauctions.com

**Wintertons Fine Arts**
Lichfield Auction Centre
Fradley Park, Lichfield, Staffordshire WS13 8NF
Tel: 01543 263 256
www.wintertons.co.uk

## STOCKTON ON TEES

**Vectis Auctions Limited**
Fleck Way, Thornaby, Stockton-on-Tees TS17 9JZ
Tel: 01642 750 616
www.vectis.co.uk

## SUFFOLK

**Diamond Mills**
117 Hamilton Road, Felixstowe, Suffolk IP11 7BL
Tel: 01394 282 281
diamondmills@easynet.co.uk

**Neal Sons & Fletcher**
26 Church Street, Woodbridge, Suffolk IP12 1DP
Tel: 01394 382 263
www.nsf.co.uk

## SURREY

**Ewbank Auctioneers**
The Burnt Common Auction Rooms, London
Road, Send, Woking, Surrey GU23 7LN
Tel: 01483 223 101
www.ewbankauctions.co.uk

**Hamptons Auctioneers**
93 High Street, Godalming, Surrey GU7 1AL
Tel: 01483 423 567
www.hamptons.co.uk

## EAST SUSSEX

**Dreweatt Neate**
46-50 South Street, Eastbourne BN21 4QJ
Tel: 01323 410 419
www.dnfa.com

**Gorringes**
15 North Street, Lewes BN7 2PD
Tel: 01273 472 503
Also at Bexhill-on-Sea
www.gorringes.co.uk

**Wallis & Wallis**
West Street Auction Galleries,
Lewes BN7 2NJ
Tel: 01273 480 208
www.wallisandwallis.co.uk

## TYNE & WEAR

**Anderson & Garland**
Marlborough House, Marlborough Crescent,
Newcastle Upon Tyne, Tyne and Wear NE1 4EE
Tel: 01912 326 278
agarland@compuserve.com

**Corbitts**
5 Mosley Street, Newcastle-upon-Tyne,
Tyne and Wear NE1 1YE
Tel: 0191 232 7268
www.corbitts.com

## WARWICKSHIRE

**Locke & England**
18 Guy Street, Leamington Spa,
Warwickshire CV32 4RT
Tel: 01926 889 100
www.leauction.co.uk

## WEST MIDLANDS

**Bonhams**
The Old House, Station Road, Knowle, Solihull,
West Midlands B93 0HT
Tel: 01564 776 151
And branches nationwide
www.bonhams.com

**Fellows & Sons**
Augusta House, 19 Augusta Street, Hockley,
Birmingham, West Midlands B18 6JA
Tel: 0121 212 2131
www.fellows.co.uk

## WEST SUSSEX

**John Bellman**
New Pound Wisborough Green, Billingshurst,
West Sussex RH14 0AZ
Tel: 01403 700 858
www.bellmans.co.uk

**Denhams**
The Auction Galleries, Warnham, Nr Horsham,
West Sussex RH12 3RZ
Tel: 01403 255 699
denhams@lineone.net

## WILTSHIRE

**Hamptons**
20 High Street, Marlborough, Wiltshire SN8 1AA
Tel: 01672 516 161
www.hamptons.co.uk

**Woolley & Wallis**
51-61 Castle Street, Salisbury, Wiltshire SP1 3SU
Tel: 01722 424 500
www.woolleyandwallis.co.uk

## WORCESTERSHIRE

**Andrew Grant**
St Mark's House, St Mark's Close, Cherry
Orchard, Worcester, Worcestershire WR5 3DJ
Tel: 01905 357 547
www.andrew-grant.co.uk

**Phillip Serrell**
The Malvern Saleroom, Barnards Green Road,
Malvern, Worcestershire WR14 3LW
Tel: 01684 892 314
www.serrell.com

## EAST YORKSHIRE

**Dee, Atkinson & Harrison**
The Exchange Saleroom, Driffield,
East Yorkshire YO25 7LJ
Tel: 01377 253 151
www.dee-atkinson-harrison.co.uk

## NORTH YORKSHIRE

**Morphets**
6 Albert Street, Harrogate, N. Yorkshire HG1 1JL
Tel: 01423 530 030
www.morphets.co.uk

**Tennants**
The Auction Centre, Leyburn, N. Yorkshire DL8 5SG
Tel: 01969 623 780
www.tennants.co.uk

## SOUTH YORKSHIRE

**A.E. Dowse & Sons**
Cornwall Galleries, Scotland Street,
Sheffield, South Yorkshire S37 7DE
Tel: 0114 272 5858
aedowse@@talk21.com

**BBR Auctions**
Elsecar Heritage Centre, 5 Ironworks Row,
Wath Road, Elsecar, Barnsley,
South Yorkshire S74 8HJ
Tel: 01226 745 156
www.bbrauctions.co.uk

## WEST YORKSHIRE

**Andrew Hartley Fine Arts**
Victoria Hall Salerooms, Little Lane, Ilkley,
West Yorkshire LS29 8EA
Tel: 01943 816 363
www.andrewhuntleyfinearts.co.uk

## SCOTLAND

**Lyon & Turnbull**
33 Broughton Place, Edinburgh EH1 3RR
Tel: 0131 557 8844
Also at Glasgow
www.lyonandturnbull.com

**Thomson, Roddick & Medcalf Ltd**
42 Moray Place, Edinburgh EH3 6BT
Tel: 0131 220 6680
www.thomsonroddick.com/trm/.index.html

## WALES

**Peter Francis**
Curiosity Salerooms, 19 King Street,
Carmarthen, South Wales
Tel: 01267 233 456
www.peterfrancis.co.uk

**Welsh Country Auctions**
2 Carmarthen Road, Cross Hands, Llanelli,
Dyfed, SA14 6SP
Tel: 01269 844 428

## IRELAND

**HOK Fine Art**
4 Main Street, Blackrock, Co. Dublin, Ireland
Tel: 00 353 1 288 1000
fineart@hok.ie

**Mealy's**
The Square, Castlecomer, County Kilkenny,
Ireland
Tel: 00 353 56 41229/41413
www.mealys.com

# CLUBS & SOCIETIES

## ADVERTISING

**The Guinness Collectors Club**
8 Hartley Road, North End,
Portsmouth, Hampshire
PO2 9HU

**The Street Jewellery Society**
André Morley, 11 Bowsden
Terrace, South Gosford,
Newcastle-Upon-Tyne NE3 1RX

## CERAMICS

**Carlton Ware Collectors'
International**
CWCI, Carlton Works,
Copeland Street, Stoke-
upon-Trent, Staffs ST4 1PU
Tel: 01782 410 504
www.carltonwarecollectorsint
ernational.com

**Chintz World International**
Tel: 01525 220 272
www.chintzworld-intl.com

**Clarice Cliff Collectors' Club**
Fantasque House,
Tennis Drive, The Park,
Nottingham, NG7 1AE
www.claricecliff.com

**The Cornish Collectors Club**
Janet Winterbottom,
PO Box 18, Glossop,
Derbyshire SK13 8FA
Tel: 01298 687 070
cornish@btconnect.com

**Hornsea Pottery Collectors**
128 Devonshire Street,
Keighley, West Yorkshire
BD21 2QJ
www.hornseacollector.co.uk

**M. I. Hummel Club (Goebel)**
Porzellanfabrik, GmbH & Co.
KG, Coburger Str.7, D-96472
Rodental, Germany
(Club Centre)
Tel: 00 49 9563 92 303

**Keith Murray Collectors' Club**
Fantasque House, Tennis
Drive, The Park,
Nottingham NG7 1AE
www.keithmurray.com

**Myott Collectors' Club**
P.O. Box 110, Sutton SM3 9YQ
www.myottcollectorsclub.com

**Noritake Collectors' Club**
13 Station Road, Ilkeston,
Derbyshire DE7 5LY
Tel: 01159 440 424

**Pendelfin Family Circle**
Cameron Mill, Howsin Street,
Burnley, Lancashire BB10 1PP
Tel: 01282 432 301
www.pendelfin.co.uk

**Poole Pottery Collectors' Club**
The Quay, Poole, Dorset
BH15 1RF
Tel: 01202 666 200
www.poolepottery.co.uk

**Portmeirion Collectors' Club**
Portmeirion Potteries Ltd,
London Road, Stoke-on-Trent
ST4 7QQ
Tel: 01782 744 721
www.portmeirion.co.uk

**Potteries of Rye Collectors'
Society**
22 Redyear Cottages,
Kennington Road, Ashford,
Kent TN24 0TF
www.potteries-of-rye-
society.co.uk

**Royal Doulton International
Collectors' Club**
Minton House, London Road,
Stoke-on-Trent,
Staffordshire ST4 7QD
Tel: 01782 292 292
www.royal-doulton.com/
collectables

**Susie Cooper Collectors'
Group**
Panorama House, 18 Oaklea
Mews, Aycliffe Village, County
Durham DL5 6JP
www.susiecooper.co.uk

**The SylvaC Collectors' Circle**
174 Portsmouth Road,
Horndean, Waterlooville,
Hampshire
www.sylvacclub.com

## COMMEMORATIVE WARE

**Commemorative Collectors'
Society**
The Gardens, Gainsborough
Road, Winthorpe, Nr Newark,
NG24 2NR
Tel: 01636 671 377
www.royalcoll.fsnet.co.uk/
collectors.htm

**Royal Commemoratives &
Collectables**
Steven N. Jackson,
The Gardens, Gainsborough
Road, Winthorpe, Nr Newark
NG24 2NR
Tel: 01636 671 377

## COSTUME & ACCESSORIES

**Costume Society**
St. Paul's House, Warwick
Lane, London EC4P 4BN
www.costumesociety.org.uk

**Headscarf Collectors'
Society**
brenda@osmetic.fsnet.co.uk

## DOLLS

**Barbie Collectors' Club**
117 Rosemount Avenue,
Acton, London W3 9LU
wdl@nipcus.co.uk

**British Doll Collectors' Club**
'The Anchorage', Wrotham
Road, Culverstone Green,
Meopham, Kent DA13 0QW
www.britishdollcollectors.com

**Doll Club of Great Britain**
PO Box 154, Cobham, Surrey
KT11 2YE

## FILM & TV & ENTERTAINMENT

**James Bond 007 Fan Club**
PO Box 007, Surrey KT15 IDY
Tel: 01483 756 007

**Fanderson - The Official Gerry Anderson Appreciation Society**
2 Romney Road, Willesborough,
Ashford, Kent TN24 0RW

## GLASS

**The Carnival Glass Society**
PO Box 14, Hayes, Middlesex
UB3 5NU
www.carnivalglasssociety.co.uk

**The Glass Association**
Broadfield House Glass
Museum, Compton Drive,
Kingswinford DY6 9NS
Tel: 01384 812 745
www.glassassociation.org.uk

**Isle Of Wight Studio Glass**
Old Park, St Lawrence,
Isle Of Wight, PO38 1XR
Tel: 01983 853526
www.isleofwightstudioglass.co.uk

## KITCHENALIA

**FoF (Friends of Fred the Homepride Man)**
Jennifer Woodward
Tel: 01925 826 158

**The British Novelty Salt & Pepper Collectors' Club**
Coleshill, Clayton Road,
Mold, Flintshire CH7 15X

## POSTCARDS

**The Postcard Club**
34 Harper House, St. James'
Crescent, London SW9 7LW

## POSTERS

**International Vintage Poster Dealer Association**
PO Box 502, Old Chelsea
Station, New York, NY,
USA 10113
Tel: 001 212 355 8391
www.ivpda.com

## RADIOS

**The British Vintage Wireless Society**
59 Dunsford Close, Swindon,
Wiltshire SN1 4PW
Tel: 01793 541 634
www.bvws.org.uk

## SMOKING

**Lighter Club of Great Britain**
Jack Bond
LCGBbond@aol.com

**Cigarette Case Collectors' Club**
19 Woodhurst North, Ray
Mead Road, Maidenhead,
Berkshire SL6 8PH

## SPORTING

**Football Postcard Collectors' Club**
6 Penstone Close, Lancing,
West Sussex BN15 9AR
Tel: 01903 764 402

## STAINLESS STEEL

**The Old Hall Stainless Steel Tableware Club**
Sandford House, Levesdale,
Staffordshire ST18 9AH
www.oldhallclub.co.uk

## SOFT TOYS

**The British Bear Club**
Freepost RCC2791, Horsham,
West Sussex RH13 8BR
Tel: 01403 711 511

**British Teddy Bear Association**
PO Box 290, Brighton, Sussex
Tel: 01273 697 974

**Merrythought International Collectors' Club**
Ironbridge, Telford,
Shropshire TF8 7NJ
Tel: 01952 433 116

**Steiff Club Office**
Margaret Steiff GmbH, Alleen
Strasse 2, D-89537
Giengen/Brenz, Germany

## TOYS

**Corgi Collectors' Club**
PO Box 323, Swansea,
Wales SA1 1BJ

**Hornby Collectors' Club**
PO Box 35, Royston,
Hertfordshire SG8 5XR
Tel: 01223 208 308
www.hornby.co.uk

**Pelham Puppets Collectors' Club**
46 The Grove,
Bedford MK40 3JN
Tel: 01234 363 336

**Train Collectors' Society**
P.O. Box 20340,
London NW11 6ZE
Tel: 020 8209 1589
www.traincollectors.org.uk

# INDEX